# CONVOY
# PQ 18
## ARCTIC VICTORY

# CONVOY
# PQ 18
# ARCTIC VICTORY

PETER C. SMITH

**NEW ENGLISH LIBRARY**
TIMES MIRROR

First published in Great Britain by William Kimber
& Co. Ltd. in 1975
© Peter Smith, 1975

*

FIRST NEL PAPERBACK EDITION FEBRUARY 1977

*

NEL Books are published by
New English Library Limited from Barnard's Inn, Holborn, London EC1N 2JR
Made and printed in Great Britain by Hunt Barnard Printing Ltd. Aylesbury, Bucks.

45003120 9

# Contents

Author's Note    7

*Chapter:*

1   Political Expediency    9
2   Against the Odds    29
3   The Golden Comb    61
4   The Phantom Fleet    95
5   War of Attrition    134
6   The Final Effort    165
7   Home is the Sailor    200

*Appendix:*

1   Composition of Convoy PQ18    219
2   Composition of the Naval Escort Forces    221
3   RAF Units and Luftwaffe Units    225
4   R/T Call Signs    226
5   Summary of Fleet Air Arm Sorties    229
6   German Naval Units    231

Sources    233

*Illustrations in the text*

Layout of Merchant Ships in Convoy PQ18    34
Route of convoy and initial U-boat dispositions    46–7
Screening Plan for Full Strength Escort    97
Submarine patrols and the route of German Forces    116–17
RAF Patrol Zones and Torpedo Strikes    135

# Author's Note

This book is a detailed account of a vital naval battle. It was not a battle in the old accepted sense of the word, not a broadside-to-broadside struggle between mighty battleships, not the high-speed clash of fast-moving flotilla craft, nor was it a carrier-to-carrier duel between the naval airmen of rival fleets whose surface ships never saw each other. It was instead both a new type of battle and yet, at the same time, the oldest battle ever waged by the Royal Navy – a convoy battle.

Over the centuries it had been the disruption of trade that had been the objective of our enemies at sea and so it remained in World War II. In the past the result of the naval setpiece battles often decided the fate of the convoys. In this conflict the enemy went straight in and attacked the merchant ships, avoiding, if he could, the protecting warships. The submarine under the sea and the bomber above added new facets to the ancient struggle but the task of the Royal Navy remained the same, the safe and timely arrival of the convoy.

There were three convoy battles which stand out above all others during World War II. All took place within the short space of three months. All are identified by the convoy code names or numbers. Two of them involved convoys to Russia, PQ 17 was a ghastly defeat, *Pedestal* a costly victory – and PQ 18? Let the reader judge.

Many other accounts have appeared on the Russia convoys, the best overall to date being *The Russian Convoys* by Admiral B. B. Schofield, and the most detailed was David Irving's book. But there are many lesser works, and the convoys are also briefly mentioned in the Official History of *The War at Sea*. It is not therefore the intention of this book to go over this well-worn ground again in any detail and the historical background to the main story is deliberately condensed.

As to the actual operation itself every effort has been made to present a factual blow-by-blow account of the battle, as it was planned and as it subsequently developed. Dialogue is, in the main, avoided, although a few quotations are given from published sources. But to try and ensure a degree of authenticity, and present a record of historical value, by far the majority of the references used are from the actual Battle Reports and War Diaries of the combatants themselves, written at the time while the events were still fresh. By going straight to source in this manner some of the delightful fantasies that have grown up around the operation have been rejected no matter how appealing. The sources have been listed accordingly to provide a firm basis for further study.

*Peter C. Smith*
*Needingworth, Huntingdon*
*1974*

# Chapter One

# Political Expediency

I

The Second World War, which broke out on 1st September, 1939, was the result, in the most simplified form, of Germany's invading Poland allegedly over the issue of Danzig, a former Germanic city incorporated into Poland by the Treaty of Versailles. Britain and France had given the Polish Government guarantees of its frontiers (including those parts it had taken from Czechoslovakia the year before), against German aggression. This latter point is of supreme importance, for Poland, although quickly conquered by German arms, was in fact divided up between Germany and the Soviet Union. Thus two large dictatorships swallowed up a third dictatorship and into the arena, in defence of a country they could not possibly help, sprang the two Western Democracies. They did not, however, do anything about the Soviet invasion but limited themselves to the German one, a fact that they found hard to explain at the time and which became an increasing embarrassment later on.

Nor was this all; other events took place in 1939 and 1940 involving uninhibited aggression by dictatorships against small neighbours which raised nothing more than righteous indignation among the two democracies. Italy absorbed Albania in April without a stir or hardly a ripple. The Soviet Union, not content with her half of Poland, proceeded to swallow whole the tiny Baltic states of Estonia and of Latvia, and when this again passed unchallenged Stalin went on to try his luck with Finland. Finland, unaided and unmourned, fought back gallantly for some months with success and her resistance eventually shamed even the two Western Governments. Moves were afoot to send her aid (but still they drew the line at war), when she eventually gave in to overwhelming pressure and ceded her only secure defence zone.

The final and inevitable result of their earlier unholy alliance was all-out ideological warfare between the Nazi and the Communist regimes, for which in 1941 Germany, although outnumbered in troops and aircraft, was none the less more prepared and experienced, and, in June of that year her legions stormed forth on their road to Moscow. The enormous casualties inflicted on the Soviet armies and air forces drained them of the strength to do much more than give ground, of which they had a premium, and hope for a miracle.

Great Britain, who had been fighting Germany and Italy on her own, since June 1940, immediately declared common cause with the nation which had helped rape her Polish ally in 1939. 'Gallant Little Poland' now appeared forgotten in the welter of goodwill toward the nation that had stabbed her in the back. Self-interest was obviously a prime motive, for without this diversion Britain's chances of survival were slim; for this reason every possible aid was offered to the Soviet leader in an attempt to keep them fighting, thus keeping the Luftwaffe and Wehrmacht away from North Africa.

There was a remarkable about-face on the part of both London and Moscow who now went to extremes to present a united front to the world. Poland's few lucky exiles, who failed to see the difference between execution at the hands of the SS or the GPU, saw things somewhat differently. As one of them was to phrase it at the time: 'The Germans will take my land, but the Russians will take my soul.'

Britain could do nothing militarily, for she had only just been thrown out of Greece and Crete, in a humiliatingly brief campaign in which the Germans had not committed more than a brief fraction of their total strength while Britain had thrown in everything she could spare. Only by the shipping of some limited amounts of arms and materials could she help and for this the Russians agreed to supply the ships. This promise, like their many others, soon fell into abeyance, the sheer volume of her requirements and demands grew and grew as the months passed and she had nowhere near the amount of shipping required to carry it. Britain volunteered to ship the cargoes in her merchant vessels and when the United States entered the war, in December 1941, she was able to throw into the arena her massive industrial strength and a large rapidly expanding mercantile marine.

Protection for these convoys, which grew into a flood of immense proportions, fell on the already over-stretched Royal Navy. Built, at best, to fight a two-ocean war, and sadly lacking in modern equipment as well as numbers, the Royal Navy had been extended beyond reasonable limits by 1942, fighting the German Navy and Air Force and the Italian Navy and Air Force in the Atlantic, the North Sea and the Mediterranean. At the end of 1941 Japan came in with a series of devastating naval victories which saw the Royal Navy fighting in the South China Sea, the Java Sea and finally in the retreat to the Indian Ocean. Now the long voyage to the Arctic ports of Archangel and Murmansk was added to their chores.

To meet this new commitment the Home Fleet had to provide the bulk of the major escorts although the local escorts were always provided by Western Approaches Command. At first the threat came only from submarines but as the Germans realised the value of these convoys to the Russians during 1942 they not only reinforced the U-boats but sent Luftwaffe units to Norway in increasing numbers. Hitler's belief that Churchill wished to re-take Norway (which, although derided, was partly true, as the Premier has admitted), had resulted in the main units of the German Navy being transferred north to Norwegian ports as a counter-measure. Although defence of Norway remained their prime function these powerful units were obviously well placed to intercept the convoys to Russia.

As well as a long and exposed flank the elements combined to make the planning of these convoys a nightmare. In winter the ice forced the convoy route closer to the German bases and in summer the perpetual daylight, or twilight, gave the Germans round-the-clock conditions in which to locate the convoys and mount repeated assaults upon them.

On paper success for the Arctic convoys seemed almost impossible. The Navy had to provide heavy ships as defence against the German fleet, but lack of aircraft-carriers and an over-sensitive complex, as a result of previous experiences, against risking heavy ships in waters dominated by the Luftwaffe, meant that they could not accompany the convoys all the way. Instead only cruiser cover could be provided, within reasonable range to intervene, but again fear of U-boats kept these vessels over the horizon where they could operate at high speeds and with a degree of immunity.

For close defence against the U-boats the small escorts, a few destroyers, corvettes and trawlers, were provided. They also served as anti-aircraft escorts against the small-scale air attacks of the early months, but against surface sorties their role was to hold on until the cruisers came to their aid. Should enemy ships come out too large for the cruisers to tackle, the same principle applied in the hope that the Home Fleet carrier would tip the scales and either cripple the German units so that they could be destroyed by British battleships or else drive the Germans away. As 1942 wore on it became increasingly clear that if the Germans cared at any time to call this bluff there was really little that could be done to aid the convoy.

All the sound arguments put forward on behalf of the Royal Navy in favour of stopping these convoys were simply ignored in the face of political expediency which dictated that Soviet Russia must be supplied no matter what. Even the reinforcement of our own colonies in the Far East was sacrificed to this end and the cost to the British nation of this policy was seen immediately in the fall of Singapore and the evacuation of Rangoon.

None the less the Royal Navy had its orders and somehow it had to carry them out. But by the early summer months of 1942 it was becoming plain that the Germans were almost ready to expose the hopelessness of the British position. A few preliminary probes had revealed to them the true state of affairs and it only remained to exploit the many weaknesses.

In March convoy PQ 13 (the thirteenth of the PQ series) sailed with an escort of a light cruiser, two destroyers and two trawlers. Light air attacks were followed by a sortie by three German destroyers which was countered by the sailing of reinforcements for the escort from Kola, three destroyers (one British and two Russian ships).

However the German destroyers found the convoy first. In a brisk fight in poor weather conditions one German boat was sunk, but they succeeded in sinking one merchant ship and in badly damaging the destroyer *Eclipse*. In addition the British cruiser *Trinidad* fired a torpedo which promptly circled round and hit her, causing severe damage!

In April a returning convoy, QP 11, escorted by six British destroyers, four corvettes, four minesweepers and a trawler, with two Russian destroyers for part of the journey in addition, was reinforced by the cruiser *Edinburgh*.

Against this force the Germans sailed another destroyer force of three ships and they gave battle to the convoy escort. The cruiser was absent, having been hit by a U-boat torpedo the previous day, and two of the destroyers were escorting her back to Russia. Despite this the three German ships were held at bay by the four British boats (who had very poor surface armaments due to their prior needs as anti-submarine escorts). Frustrated in their attempts to get at the convoy they turned their attentions to the *Edinburgh* and sent her to the bottom with a torpedo. They also badly damaged the destroyers *Forester* and *Foresight*, losing one of their own number, *Hermann Schoemann*, in the exchange. The four British minesweepers appeared on the scene and were mistaken for destroyers so the two remaining German boats withdrew.

Soon after this the *Trinidad*, heading home after repairs, was caught by Ju. 88s and sent to the bottom. At the end of May an even larger convoy, with the strongest escort yet, sailed, PQ 16. U-boats and aircraft sank seven of the merchant ships. Despite repeated warnings about the feasibility of such an operation in midsummer, PQ 17, which sailed at the end of July, was even larger.

The result of this refusal to face realistic facts by the British and American leaders is well-known. The threat of the intervention of the German battle fleet led to a series of signals which led the escort commanders to believe that surface attack upon the convoy was imminent.

However London, and *not* the commanders on the spot, ordered the convoy to scatter. The warships of the escort formed up to offer forlorn battle in the hope that while they were being blown asunder the merchant ships could escape. But no enemy warships appeared and the isolated merchant vessels, not knowing what was going on, were subsequently slaughtered wholesale by U-boats and aircraft operating with little or no opposition.

Far from showing the Western leaders the errors of their policy the massacre of PQ 17 merely led to an even larger convoy, but this, PQ 18, had to be delayed for a time as the survival of Malta was in the balance in August, 1942, and in order to fight through the vital *Pedestal* convoy to that island all available units of the Home Fleet had to be transferred south. Not until September could they reassemble in sufficient numbers to take part in PQ 18.

This was however a fortunate occurrence for not only did it give the C-in-C, Home Fleet, Admiral Sir J. C. Tovey, KCB, KBE, DSO, and his staff time to plan the operation in detail but it also pre-empted the Germans' planned counter-moves for a time.

Before we examine in detail just how the defence of convoy PQ 18 was to be carried out in the face of the almost insoluble problems, let us briefly examine how the conclusions drawn from their July victory affected German plans against PQ 18.


## II

The PQ 17 episode was hailed in the German press as a great achievement for the Luftwaffe and U-boat crews but, in general, the respective Air and Naval Commands had drawn very different conclusions as to how this achievement had come to pass.

The Luftwaffe did not much concern themselves with the claims or the sinkings of the submarine arm; instead they shouted aloud that the victory had been due entirely to their efforts. It had been *their* torpedo bomber attacks which had so demoralised the convoy and its escort that they had broken formation and it had been the subsequent air strikes directed against the individual merchantmen that had sent the greater proportion of the convoy to the bottom of the ocean.

As usual therefore the reports of airmen were wildly blown up and distorted and little or no allowance made for visual error, even though it was known that this was common among aircrew of all nations when attacks on ships were being analysed. As a result Colonel-General Stumpff was able to deliver an ego-building report to Reichsmarschall Goering on July 12th. It began with no false modesty:

I beg to report the destruction of convoy PQ 17. I report the sinking by the Fifth Air Force of one cruiser, one destroyer, two small escorts totalling 4,000 tons.* 22 merchant ships totalling 142,216 tons.

In fact the convoy had lost some 23 ships out of a total of 34 and of these 23 *ten* at least were sunk by U-boats. But the most important point of all was ignored and this was the fact that it had been the fear of intervention by the powerful surface fleet that led to the convoy's disbandment into a melee of undefended victims *not* the torpedo bomber assault, no matter how bravely this had been driven home. As the Germans drew up their plans of attacks against PQ 18 on such an obviously false base, it was little wonder that their operations against it lacked cohesion.

However, the confidence all arms of the German forces in Norway now felt in their powers was reflected in the eager manner that plans were prepared against PQ 18 and the keenness in which searches were made to locate it early on so that the maximum time could be spent sending it to the bottom along with its unhappy predecessor.

The German Naval Command was more modest than the Luftwaffe in its claims and more generous in its distribution of accolades. In striking contrast to the selfish bombast delivered by Stumpff to Goering (perhaps he was playing to his audience for it even *sounds* like Goering), the Navy reported that the victory over PQ 17 ' . . . was achieved by exemplary co-operation between aircraft and U-boats.' This despite the fact that several U-boat commanders had complained bitterly about the dangers they had been exposed to by the bomb-happy antics of the Ju 88s who straffed anything that moved in the Barents Sea during the pulverisation of the merchantmen.

They therefore decided to leave the attacks on PQ 18 to the underwater and airborne arms while the surface ships would instead only sortie out against the homeward, and less well defended, QP convoy. The full details of how this decision was made we shall describe later but again the Navy Command fell into the same trap of underrating the effect of the battle fleet.

In their eagerness to repeat the performance the Germans set in train wide-ranging movements well before the end of July when they expected PQ 18 to put to sea. No less than five submarines were sent to patrol north of Bear Island while others

* It is difficult to understand how this tonnage was arrived at for even the smallest cruiser in the Royal Navy was of almost 4,000 tons alone.

were held at instant readiness to take up assigned patrol lines. This group was designated the 'Ice Palace' patrol group and, although its composition changed constantly, up to the actual operation, its plans remained constant, as did its confidence.

Air searches were flown by Stumpff's long-range FW 200s and the harbours of Iceland were kept under special watch. When a small force of four destroyers was picked up south-west of Spitzbergen, while en route to carry supplies through to the ships locked up at Archangel, it was assumed that these islands would be used as a fuelling base for the expected PQ 18. Tension was screwed up to maximum pitch at Oslo on 6th August when the submarine *U-405* (Lieutenant-Commander Hopmann) reported the sighting of a convoy in the Denmark Strait.

Naval Group North had just come under the command of Admiral Klüber, who relieved Admiral Schmundt, and he at once ordered the ten waiting submarines to sea to their waiting positions in readiness for the attack. To further keep the German Commands on tenterhooks the weather worsened during this period and air reconnaissance, although stepped up, failed to relocate this convoy along its expected route. On August 12th some 140 aircraft were despatched to locate the phantom PQ 18 but when they returned empty handed it was realised that Hopmann's sighting was not the real thing and the operation was aborted.

If the Germans were disappointed because PQ 18 did not sail on schedule then our Allies were appalled. Churchill had tried to explain away this prudence to Marshal Stalin but he was not the slightest bit interested in the reasoning behind the decision. The Soviet authorities cared not a jot that a few merchant ships had been slaughtered the previous week trying to reach them with aid. Fighting for their life against their recent ally, the only thing which concerned them was the sending of more supplies and yet more supplies. The more the British sailors pointed out the dangers the more Stalin closed his mind and repeated his call for more and more convoys.

Churchill himself of course was not too accommodating to the advice of his Naval advisers. No doubt his experience in the Great War had led him to believe that he was a naval genius, just as Hitler became convinced that he was a better general than his staff officers. He was extremely loath to stop, or even delay the convoys, no matter what the reason, but eventually he, and the even more naïve Roosevelt, had it spelled out to them with sufficient clarity to bring a note of reality into their planning.

'In defeat, defiance,' maintained Churchill proudly, but stirring slogans like this became meaningless in the ghastly aftermath of PQ 17, and certainly the survivors of that episode might not have agreed with his policy. His first reaction was to propose that for the next Arctic convoy two of Admiral Tovey's precious battle-ships should accompany the merchantmen all the way to Russia, keeping well to the south and not clinging to the ice packs. With the clear example of this type of strategy before them in the loss of the *Prince* of *Wales* and *Repulse*, the Admiralty were, not surprisingly, exceedingly luke-warm about this weird scheme and it was quickly dropped.

Churchill therefore cabled Stalin the unhappy news that, 'with the greatest respect', PQ 18 would not be sailing as planned. In his message of July 17th he added in explanation that this was due to the German dominance of the Barents Sea. He did not add that this was being exercised on Russia's doorstep and a long way from Great Britain, but he could have done. Even had he have done so it would have made little difference. Stalin was not interested in excuses, nor in the fact that the Royal Navy had certain other commitments of slightly longer standing than a sudden and unexpected alliance with Russia – Malta's survival and keeping the Indian Ocean free from the Japanese Navy and, above everything else, Great Britain's own survival in the Atlantic, were factors that counted as nothing to him.

The *Tirpitz*, *Scheer*, *Hipper*, and the 'Ice Palace' submarine-pack were dismissed in the same breath as the Fifth Air Force's dive- and torpedo bombers as 'wholly unconvincing', reasons for delaying the sailing of PQ 18. Against such a wealth of ignorance, of self-interest, there was really no logical answer to be made. 'Has the Royal Navy no sense of honour?' asked this mass-murderer in all seriousness.


III

With the Premier's idea quietly deposited in the waste-paper basket the Admiralty and Admiral Tovey's Staff were able to get on with making more realistic plans for the defence of convoy

PQ 18, which was now due to sail at the beginning of September. To overall command of the very strong escort was assigned Rear-Admiral Robert Burnett, a PT specialist in the pre-war Navy who had recently become Rear-Admiral(D) in command of the Home Fleet's Destroyer Flotillas.

Robert Lindsay Burnett entered the Royal Navy in 1902, serving as a midshipman aboard the cruiser *Amphitrite* on the China Station in 1904–5. In 1911 he became the physical training officer of Shotley and in 1913 at Portsmouth. As a 'Springer', as PT specialists were called in the service, he was outstanding and he became also an all-round sportsman in the fields of football, hockey and water-polo. He also became the sabre champion of the Navy.

He went to war in 1914 as a Lieutenant of the destroyer *Laertes* of the Harwich Force and soon saw action, his first command being the torpedo boat *No 26*. He later graduated to destroyer commands, the *Acheron* and the *Nessus*. After the war he resumed his PT duties becoming fleet PT officer in the Mediterranean in 1922 and Assistant Director of Physical Training and Sports at the Admiralty a year later. Promoted to Commander in 1928 he became executive officer of the battleship *Rodney*.

In the early 1930s he renewed his contact with the Destroyer service by becoming Captain(D) Eighth Flotilla on the China Station in the Flotilla Leader *Keppel* when she was in her heyday. After this he was appointed Director of PT and Sports and in command of the Portsmouth PRT School. Command of the new cruiser *Amphion* in the mid-thirties before she was given to Australia was followed by a post as flag-captain and chief of staff to C-in-C Africa Station in 1936–38. By March, 1939, Burnett had become commodore of the RN Barracks, Chatham, but later joined the minelaying squadron in late 1940 as acting Rear-Admiral.

A strong personality, he was not universally loved in the destroyer service, but to those who did follow him he was known, affectionately, as 'Uncle Bob'. He had been itching to get into the action and the appointment to the command of PQ 18's escorting force was welcomed by him as a chance to get to sea again with the bit between his teeth. The date of sailing was later put back again but, following the visit to Moscow by Churchill and the constant urgings from Americans, PQ 18, when it did sail, was to be even larger than the ill-fated PQ 17. Despite PQ 17's losses, this was decided upon at the highest level. Some very special measures had therefore to be organised in its defence. What these were we shall now examine.

On 24th August, 1942, a 'Most Secret' Memorandum was prepared by the Admiralty which gave the pre-sailing Intelligence of German dispositions and strengths as then assessed in Whitehall. Bearing the words, 'To be burnt on completion of the Operation or if there is any possibility of it falling into enemy hands', it nonetheless still survives in the file at the Public Records Office, and from it can be seen that British Intelligence was very good indeed, both as to the numbers, and dispositions, of the German forces likely to be available to oppose PQ 18.

Of the surface forces available to the Germans the *Tirpitz*, *Scheer*, *Hipper*, *Köln* and about seven large destroyers (of the so-called *Narvik* and *Maas* classes), were reported based on North Norway. The main force was normally based on Narvik. The submarine strength was put at approximately twenty U-boats. They were reported to start usually with one group in the Iceland-Jan Mayan area with a second near Bear Island. German air strength was put at forty long-range bombers (Ju 88 and He 111) and seventy-five torpedo bombers (He 115, He 111 and Ju 88s). A few Ju 87 (Stuka) dive-bombers were known to be based at Kirkenes and in addition shadowing by FW 200 and BV 138 aircraft was expected from the vicinity of Jan Mayan island all the way through to Russia. The torpedo bombers however were, 'believed to be able to operate only from Bardufoss . . . '

To counter these concentrations Admiral Tovey spelt out his counter-measures in his own report dated 8th October, 1942. In retrospect he summarised the situation as he had seen it and detailed his actions.

. He pointed out that the plan he had made differed from that used on previous occasions in several very important respects. The traditional use of a heavy covering force, with a carrier in company and the cruiser squadron closer-in just over the horizon, he rejected as being now far too dangerous.

The protection against surface attack in that area was thus virtually non-existent, except for that afforded by submarine patrols.[1]

He concluded on pointing out the dangers to these invaluable ships from U-boat attacks or torpedo bombers. Although he admitted that the enemy might have been deterred by the threat of a carrier-borne air strike force, on this occasion the Home Fleet had no aircraft carrier of the large fleet type available.*

As the example of PQ 17 had shown (or appeared to have shown), the Germans were now prepared to risk their big ships against these convoys, despite this aerial threat, and it was therefore necessary to take more positive measures to counter this eventuality while at the same time extending an equal degree of protection to the home bound QP convoy. In order to do this the routing of QP 14 had to be changed so that the two convoys no longer crossed over in the vicinity of Bear Island. This in turn meant complications of fuelling for the new-style escort that was envisaged.

It was decided that the answer to the threat of surface attack could be best met by the provision of a very strong destroyer covering force, composed of all available Fleet destroyers which still maintained their heavy torpedo outfits. To do this would naturally impair the mobility of the battlefleet proper but this was accepted as the lesser evil, for there were just not enough destroyers to go round, a rather common problem in this war and one that was not to be resolved for another two years.

The operation (Codenamed 'EV'), therefore would cover a long and extended period of time and the cruiser covering force could not cover both outward and homeward convoys as they usually did. Furthermore the need for ships of that force to help in the supply of Spitzbergen itself further complicated their programme. It was therefore decided that the cruisers would only provide cover for the homeward convoy west of Bear Island.

To try and prevent just the early sighting that we have seen the Germans were straining every nerve to obtain, the convoy, which normally would have been expected to sail from Reykjavik, would start from Loch Ewe in Northern Scotland, and it was hoped that this unexpected switch would prevent the usual detection of the assembly and departure of the convoy. However, not all the merchantmen had completed embarkations and a

* During Operation *Pedestal* that August *Eagle* was sunk, *Indomitable* was severely damaged, *Victorious* slightly damaged and *Furious* was engaged in running in more aircraft to Malta.

few, mainly Soviet vessels, remained at Reykjavik and would sail to join the main convoy later.

As a bonus for the escort, and an especially welcome addition against the expected air assaults, PQ 18 would be accompanied on its voyage by one of the new little escort carriers that were just starting to come into service and from which great things were expected following the early happy, but brief, experience with the *Audacity*.

For the first time the RAF was to take a major part and arrangements were agreed, after protracted bargaining, for an air striking force to be based in Russia as a further deterrent. The usual submarine patrols were to be mounted off the principal German bases in the hope that one of the big ships could be crippled once they sallied forth to give battle.

But another large-scale alteration to the normal plan was that Admiral Tovey himself was to stay at Scapa Flow in the Fleet Flagship *King George V* and direct operations from there. Contrary to the vivid imaginations of popular fiction writers on the Arctic Convoys, the battleships of the Home Fleet did *not* spend the war swinging around the buoy only putting to sea when there were submarine alarms on the Flow. On the contrary, they were out on patrol as often as the smaller vessels. However, on this operation, as we have seen, the screen was insufficient to allow the whole fleet of three battleships to put to sea and so the Second-in-Command, Admiral Sir Bruce Fraser, was to make two sorties out from Iceland to give distance support while Admiral Tovey remained in direct contact with London over his scrambled phone link from *King George V*. This would, he hoped, avert any unnecessary intervention by Whitehall into the actions of the men on the spot. Unlike Rear-Admiral Hamilton and Commander Broome of PQ 17, Rear-Admiral Burnett and Commander A. Russell were to be shielded from such irksome direction.

Such was Operation 'EV's' overall plan. Let us now examine in more detail the operation and the ships assigned to carry out the task.

The merchantmen were a very mixed bunch in all respects. The British ships were, in the main, large and crewed by the most experienced seamen. They were used to war and used to discipline. They had been working in close harmony with the Royal Navy now for three years of total warfare and knew and trusted them. They also realised how much their fate depended on a mutual reliance of each other's skills and common sense. The convoy commodore was Rear-Admiral E. K. Boddam-Whetham, an ex-serving officer of great wisdom and strength, called back into active duty to perform this vital function. Boddam-Whetham had a proud fighting record in the service of the Royal Navy. He had entered the old *Britannia* as a cadet in 1901 and became a lieutenant in 1908. From the start he was a destroyer man showing the dash and courage of that select breed of naval officers.

During the Great War his destroyer commands had included the *Locust*, *Lennox* and *Sharpshooter* and he saw considerable action. His most modern command was the destroyer *Ulleswater* which he operated from Dover and Harwich and he survived when she was torpedoed and sunk off the Dutch coast in 1918. Postwar he continued to command flotilla craft, taking the new destroyer *Swallow* out to the Mediterranean and the Black Sea during the final actions of the Russian Revolutionary war.

Not content with this he became the first Commander to qualify as an observer in the Fleet Air Arm and served in that capacity aboard the aircraft carrier *Argus* and the battleship *Queen Elizabeth*. Following a course at the RAF Staff College, Andover, Boddam-Whetham held an appointment at the Air Ministry during the 1920s but in 1926 he returned once more to his first love, destroyers, and was made Captain in 1928.

Between 1929 and 1931 this remarkable officer was the senior officer of the little flotilla of river gunboats that were stationed on the West River in China during the troubles there, and in 1932 became Captain(D) 2nd Destroyer Flotilla, Home Fleet. After a period as Captain-in-charge of Bermuda and Chatham Dockyards Boddam-Whetham was placed on the retired list as a Rear-Admiral in 1939.

Within five weeks he was recalled as a Convoy Commodore

where his great knowledge and wisdom were once more to be actively re-employed in the service of the nation.

With such a man there was every chance of achieving perfect harmony, and indeed there is no doubt it would have been, had all his ships been British. Unfortunately only a quarter were, eleven ships in all. The remainder were from the mercantile marines of the United States, the Soviet Union, while a few more flew the flag of Panama.

For the most part the Russian ships kept good discipline and were crewed by good seamen. They had a reputation second to none for courage and would not give up their ships if there was the least chance of bringing them in. Love of their country, pride in the task, plus the ever watchful eye of the Commissars, ensured that the Soviet vessels would have equally fitted into the convoy but for the fact that most of them were small, old and slow coal-burning vessels which did not, no matter how earnest their efforts, make for efficient station-keeping in a convoy of modern oil burning ships.

The American and Panamanian ships conversely were mainly fine, brand-new vessels, many of them on their maiden voyages, including the famous Liberty ships, with sleek, attractive hull line, efficient navigational aids and every modern device. Their crews were mixed and totally inexperienced however, and despite astronomical wages and every possible comfort, had not yet been blooded. Nor were many of them very willing to learn from those that had been fighting. Brimming with confidence in their splendid vessels, their ships bristling with more anti-aircraft guns and devices than the British escorts had seen in all their years of weary fighting, the Americans sailed to do battle confident that they could overcome anything that the Germans could throw at them. Confidence is a good asset in time of war but not when it crosses the gap to become complaisancy.

Of course the merchant ships' crews had to take everything on trust. Their immediate defences were the guns manned by the 'Armed Guard Crews' of regular United States Navy personnel, usually under the command of young lieutenants and ensigns. These gun crews imparted a great sense of stability into the crews but despite their steadiness and their eagerness to make their mark in the war proper they were equally as inexperienced as the crews themselves.

After the long voyage across the Atlantic, loaded with what they were told were vital war supplies for their gallant Soviet Allies, many were perplexed and bewildered that they should have to lay idle at anchorages in Iceland and not be pressing on to Russia with all despatch. The diversionary voyage south to Loch Ewe which added many many hundreds of miles to their route, with no effect that they could see, also, quite understandably, puzzled them further. This was one of the Armed Guard's comments at the time:

Fuelled ship on 4th April and shifted to Pier 100 South, Philadelphia, PA, where we commenced loading a cargo of war goods consigned to the USSR. Loading was complete 15 April and we got underway at 0300, 16 April. At 0530 the ship grounded off Marcus Hook, PA doing moderate damage to ships bottom.[36]

It was an unauspicious start to such a long and dangerous journey for the *Virginia Dare* but, as Lieutenant John Landers Laird, reported, things got worse. After reaching New York –

April 20, we shifted to Pier 3, Hoboken, NJ and commenced discharging cargo. Discharging complete 29 April and we entered drydock. Emergency repairs completed 5 May and we commenced re-loading. Loading was complete 14 May and we lay idle awaiting orders until May 20 when we commenced discharging cargo. Discharging was completed 29 May and we began to re-load again.[36]

Extra gun positions were mounted and on 15th June she got underway once more but missed the rendezvous with the convoy and proceeded to Halifax, NS on her own. They sailed from Halifax on 23rd June and again lost their convoy in the fog. Arriving at Sydney, NS on the 25th they stood out sea once more on the 26th en route to Iceland. The ship kept station very poorly, 'and was called for it several times, both by the convoy Commodore and the escorting vessels.'

The *Virginia Dare* anchored at Hvalfiord on 9th July. Then they discharged one gunner who was showing signs of mental instability.

For reasons unknown, we, and about thirty other ships were detained in Hvalfjordur [sic], until 3 August when we got underway for an unknown destination. After a rainy and foggy trip we anchored in Loch Long [sic], Scotland, on 8 August. The reason for this trip is obscure; we changed neither our cargo nor our eventual destination.[36]

Little wonder then, after such frustration, the American gunners were anxious to get into the fight and vent their wrath on the enemy. We can therefore surely sympathise with Laird's summary of the operations when he bemoans that

> the long unexplained periods of idleness did not exactly benefit our morale. It seemed very odd for whole convoys to be tied up for weeks at a time when their cargoes were so desperately needed.

For the keyed up gun crews on the Liberty ship and for the sullen dictator in Moscow the picture seemed simple enough. Only the few, overworked, men in the Admiralty knew the true picture and the true reasons for these delays. Moving their far too few counters about the globe to fulfil the ever increasing needs and commitments of global war, after the decades of naval retrenchment had left them almost empty-handed, their tasks were almost insoluble. However these grim facts remained a secret for all but a few, the effect on morale was accepted as just one more minus facet in the balance of sea-power.

It should also be remembered that the crews of the British warships were not often informed of their missions either, as Commander Jack Broome was to recall of PQ 17 earlier:

> I don't remember exactly how or when I first heard that my Group was to escort the next Russian convoy. It must have been about mid-June 1942, but whether the news came by signal, telephone or bush telegraph, my reactions are still quite clear. We all knew about these hazardous runs; many friends who had sampled them. As a fairly seasoned escort commander, I must have realised that, all things being equal, my time would come. When it did, I thanked God it was summer. Before weighing up the relative disadvantages of permanent darkness and permanent daylight, creature comforts, I must confess, came first. It would certainly be a change from slow merchant- or fast troop-convoys, and besides, we were naïve enough to think it was a challenge. Dammit, someone must have chosen us. We found this part stimulating without stopping to consider that the escort 'barrel' was probably so empty that all there was to scrape out

was my group. If that was the case, the crafty Planners had at least been kind enough not to say so.[63] *

This was the custom rather than the exception; it was only afterwards that participants were able to look back and assess things, and say, yes, I was on that show, and often a succession of tough incidents would make everything run into a blur of actions and events with particular operations hard to distinguish even if they were not too tired to bother one way or the other. As has already been pointed out, the Royal Navy was so short of warships of all kinds that the ships that were capable of steaming just kept going until they were sunk or damaged.

The overall plan decided upon, Rear-Admiral Burnett and his staff got down to planning the operation in tiny detail. The Rear-Admiral decided to adopt the old system of flotilla control and lead his ships from a light cruiser. Although he had four full flotillas to select his vessels from with the Home Fleet units, many of them were refitting or engaged on other vital tasks and in the end his sixteen destroyers were drawn from all four flotillas, four boats from each. His flag was to be flown in the brand-new light cruiser *Scylla*.

Originally to be one of the original 'Dido' class of anti-aircraft cruisers, mounting ten of the new type 5.25-inch dual purpose guns in five twin turrets, the *Scylla* and her sister, *Charybdis*, had been completed, due to wartime shortages of the new guns, with eight smaller 4.5-inch guns in open shields. As such, with the smaller weapons dwarfed by her hull, she was known as 'The Toothless Terror'. However, although equipped with inferior guns, the *Scylla* was to win for herself an enviable reputation on her very first operation.

The *Avenger*, the little escort carrier, had just completed her working up programme. Of some 8,200-tons displacement and built in the USA for the Royal Navy under the Lease-Lend arrangement, the stubby and ungraceful little ship had a maximum speed of only seventeen knots and an overall length of some 468½ feet. She could carry a maximum of fifteen aircraft but only had a half-hangar under the after end of her flight deck. She embarked twelve Sea Hurricane fighters and three Fairey Swordfish biplanes, these ancient torpedo bombers now being tried out as anti-submarine aircraft. Certainly their slow speed and easy

* *Convoy is to Scatter*, William Kimber, 1972.

handling made them very suitable indeed for escort work, but all such operations were, at this stage of the war, very much in the nature of experiments. The young Fleet Air Arm pilots would have to work out their own tactics as they went along and learn the hard way. In this respect then they were as much novices as the US gun crews.

To add to the carrier's own protection two of the little 'Hunt' class destroyers were assigned to her for her own very personal escort. They were to stick to her flanks like glue, follow her on her eccentric course when she flew off and landed her aircraft according to the dictates of the wind and weather.

Finally, two fleet oilers were to accompany the convoy for refuelling, with a further stationed at Spitzbergen to top up the 'Fighting Destroyer Escort'. This latter was to provide PQ 18 with their additional strength as far as latitude 73° 30′ N. It would then transfer its protection to the homeward bound QP 14 whose sailing date would be held back to fit in with this movement.

While they were with the convoy Rear-Admiral Burnett would assume control of the force as a whole, and in the absence of the *Scylla* the Senior Destroyer skipper of whatever flotillas remained would take over. At all other times the Senior Officer of the Close Escort, Commander Russell aboard the destroyer *Malcolm*, would take over. [This is clearer if Appendix Two is consulted on page 221 where the respective forces are listed and commanding officers given in detail.]

For the bulk of the convoy waiting patiently in Loch Ewe the first indication of their destination came at the convoy conference held on 2nd September, during which Rear-Admiral Burnett in person explained to the skippers of the merchantmen the details and escort for the passage of PQ 18.

At long last Ensign Rooker of the *Campfire* was able to write tersely:

Convoy conference held ashore at the naval base for Convoy PQ 18, destination-Archangel.[34]

Rear-Admiral Burnett himself was to recall that:

The news that a cruiser, an aircraft carrier and sixteen Home Fleet destroyers were to accompany the convoy obviously had a heartening effect on the masters who I found to be cheerful and confident.[2]

From this briefing Rear-Admiral Burnett proceeded to Iceland, and after his arrival at Hvalfiord on 4th September he discussed arrangements with Vice-Admiral Bonham-Carter, the Vice-Admiral Commanding 18th Cruiser Squadron, which were the heavy cruisers of the covering force.

Later a further conference was held with the commanding officers of some of the destroyers, the two AA ships *Ulster Queen* and *Alynbank* and the remaining ships of the close escort. The two AA ships were, like the escort carrier, converted merchant ships fitted out with directors and radar and a heavy punch of anti-aircraft guns that almost matched the *Scylla* herself, although of course they lacked her speed and armour.

Two submarines were to accompany the convoy on the surface under the care and protection of a smaller escort. This had been tried before and was thought to be an effective deterrent against surface attack. Care had to be taken that these two were not mistaken for enemy boats of course, but their young commanders seemed eager only that an attack would give them the chance to have a shot at the *Tirpitz*. The remainder of the escort probably were of the opinion that this experience would be better gained elsewhere!

And so, by the evening of 2nd September, everything was ready. Forty merchant ships were laden down with war goods of every description, tanks, aircraft, ammunition and the like. More than ninety British warships from battleship to trawler were standing ready to give them protection on their long voyage north. Arrayed against them, in equal confidence and readiness, were twelve U-boats, two hundred aircraft and the great bulks of the German Battle Fleet lurking in their fiords ready to slip their cables.

The battle lines were evenly matched, the stakes were the fates, not only of the several hundred merchant seamen, but of countless thousands of soldiers on the ghastly Eastern Front, either Russian or German depending on the course of the battle and the arrival or non-arrival of those vital cargoes along the banks of the Volga.

The gamble that was Operation 'EV' was ready for the fateful throw.

Chapter Two

# Against the Odds

I

Operation 'EV' got under way for the bulk of the convoy when, during the late afternoon of 2nd September, 1942, the forty freighters sailed from the protective haven of Loch Ewe on the north-west coast of Scotland and headed out into the Minches, north-bound for the rendezvous with the various other forces that would make up PQ 18. The merchantmen were stationed in two columns for the night passage – it was 1610 when the ships first weighed anchor at dusk. Speed was set at eight knots. They were bound for Archangel and the unknown and, as an indication of something of what they were in for, as they left the haven of the Scottish sea-loch the barometer started to go down rapidly. It looked as if their long-delayed voyage would start with a dusting. It did.

The initial escort, as far as the rendezvous, was quite small; the local escort was provided by two 'Hunt' class destroyers, *Eskdale* (with Lieutenant M. J. W. Paussey under Norwegian command and with a Norwegian Commander as Senior Officer), and *Farndale* (Lieutenant David Trentham), two old destroyers, *Campbell* and *Mackay*, the five trawlers, *Paynter*, *King Sol*, *Arab*, *Hugh Walpole* and *Duncton*. The 'Hunts' were stationed ahead and astern of the long columns with the *Campbell* abreast the rear ships to starboard and the *Mackay* to port, with the trawlers forming a loose circle and filling the gaps ahead.

The weather was rough and worsening and, at dawn on the 3rd, it was found that the *John Penn* and the *Beauregard* were both missing from the convoy. Somewhat concerned at losing two ships within the first few miles of the operation the *Eskdale* cast astern for them but found no sign of the two United States ships. However some time later a signal was received to the effect that *Beauregard* had put back into harbour with engine trouble.

Daytime screening positions were adopted with the destroyers stationed 4,000 yards and the trawlers 1,500 yards from the convoy which was re-formed by Commodore Boddham-Whetham into ten columns now that they had ample sea-room. These columns were far from rule-straight however, and the Commodore had endless trouble with signals and orders to get the American vessels to comply. Tempers became very frayed over the next few days as the Commodore sought to impose some sort of order on the chaotic lines of the convoy. In this he was severely hampered, for, during the next night, the weather further deteriorated and soon the straggling convoy was beset by a full gale. Out beyond the lee of the Outer Hebrides there was nothing between them and the gale at all and soon what little semblance there remained of a well-ordered convoy vanished in the wild spray and howling wind of the night.

The merchant ships were soon in trouble, the *Campfire* reporting 'South easternly gale, very heavy seas. Two ships observed hoisting out of command signals'. Aboard the *Patrick Henry*, an American Liberty ship, the wind was reported as force 9-10 with a rough beam sea. The fo'c'sle gun crew was taken off duty because it was too rough for them to maintain their exposed positions. By 2000 that evening her master had had enough of trying to maintain his allotted place in line. Speed was reduced and *Patrick Henry*'s helm was put over to port as she left the convoy. She re-joined the next morning, but she was far from being the only freighter to be left behind or to choose her own course that night.

Dawn revealed the unhappy fact that no less than nine of the merchantmen were missing together with three of the escort, the destroyers *Campbell* and *Mackay* and the rescue ship *Duncton*, all of whom had used their initiative and gone after groups of scattered freighters in their vicinity. The general speed of the convoy, due to the ferocious weather, was never more than five knots at best.

Three of the missing ships re-joined of their own accord during the day and the two destroyers brought word that they had found a further group of five which was being shepherded along by the *Duncton* some fifteen miles off the port quarter. *Mackay* was sent back to them for the night of the 4th/5th with orders to re-join with them at dawn.

Fortunately weather conditions eased after this to such an extent that, by 1100 on the 5th, all the ships had re-joined the convoy with the exception of the *John Penn* and the rescue ships *Duncton* and *Copeland*. The latter had been with *Mackay*'s group but apparently slipped off on her own to re-coal at Reykjavik for she later re-joined with the Iceland portion of the convoy. The *Duncton* had meanwhile found the wayward *John Penn* and was guiding her back into the fold that afternoon. The *Empire Tristram* reported that due to weather damage only one serviceable lifeboat remained to her. This had a maximum capacity of thirty men to accommodate a crew of seventy. Commodore Boddam-Whetham asked whether she should be allowed to proceed and this information was passed to the first of the patrolling Catalina flying boats when it arrived over the convoy at 1400.

The Catalina replied with a disturbing signal which reported the sighting of a U-boat on the surface some thirty-eight miles to the north. Further sightings were also received which led the Senior Officer of the escort to understand that four or five German submarines were patrolling a line across the convoy's route. To have been discovered so early in the operation seemed uncanny, especially when the weather conditions were taken into account, but it was a fact that the Germans had established U-boat patrols very early in the month in readiness for PQ 18.

The convoy was now about thirty-six hours behind schedule, but none the less it was decided to carry out an evasive alteration of course to the southward while the *Farndale*, *Campbell* and *Mackay* were sent to carry out a dusk anti-submarine sweep to put down any possible shadowers. This soon produced results which showed that the Catalina's warning was not unfounded.

At 1956 the *Farndale* reported sighting a surfaced U-boat on the Fleet wave. There was some doubt about where this was however, as her position was worked out to be sixty miles away on the starboard quarter of the convoy. The broadcast version, received by *Eskdale* just before midnight, put her as only twelve miles away at the time and on the port quarter. In fact the *Farndale* sighted her quarry, the *U-456* (Lieutenant-Commander Teichert), briefly through the murk. The alarm rattlers were sounded, even though the guns' crews were at defence stations, and the forward twin 4-inch should have commenced firing, but they failed to do so, having only a very fleeting glimpse of their target. The submarine submerged with the range down to only 500 yards but although an attack was carried out no contact could be picked up by the asdic. However this was not thought surprising due to the 'quenching' effect the rough weather conditions had on the set.

The U-boat therefore survived this encounter and lived to fight another day, but as *Farndale* had only been working up at Scapa for eleven days prior to this operation it was not expected that her inexperienced guns' crews would have fully worked up their gunnery efficiency to enable them to carry off a surprise operation of that nature and no blame was attached to them. The close shave she received did not apparently put *U-456* on the track of PQ 18, although by this time the *Avenger* (reported as the *Argus*), the *Scylla* (reported as a 'Dido'-class cruiser), and the 'Fighting Destroyer Escort' had all been identified at Seidesfiord from aerial-reconnaissance so the Germans were well aware of what was coming.

Meanwhile PQ 18 had altered course thirty degrees to port at 2100 and after five hours back again to the original course. The night passed without any further alarms and by dawn on the 6th even the *John Penn* had re-joined the convoy's ranks once more. Because of the potential threat of the submarine line three more destroyers were sent out from Iceland to reinforce the slender escort and these, *Echo*, *Montrose* and *Walpole*, joined forces at 1300. These welcome reinforcements enabled the screen to be adjusted. The *Farndale*'s asdic was out of action following her encounter and so her place astern the convoy was taken by the *Walpole* (Lieutenant A. S. Pomeroy, DSC), *Campbell* and *Mackay* were dropped back on the beam of the convoy and the *Echo*, *Farndale*, *Eskdale* and *Montrose* formed line abreast some 2,500 yards apart ahead.

The convoy had been making very good progress in catching up on their original timetable, so much so that the Commodore thought it advisable to wait until the morning of the 7th before forming the still undisciplined convoy into two lines again to pass through the Reykjanes Passage. This was done at 1900 and, after passage had been safely effected, the *Oremar*, *San Zotica* and *Gateway City*, who were due to travel no further, were accordingly sent into Reykjavik with the trawler *Arab* as escort after she had embarked a passenger from the *Empire Tristram* for passage back to the UK.

Meanwhile the Iceland portion of the convoy, eight merchant ships, including the Russian vessels *Andre Marti*, *Komiles*, *Petrovsky*, *Tbitisi*, *Stalingrad* and *Sukhona*, had sailed at 0700 to rendezvous with the bulk of the convoy. Escorting them were the destroyers *Malcolm*, *Achales* and *Amazon*, anti-aircraft ships *Ulster Queen* and *Alynbank*, minesweepers *Harrier* and *Gleaner*, corvettes *Bryony*, *Bergamot*, *Bluebell* and *Camelia* and the trawlers *Cape Mariato*, *Cape Argona*, *St Kenan* and *Daneman* under the command of Commander A. B. Russell, Senior Officer of the Close Escort. The trawlers had in tow the three little motor minesweepers, *MMS 90*, *MMS 203* and *MMS 212* who were not thought capable of facing the long hazardous voyage under their own power. They were soon to dispute this fact however.

At 1100 the destroyer *Amazon* (Lieutenant Commander Lord Teynham), was forced to return with condenser trouble but an hour later the main body of the convoy was sighted and the new escort and the old now helped manoeuvre them into their new sailing formation. (See Diagram 1.)

While the convoy was sorting itself out from two columns into ten, with the two fleet oilers prolonging the formation, the Commodore and the escort commanders had to decide which ship to send into Iceland, for Boddam-Whetham had strict instructions from Admiral Tovey that not more than forty ships were to sail with PQ 18. Furthermore both men thought even this number far too many to handle and so this ruling was strictly enforced.

The first choice lay with the *John Penn* for that unpredictable vessel had again reported herself in difficulties, this time because her steering gear had broken down the previous night. She was accordingly sent in, but shortly after leaving the convoy she reported that her repairs had been effected and that she could therefore proceed if necessary. After some lengthy discussions the *John Penn* was recalled and the *Richard Basset*, one of the Icelandic portion of the convoy which had just joined, was detailed to return to Hvalfiord under the escort of the *Eskdale* and *Farndale* as far as the swept channel. For the *John Penn* this decision was to be a fateful one.

Earlier, at 1800, the *Campbell*, *Mackay* and the trawlers of the

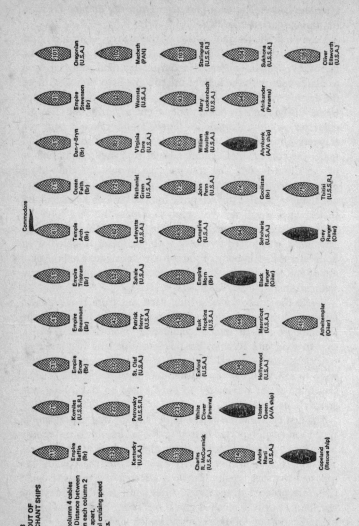

**PQ 18
LAYOUT OF
MERCHANT SHIPS**

Each column 4 cables apart. Distance between ships in each column 2 cables apart. Normal cruising speed 8 knots.

Commodore

| | | | | | | | | | |
|---|---|---|---|---|---|---|---|---|---|
| Oregonian (U.S.A.) | Empire Stevenson (Br.) | Dan-y-Bryn (Br.) | Ocean Faith (Br.) | | Temple Arch (Br.) | Empire Tristram (Br.) | Empire Beaumont (Br.) | Empire Snow (Br.) | Komiles (U.S.S.R.) |
| Macbeth (PAN.) | Wacosta (U.S.A.) | Virginia Dare (U.S.A.) | Nathaniel Green (U.S.A.) | | Lafayette (U.S.A.) | Sahale (U.S.A.) | Patrick Henry (U.S.A.) | St. Olaf (U.S.A.) | Petrovsky (U.S.S.R.) |
| Stalingrad (U.S.S.R.) | Mary Luckenbach (U.S.A.) | William Moultrie (U.S.A.) | John Penn (U.S.A.) | | Campfire (U.S.A.) | Empire Morn (Br.) | Esek Hopkins (U.S.A.) | Exford (U.S.A.) | White Clover (Panama) |
| Sukhona (U.S.S.R.) | Afrikander (Panama) | Alynbank (A/A ship) | Goolistan (Br.) | | Schoharie (U.S.A.) | Black Ranger (Oiler) | Meanticut (U.S.A.) | Hollywood (U.S.A.) | Ulster Queen (A/A ship) |
| Oliver Ellsworth (U.S.A.) | | | Tbilisi (U.S.S.R.) | | Grey Ranger (Oiler) | | Atheltemplar (Oiler) | | |

Empire Baffin (Br.)
Kentucky (U.S.A.)
Charles R. McCormick (U.S.A.)
Andre Marti (U.S.A.)
Copeland (Rescue Ship)

initial escort had been detached by Hvalfiord to fuel and only the *Montrose* and *Echo* remained to reinforce the close escort for the next stage of the journey until the *Amazon* could re-join. Meanwhile, having passed the Straumnes minefields, the convoy had formed up and the remaining escorts adopted a protective screen. However the seas remained heavy and soon the little minesweepers astern the trawlers were reporting impossible conditions, tied as they were and unable to adopt suitable courses. Accordingly they were allowed to slip their tows and proceed at their own best speed. This proved a blessing, both to the crews of the motor minesweepers themselves, giving them freedom of action but, also later to the convoy as a whole for these three little vessels performed valiantly and were invaluable as additional rescue ships.

At 1230 on the 8th the *Amazon* rejoined the convoy again looking smug and aggressive but, unfortunately for the proud old lady's reputation, she almost immediately had to part company again with dynamo defects. She was feeling the effects of her fifteen years at sea, but despite this set-back did manage later to play a small but vital role in the safe passage of PQ 18. The convoy meanwhile changed course to 044 degrees at eight knots, but any hopes of an undetected start on their long haul were dashed soon afterwards when the first long-range Focke-Wulf *Condor*, FW 200, appeared in the grey sky overhead, its four great engines beating out a muffled rhythm of triumph and its wireless chattering its excited message to the waiting commanders in Oslo. PQ 18 was on its way, they learned at last.

As Commander Russell recalled it, this sighting upset their calculations and more, their hopes, for it was earlier than expected. None the less he decided to keep wireless and radar silence for the time being in order not to give the Germans too much to work on. One of the patrolling Catalinas passed on the report of this sighting to the ACIC.

The German sighting report was quite comprehensive and listed:

Pinpoint 2950, 36 West. One Battleship, two cruisers six escorts and thirty-five merchant ships.[40]

Apart from the usual aerial reconnaissance error of upgrading all the escorts several times (anti-aircraft ships become battleships, large destroyers become cruisers and so on; all air forces made the identical mistake all through the war), the count of merchant ships was not far short of correct and the eager recipients of the signal at OKM and Group North could have no doubt that this was in fact the long awaited follow-up to PQ 17. The Luftwaffe in particular felt very keyed up and confident that they would inflict an equally severe drubbing on PQ 18.

With regard to the U-boats, as we have seen patrol lines had been established for some time and on the 7th the 'Ice Palace' attack group consisted of only a few scattered vessels but with others in reserve awaiting their opportunity. *U-255* (Lieutenant-Commander Reche) was speeding up her refuelling at Kirkenes, *U-251* (Lieutenant-Commander Timm) was occupying an ice-edge patrol off Novaya Zemlya while *U-601* (Lieutenant-Commander Grau) remained transmitting data in the main convoy zone. All available U-boats at Narvik were completing their arming in readiness for sea while the *U-456* (Lieutenant-Commander Teichert) still kept watch to the south undaunted by her brush with *Farndale* earlier.

Having been given this tantalising glimpse of their intended prey, the Germans now had it snatched away from them, for the shadowing aircraft lost touch with PQ 18 again, and they did not regain it for some considerable time. Fortunately for the complicated moves planned by the Oslo command and Group North their U-boats only needed this one brief sighting to home themselves and they were in touch much sooner. None the less it proved the wisdom of Commander Russell's retention of wireless silence for a little while longer, for the thick clouds and low visibility of the next few days kept the air reconnaissance at bay and thus the convoy was granted some respite before the Junkers and Heinkels got down to work in earnest.

Meanwhile the convoy received extra reinforcements, for, at 0600 on the 8th, the two British submarines *P.614* and *P.615* had sailed from Seidesfiord escorted by the *Sharpshooter* and, at 1200 on the 9th, these vessels joined in position 60° 36′ N, 17° 55′ W. From then onward the *Bryony* took over and her two surfaced submarine charges occupied stern positions, to port or starboard, according to the movements of the *Avenger* and her two Hunts when they later joined, the two groups alternating according to flying conditions.

Rear-Admiral Burnett and the Fighting Destroyer Escort did not put in an appearance until the 9th, but earlier had put in motion the complicated pattern of fuelling and high-speed steaming that would ensure their maximum support for the most critical part of the voyage.

Rear-Admiral Burnett's flagship, the *Scylla*, had arrived at Seidesfiord on 5th September, having been sighted by a Focke-Wulf FW 200 en route, and on his arrival it was confirmed by Commander Colthurst of the *Avenger* that the assembled warships had been sighted there the same day, for a FW 200 had made a bombing attack, dropping two bombs close to the carrier. *Avenger* also reported the first casualty of the operation – one Sea Hurricane had gone over the side in the rough weather during her voyage north to Iceland from Scapa Flow.

The C-in-C Home Fleet had meanwhile forwarded the information that PQ 18 was still running twenty-four hours late and Burnett therefore put off his conference with the Commanding Officers of his destroyers until the 7th. Meanwhile the patrolling by the Germans continued and full reports were being fed back to Norway on this force. The aircraft were usually too high for interception by the available fighters, although once the *Wheatland* loosened off a couple of rounds of 4-inch perhaps to relieve the feelings at being thus exposed without chance reply.

On the 7th a further message was received from Admiral Tovey informing Burnett that the convoy was now thirty-six hours late and on the 8th came confirmation that the *Sharpshooter* and the two submarines had also been sighted by the very vigilant FW 200s.

It was not until 2030 that the *Scylla*, *Avenger*, the two Hunts and the eight destroyers of the 8th and 13th flotillas sailed from Seidesfiord and headed north to join the impending combat. They were soon in trouble, for at midnight the *Avenger* reported that she would have to stop for an hour owing to defects in her main engines. This was a blow, for not only was it extremely dangerous for the carrier but the threat of the loss of their air cover before the operation had got underway was depressing.

It must be remembered that the *Avenger* was one of the very first products of the Lease-Lend agreement whereby warships were being built in United States shipyards for the Royal Navy and it is not to be wondered at that there were teething troubles. For a start the *Avenger* was in fact the first of her particular class to be taken over. The need for aircraft-carriers of any type, large or small, was desperate and the work was rushed through by the Sun Shipbuilding company to meet the demand, although the workmanship was of a high quality. None the less the converting of a mercantile hull (the original vessel was the *Rio Hudson*) meant that specifications were of a mercantile and not a naval standard in many areas. This was of course accepted as inevitable but some degree of low standard or differences of opinion naturally arose. (This later came to a head with the loss of the sister ship of *Avenger*, the *Dasher*, and the fault and remedy was never agreed upon.)

As Commander Colthurst was to point out however, things went surprisingly well for a new type of warship and a new type of programme to work out while subjected to a heavy scale of attack.

> The work of the T.12X Engineroom Department was excellent. They had no easy task to keep running the American machinery with which they were not yet fully conversant and which was certainly not designed for operations of this nature.[16]

Rear-Admiral Burnett left the destroyers, *Meteor*, *Impulsive* and the two Hunts to give the carrier protection while she carried out her repairs and hurried on with the *Scylla* and the remaining six boats. For three hours *Avenger* hove to while her engineers struggled to get her mobile again. It was a nerve-wracking wait, for though the four escorts kept up a constant watch and patrol around her, it was felt that at any moment this dream target for any submarine skipper would receive the blast of a U-boat torpedo in her very paunchy belly. However her luck held out. The fault was found to be water sludge and sand in her oil fuel and certain modifications were thought to be essential to her fuel storage for future operations. Thankfully they got underway again to catch up with the rest of the force.

Meanwhile Bob Burnett was having second thoughts about leaving his only carrier thus and had turned back to meet her. Therefore it was in company that the combined force shaped course at 0415 to meet the convoy. The ubiquitous FW 200 spotted them during the forenoon and again in the afternoon, and as a reminder that they were now in very dangerous waters and that the battle had already commenced, both the *Faulknor* and the *Milne* obtained submarine contacts on their asdics and dropped depth charges, although later losing their echo reports.

Visibility was poor but at 2010 PQ 18 was eventually sighted through the murk in position 69° 21′ N, 16° 10′ W and the *Scylla* took up her station with a flourish at the head of the centre column on the port hand of the Commodore, while the destroyers took up their pre-arranged screening diagram. The arrival of even half the Fighting Destroyer Escort was a stirring sight to the ships of the convoy who now felt very exposed and on the edge of great dangers, as indeed they were. With the arrival of these ships the destroyers *Montrose* and *Echo* parted company, although, as in the case of the *Amazon*, both were to play further minor but essential roles in the operation.

John Currant was one of the US Navy Armed Guard crews aboard the freighter *Exford*, one of the ships that had joined from Iceland, and he recorded the passage of the convoy at this early stage through the heavy seas and low visibility towards the waiting enemy.

> We lost our position during the night (7/8th) so we are taking position again. Most of the convoy is mixed up and they are doing as we are. One ship was in some kind of trouble so it turned back. After running all night in the fog (8/9th) we got out of position again.[30]

Meanwhile the eight destroyers of the 6th and 17th flotillas had sailed ahead to Spitzbergen to fuel from the tankers *Oligarch* and *Blue Ranger* which had been located there with the four destroyers of their escort.

Early on the 10th the convoy ran into repeated snow squalls before the weather closed down even further and they ran into fog which was thick from midday until dark. Before it closed right in a Catalina was observed overhead on patrol. The *Avenger* flew off a single Swordfish to assist with the aerial patrol at 0725, but an hour later this aircraft was recalled due to the poor visibility and was damaged on landing. However the aircraft was operational again with three hours. This fog did prevent the submarines making contact and keeping in touch however, for at 1215 the *Harrier* obtained a firm asdic echo astern of the convoy.

Both *Harrier* and *Sharpshooter* made depth charge attacks and they reported a great deal of oil on the surface afterwards but no submarine was damaged by these ships. Equally sobering was the report received in from two of the British submarines on patrol off the Norwegian coast, the *Tigris* and *Tribune*. They signalled that a battleship, two cruisers and six destroyers had sailed from Narvik. This was obviously a move north by the main German fleet and it seemed certain that their ultimate target was PQ 18. We shall return to these reports later but at the time there was little that Burnett could do except trust in the soundness of his plans and the strength of the various forces assigned to help him.

The 11th was in large part a repetition of the 10th although the fog cleared slightly but frequent rain squalls shut down visibility just as effectively and the convoy plodded its way northward in the murk and gloom. A warning signal of a concentration of U-boats forming across the convoy's route was received from the Intelligence in London via the C-in-C, Home Fleet and the convoy was accordingly switched on to a new course in an attempt to avoid this. But their diversion proved to be in vain. Their only sign of friendly or hostile aerial activity was when a Liberator was sighted briefly at dawn. Her sudden appearance out of the mist caused some alarm but she was soon identified as friendly. The *Avenger* flew off no aircraft this day because of the conditions.

Meanwhile the discipline of the convoy had improved slightly but still was far from satisfactory. The commanding officer of the *Bryony* reported how the *Oliver Ellsworth* kept dropping back.

The ship had been warned by *Bryony*, repeated *Malcolm*, that she was in danger and that she was decreasing the effectiveness of the screen.[19]

Other vessels also fell back, and some of the American skippers complained that their brand new vessels had to drop out of formation because of poor station keeping by the more ancient coal burners stationed ahead of them which could not keep up. There was some justification in this and the *Bryony's* skipper conceded this point describing how the *Atheltemplar* had also been inclined to straggle, 'handicapped by the ships ahead of her who were also to a certain extent guilty.'

John Currant continued his diary aboard the *Exford*:

We are still going along in a rough sea and the wind is blowing just as hard as ever. Light snow flurries and fog banks. We have a hard time keeping our guns clean, this bad weather is hard to beat. Once in a while we hear depth charges go off, but outside of that it is quiet. Weather still fog and snow and rain.[30]

Aboard another Liberty ship, the *Patrick Henry*, Ensign Blake Hughes recorded that the Commodore sent all the ships a signal this day to prepare them for tougher opponents than the weather in the near future.

Enemy attack certain within day or so. Ships should keep closed up to two cables and be prepared to help with mass fire.[35]

All through this period of course the constant high speed steaming and resultant heavy fuel consumption of the destroyers, and especially the Hunts, meant that the dominant problem for them was the need to keep constantly topped up with oil fuel. Earlier convoys had suffered from this and PQ 18 was particularly well provided for with the two big fleet auxiliaries accompanying the convoy and the two others tucked away at Spitzbergen. None the less the safety of these vessels was a constant source of anxiety to the escort commanders and fuelling alongside these vessels was no sinecure either.

At this stage of the war the development of ship to ship refuelling was still at a very basic and elementary stage in the Royal Navy. Despite the fact that experiments of fuelling ships under way had been carried out ever since the early days of World War I, the practice of employing fleet auxiliaries flying the Blue Ensign meant that these ships were crewed by mercantile officers and men rather than navy personnel.

The tankers available to the Royal Navy at this period were therefore deficient in two ways, that were far from large enough for the job in hand and did not have a high enough speed to accompany a battle fleet. Their gear was somewhat lacking also and the methods used were not so efficient as those already in use by the German and United States navies. Both these services had accepted the fact that geographical conditions would affect their fleets in that they would be operating across vast distances a long way from their home bases, the Germans all over the world and the Americans with a view to Pacific operations. Both had therefore devoted some considerable time and effort to develop an efficient afloat support system. The Royal Navy on the other hand, had had centuries of world wide operations in which to develop bases all round the globe, perhaps because of these the spur to develop in a similar manner was lacking.

All this was fully realised and as a result every effort had been made with PQ 18 to fully ensure that everything that could be done to make this complicated procedure work smoothly was done. Initially it was stressed to all escorts that the conservation of oil fuel, especially by the destroyers the heaviest consumers, was essential and that every opportunity should be taken to keep their tanks topped up during lulls in the action.

The two fleet oilers that would accompany PQ 18, *Black Ranger* and *Grey Ranger*, were to transfer over to QP 14 with the Fighting Destroyer Escort when the time came. The additional oilers, *Oligarch* and *Blue Ranger*, were, as we have seen, stationed at Lowe Sound in Spitzbergen to enable the destroyers of the covering force to fuel on their outward and return journeys.

These oilers all embarked an extra working party over and above their normal complements consisting of a leading seaman and seven ratings to assist in working wires. All the oilers were fitted with sufficient hoses to oil by both trough and stirrup method at the same time thus enabling more than one vessel to be refuelled by each oiler if required. The *Oligarch*, *Blue Ranger* and *Grey Ranger* were unfortunately fitted with the British floating rubber hoses which were notoriously inefficient and prone to breakages and leaks, the *Black Ranger* was better equipped having the improved German floating rubber hose. This was based on designs found aboard German tankers captured when acting as supply ships to raiders in the distant oceans and was so superior to British types that even during the war they were named the 'German Type' hose to differentiate between them and the inferior British type.

It was therefore the practice for two destroyers to oil at sea from each oiler while weather conditions allowed and to further smooth the flow of this operation every Home Fleet destroyer was issued with a special spanner for working with the rubber hose. For those destroyers not so issued the oilers were instructed to attach a spare to the end of the rubber hose which the destroyer would re-attach to the end of the hose on completion of oiling. For those units which were using the trough method of oiling the oilers began to suck back after the valves in the destroyers had been shut off, whereas those utilising the rubber hoses ceased pumping when some five tons short on signal from the destroyer; the oiler would then blow the remaining contents in the hose into the destroyer's tanks before disconnecting. This ensured that every drop of the precious fluid was used and not wasted.

The destroyers were further instructed that as they would be required to top up on several occasions that they must make themselves proficient in the handling of wires and hoses to avoid any damage because the oilers could only carry so many spare sets.

With a final view to the safety of ship-to-ship fuelling during hostile attack the destroyers were given freedom at their discretion with regard to casting off and suspending fuelling operations while an air raid was in progress. Few, in the event, chose to spend this type of period dawdling along in tow of a floating inferno!

With refuelling so vital and the timing essential the forenoon of the 11th saw Admiral Burnett parting company with the convoy once more in order to set off for Bell Sound to refuel the two flotillas. However in view of the constant submarine alerts and warnings he decided not to take every destroyer he had but to leave three of them, the *Faulknor*, *Fury* and *Impulsive* of the 8th Flotilla, the most experienced and well equipped flotilla for anti-submarine operations, to further strengthen the close escort until the 6th and 17th Flotillas joined forces and he returned.

Accordingly, at 1140, the *Scylla* led the *Milne*, *Martin*, *Marne*, *Meteor* and *Intrepid* off to the northward. With the escort thus reduced, although under the skilled control of Allan Scott-Moncrieff, the first line of submarines began to close in on the convoy with fresh confidence.

In all some twelve U-boats were assigned to the 'Ice Palace' striking force that the Germans had ready to attack PQ 18, although British estimates later put the number at around thirty so effective and persistent were the efforts of these dozen. Despite having to face the most massive destroyer screen, when at full strength, of any Arctic convoy, or indeed any convoy with the exception of the *Pedestal* operation the previous month in the Mediterranean, the German submarine captains constantly took their craft in towards the convoy in repeated attempts to penetrate the ranks of the escorts.

Three U-boats formed the first line to give battle and they had been assigned the area between Spitzbergen and the Barents Sea so were quickly able to home on the early sighting reports. These boats were the *U-88* (Lieutenant-Commander Heinx Bohmann), *U-403* (Lieutenant-Commander Claussen) and *U-405* (Lieutenant-Commander Hopmann) but of these *U-88* was the closest and so were the four boats of the second line which therefore made contact earlier. These four were *U-377* (Lieutenant-Commander Koehler), *U-408* (Lieutenant-Commander von Hymmen), *U-589* (Lieutenant-Commander Horrer) and *U-592* (Lieutenant-Commander Bora).

A third line was being prepared consisting of boats at present hastily refuelling, *U-703* (Lieutenant-Commander Bielfeld), and *U-378* (Lieutenant-Commander Zetsche), with the two others already at sea and in their positions, *U-435* (Lieutenant-Commander Strelow) and *U-457* (Lieutenant-Commander Brandenburg). As has been recorded the twelve were completed by *U-456* (Lieutenant-Commander Teichert) initially stationed in an advance position, but now left well behind. It was on these boats that the main German naval effort against PQ 18 was to rest. Opposing them were some twenty destroyers, four corvettes, three minesweeping sloops, and four trawlers plus the *Avenger*'s three Swordfish and a few odd long-range aircraft from time to time along the route.

The fight for PQ 18 now began.


II


As if to mark the new phase of the operation soon after the departure of Rear-Admiral Burnett's force, both the *Fury* and the *Achates* reported anti-submarine contacts. At 1885 in position 70° 03′ N, 07° 18′ E the *Achates* dropped one depth charge

44

but this echo was later confirmed as a school of fish. Likewise the *Fury* attacked a contact at 1912 but no visible result of these attacks came to light and this was also called later a 'non-sub' contact.

Saturday, 12th September brought further indications that the Germans were now in close contact both underwater and in the air. The convoy varied speed and made several emergency turns and a large number of depth charges were dropped. The wind still blew from the north-west, force three. Fog in the morning gave way to low grey skies and good visibility in the afternoon. This had the inevitable result of bringing with it the Luftwaffe again after a long absence.

At 1235 a BV 138 float plane was observed which had obviously spotted the convoy. The weather conditions earlier had meant that *Avenger* had not flown off Swordfish patrols, but at 1245 the alarm bells sounded throughout the little carrier and at 1304 two sections of Sea Hurricanes were flown off to try and intercept this lumbering shadower; as they had been fully reported by this time, radar and wireless silence was relaxed to give the defences a chance to prepare for the expected attacks.

The four Sea Hurricanes found this first taste of combat an embarrassment rather than an ideal chance to cut their teeth, for despite their best efforts the BV 138 escaped unharmed. Both sections intercepted the shadower but could not get within range. One of the Sea Hurricanes did fire some twenty rounds per gun at a range of 400 yards but without effect and the German seaplane retired to the cover of the clouds which in places were reported down to sea level. The die was now cast for the forty merchantmen were now accurately pinpointed on the big operations maps at Banak and Bardufoss.

Although the convoy's route was to take them over 450 miles from these air bases to the limit of the summer ice caps, even this was to prove an insufficient detour to save them from the might of the Luftwaffe. However, no attack developed this day from the air although tension was screwed up to a new level.

Perhaps as a result of this there were some very odd reports. The Liberty ship *Virginia Dare* for example reported to the Commodore that they had intercepted on 165 kilocycles, close to a Finnish station, a series of Italian code-word messages. These were also apparently being broadcast in the vicinity of

45

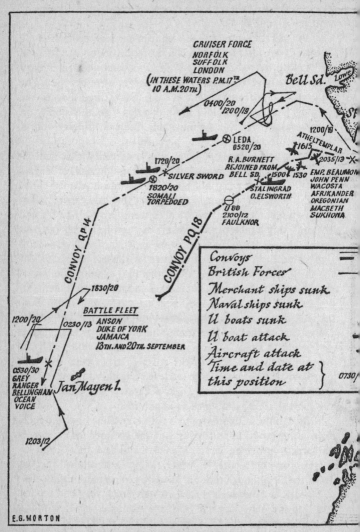

CRUISER FORCE
NORFOLK
SUFFOLK
LONDON
(IN THESE WATERS P.M.17TH
10 A.M.20TH.)

Bell Sd.

0400/20
1200/19

1200/19

ATHELTEMPLAR
1615

2035/13

LEDA
0520/20

R.A.BURNETT
REJOINED FROM
BELL SD.    1500    1530

EMP. BEAUMON
JOHN PENN
WACOSTA
AFRIKANDER
OREGONIAN
MACBETH
SUKHONA

1720/20
SILVER SWORD

1820/20
SOMALI
TORPEDOED

STALINGRAD
O.ELSWORTH

U88
2100/12
FAULKNOR

CONVOY QP 14

CONVOY PQ 18

1830/20

1200/20      0230/13

BATTLE FLEET
ANSON
DUKE OF YORK
JAMAICA
13TH. AND 20TH. SEPTEMBER

0530/30
GREY
RANGER
BELLINGHAM
OCEAN
VOICE

Jan Mayen I.

1203/12

Convoys
British Forces
Merchant ships sunk
Naval ships sunk
U boats sunk
U boat attack
Aircraft attack
Time and date at
this position

0730/

E.G. MORTON

Route of convoy and initial U-boat dispositions

# PQ 18–QP 14 SEPTEMBER 1942

ERGEN

Cape          Hope Island

1200/16          CONVOY QP 14

R.A. BURNETT –
JOINED
0300/17

89          M.LUCHENBACK          CONVOY PQ 18
5/14          1235/14
SLOW          1300                          1245–1535/15
1410
1430                                                    IMPULSIVE          0300/16
                                                        U 457

Bear Island

R.A.BURNETT
PARTED
COMPANY
1500/16

North Cape

Alten Fiord          Kola Inlet

dufoss                                                      Kolguev
vik                          0820–1030/18          C. Kanin
                            KENTUCKY

100          200 Miles

the convoy and were positively identified as Italian by a deck cadet of Italian origin who spoke the language. It was thought significant that submarines were near the convoy on both occasions.

Commander Russell aboard the *Malcolm* and Captain Scott-Moncrieff aboard the *Faulknor*, both veteran and expert U-boat hunters, confirmed that there were frequent H/F and M/F D/F bearings obtained from evening onward indicating the first wolf-pack was preparing for its first effort. In view of these reports the *Avenger* re-commenced her Swordfish patrols, and these were rewarded at 1955 when one of the 'Stringbags' sighted a U-boat with her conning tower awash some five miles ahead of the port wing column of the convoy. The Swordfish contacted Commander Russell by visual signal and the *Malcolm* increased speed and sped ahead to investigate.

*Malcolm* soon obtained a firm contact and one five-charge depth-charge pattern was dropped with the charges set to medium depth. This was followed by a ten-charge pattern set deep. When she was joined by the *Impulsive*, the contact was lost and therefore both ships re-joined the screen at 2200.

Meanwhile the *Faulknor* had been more successful. At 2103 in 75° 04' N, 04° 49' E, while Scott-Moncrieff was taking his destroyer over to reinforce the starboard side of the screen, his asdic operator reported a firm contact, classified as 'Submarine', bearing 345 degrees at a range of 2,100 yards. The echo was moderate low and the submarine appeared to be steering away with a slight zig-zag. This was the *U-88* and Lieutenant-Commander Bohmann was apparently trying to cross across the screen to position himself for an attack when he sighted *Faulknor* bearing down upon him and tried to hastily extradite his boat from a very dangerous position. In this he failed for the veteran team aboard the *Faulknor* had him firmly fixed.

A five-charge pattern was dropped at 2109 with the first and last charges set to 250 feet, the throwers to 150 feet and the centre charge at 100 feet. Some fifteen seconds after this pattern had exploded in *Faulknor*'s wake there was picked up a very loud noise of submarine tanks being blown or vented. It would appear that Scott-Moncrieff's first attack was deadly and the doomed Bohmann was desperately trying to blow his crippled command to the surface to save at least part of his crew.

The British destroyer had meanwhile swung round for a second attack but found that the echo was not so clear as before and only one depth charge was sent down, set to one hundred feet. Far below their keel the pulverised hull of *U-88* was already a lifeless hulk settling on the bottom of the ocean. The *Faulknor* steamed around the area through a large patch of strongly smelling oil and picked up a sample of it, which, when it was subsequently analysed, proved to be diesel. After searching for some fifteen minutes during which time no further contact was gained Scott-Moncrieff set course to re-join the convoy, leaving behind her the large and ever expanding pool of oil as the marker on the grave of forty men.

It was first blood to the escort but *U-88* was soon to be avenged.

At 0430 the next morning the 6th and 17th flotillas joined the convoy from Bell Sound but even before this, at 0345, the *Avenger* had flown off her first Swordfish for an early patrol. At 0600 this aircraft was rewarded with the sighting of a U-boat on the surface some twelve miles on the starboard quarter of the convoy. It dived on being sighted and was attacked with depth charges by the Swordfish without any visible result. The *Onslow* also made an attack on his contact in position 73° 35′ N, 06° 02′ E, again without result.

At 0745 a BV 138 shadower appeared and two sections of Sea Hurricanes were once again sent aloft to try and intercept her. This proved to be a repetition of the earlier fiasco and although the leading Sea Hurricane opened fire at 500 yards the seaplane escaped into the clouds once more. From this time onward the convoy was under continual air observation.

At 0815 one of the Swordfish spotted another U-boat on the surface some twenty miles astern of the convoy patiently following it and transmitting homing signals in the classic manner. This U-boat dived when the Swordfish was still some three miles distant and no accurate position could be selected for a depth charge attack. The approximate position of this contact was passed by visual signal to one of the escorts but no action was taken by them.

By this time no less than two of the pack were submerged at periscope depth in good attacking positions astern of the convoy. Both the *U-408* and *U-589*'s captains chose almost identical moments to press the firing button and their targets were ships in column ten. At 0855 two of their torpedoes struck home on ships of the convoy.

Although it was thought at the time that a single submarine had fired browning shots from outside the screen, subsequent analysis seemed to indicate the contrary and indeed the two U-boat skippers made their claims quite independently of each other in their subsequent broadcasts. Von Hymmen claimed a single steamer of 7,000 tons sunk in pinpoint 2569, while Horrer claimed he had sunk a 7,000 ton steamer in pinpoint 2566.

The Stalingrad was apparently hit by a single torpedo on the starboard side and she sank within fifteen minutes. A woman mate aboard the Soviet ship was pregnant and went into labour at the time of the attack. Her child was stillborn. This was the only casualty and rescue ships and escorts were soon on the scene to pick up the survivors. There had been no chance of saving the vessel. Lieutenant Blake Hughes aboard the *Patrick Henry* thought she was hit by *two* torpedoes and reported that she sank, 'rapidly', while Lieutenant De Foe of the *Esek Hopkins* recalled that she sank in five minutes. The Stalingrad was only a small freighter, of some 3,560 tons, and would certainly not stand up to two torpedoes.

The second victim was the large Liberty ship *Oliver Ellsworth*, of about double the tonnage, and she was hit by a single torpedo. She was proceeding at a speed of nine knots and had a full cargo of aircraft and munitions aboard. The torpedo struck her on the starboard side between numbers four and five holds and the damage was almost entirely below the waterline and invisible. Her engines were secured within three minutes. Because of the torpedoing of the *Stalingrad* ahead of her just minutes before, the *Oliver Ellsworth* was under hard left rudder to avoid hitting her when she herself was struck.

The captain gave the order to abandon ship when hit and all hands, with the exception of one of the Armed Guard party, got safely aboard the lifeboats.

Among the vessels which closed and picked up these was the trawler *St Kenan*. The convoy commodore had ordered an immediate emergency turn when *Stalingrad* had been hit but this was too late to save the *Oliver Ellsworth*. None the less she showed little sign of sinking immediately and her master protested that it was impossible to sink a Liberty ship with just one torpedo and that she might be saved yet.

However with no rescue tug to take her in tow there was little chance of this. Observers reported that this Liberty ship sank very slowly by the stern. Lieutenant Mackay of the *St Kenan* picked up the Master and three other survivors from a raft; he agreed that the *Ellsworth* could perhaps have been saved and kept afloat had provision been made for it, but in view of subsequent air attacks she would have been a sitting duck and would not have lasted very long. The minesweeper *Sharpshooter* picked up another thirty of the *Ellsworth*'s crew. There was nothing for it but to send her and her valuable cargo to the bottom and, an hour after she had been hit, she finally went down after being shelled.

Meanwhile the destroyers *Offa*, *Onslaught* and *Opportune* were sent back to carry out an anti-submarine sweep but without result. In the convoy this attack caused some alarm. The *Nathaniel Green* reported the sighting of a periscope about one hundred yards off her starboard beam. Fire was immediately opened up on this object with machine-gun, but her Armed Guard reported that the periscope was so close that the oerlikons would not bear. This contact vanished, only to re-appear about five hundred yards away off the starboard bow of the *Virginia Dare* and the *Nathaniel Green* commenced firing again. The object again vanished soon after this and three destroyers arrived over the spot and dropped a number of depth charges.

At 0945 the *Onslaught* out ahead of the starboard wing ship of the convoy some 2,200 yards obtained a distant asdic contact at about 2,000 yards range, classified as 'doubtful'. None the less a counter-attack was made and on her run-in to the target the echo was reaffirmed as 'submarine'. In position 75° 54′ N, 07° 50′ *Onslaught* attacked with a five-charge pattern set at fifty feet. There was no apparent result of this attack and contact was subsequently lost when the convoy passed over the spot a few minutes later but it was thought that a submarine was detected whilst endeavouring to penetrate the screen and that *Onslaught*'s counter attack had prevented a torpedo attack on the convoy's starboard wing ships.

There were now estimated to be eight U-boats in contact with PQ 18 and contact quickly followed contact. At 1050 the

*Avenger* had flown off two sections of fighters to intercept the total of five shadowers that were now in sight around the horizon. Several interceptions were made and fire was opened but all the shadowers melted away into the low cloud before they could be brought under effective attack.

At 1100 one of the Swordfish reported that she had observed one of the BV 138s dropping an object into the sea some fifteen miles ahead of the convoy. Thinking that this might be a floating mine, several of which had been observed earlier, Captain Scott-Moncrieff suggested that the convoy make an emergency turn to port of 45° and this was in fact carried out.

Meanwhile the same Swordfish sighted a surfaced U-boat ten miles ahead of the convoy. She reported this sighting by V/S but her attempts to keep in contact with the submarine were frustrated by the unwelcome attentions of the BV 138 which drove the old 'Stringbag' away and then patrolled over the U-boat.

Back in the convoy itself the minesweeper *Sharpshooter* obtained a good asdic contact at 1215 and counter-attacked with a three-charge depth-charge pattern. After five minutes contact was regained and a hunt was commenced. The destroyer *Tartar* was sent to assist in this search astern of the convoy, and she definitely confirmed the contact as 'submarine'. Meanwhile after the first contact *Sharpshooter* observed the U-boat's conning tower partially break the surface and then submerge. *Sharpshooter* delivered three more attacks herself and the *Tartar* made two, with three- and five-charge patterns. There was no visible result from *Tartar*'s attacks but *Sharpshooter* reported that she had another sighting of a conning tower and air bubbles were seen on the surface. Contact was finally lost with this promising target at 1219 and the *Sharpshooter* returned to catch up with the convoy.

Still further contacts had been obtained during her absence, the *Onslaught* counter-attacking another in position 75° 2′ N, 09° 8′ E with two depth charges from her traps set at 50 and 150 feet respectively. After her depth charges had exploded a large amount of periscope was sighted abeam of the leading ships of the starboard wing column. Asdic contact was regained between the two convoy columns and the attack went on between the watching freighters.

Because of the close proximity of the merchantmen however, an accurate attack was impossible nor could the full spread of the throwers be used. Instead *Onslaught* fired two charges from the traps astern at 1216 with the same staggered depth settings. After this all contact was lost in the middle of the convoy lanes amidst the churning wakes of thrashing propellers of forty merchant ships. Again it was thought certain that prompt action by *Onslaught* had prevented a determined attack. The *Faulknor* also briefly confirmed a contact at this time.

At 1357 a Swordfish once again sighted a surfaced U-boat some twelve miles on the port bow of the convoy. It dived and was attacked with depth-charges and its position was reported by V/S to the nearest destroyer which took no action. The Swordfish did not tarry for she sighted warships coming up over the horizon and scurried off to investigate them.

The persistence of the U-boats in attempting to penetrate the strong screen was certainly matched by the skill and alertness of the destroyers themselves, and the two merchantmen were their only rewards this day. There is no doubt that the use of lightly trained destroyer units to supplement the escort was a great boon for PQ 18 even though, as we shall see, their principal function was to deter surface attack. The well planned and executed anti-submarine measures derived from the detailed plans laid down for Operation 'EV' by the staff of the Home Fleet Flotillas.

These stipulated that, if a contact was obtained outside the screen the ship next but one outwards from that obtaining the contact was to join the hunting ship while the destroyers positioned astern where to move up and fill the gaps thus left. If the contact was gained inside the screen then these spare destroyers were to assist in the hunt.

Positive contacts were to be hunted by Home Fleet destroyers for two hours only to conserve fuel, or by Western Approaches destroyers or escorts for one hour, and the slow trawlers were given strict instructions not to allow themselves to drop back more than three miles in any search. Furthermore, with the fuel situation uppermost in his mind, Rear-Admiral Burnett had instructed that no hunt was to be continued longer than an hour and a half after contact had been lost.

Distant sightings of U-boats by the aircraft patrols were to be dealt with according to the prevailing situation; if possible a striking force of three destroyers would be sent out. But the most frequently used operation of this anti-submarine plan was that given the code name 'GRAB'. This went into effect if any ship on the screen had reason to suspect that a submarine had penetrated the screen and was diving under the convoy. On receipt of this code word all the rear escorts were to move up towards the convoy dropping not more than two depth-charges at spaced intervals to keep such a submarine down. As we have seen, this routine worked well as a deterrent and the only other claim made by the German submarines this day was one by *U-589* that she had fired two torpedoes at the aircraft carrier and might have scored a hit. However, this information was soon digested by Oslo command and subsequent reports from the numerous shadowing aircraft quickly confirmed that the *Avenger* was still very much among those present.

Meanwhile what of Rear-Admiral Burnett and his remaining destroyers?

## III

After leaving the convoy on the 11th he had set course for Bell Sound with the *Scylla*, the destroyers of the 3rd flotilla and *Intrepid*. He later admitted that he had a great feeling of insecurity during this passage for he had no means of communicating with the convoy's remaining screen during the many thick patches for he was extremely reluctant to use the Fleet wave, low power. The reason for this was that on many previous occasions such transmissions had been picked up considerably further than was intended and could easily be located and used as D/F beacons by the wolf packs. Rear-Admiral Burnett later commented that a good means of VHF communication would have been invaluable as so often before.

On Saturday 12th the weather became very cold with some fog and snow showers but one tiny morsel of good news was that aerial reconnaissance had revealed that at the moment the *Scheer*, *Hipper* and *Köln* were still snugly in Altenfiord.

At 2010 the force passed through the entrance to Bell Sound, which was reported as narrow and beset by strong tidal streams. It was therefore suited to defence and ideal for the purpose to which it was being put. Here they found the destroyer *Windsor* anchored just inside Axelfiord and she had also established a signal station at the entrance. By 2145 the head of the fiord was reached and there, tucked safely away from prying eyes, they found Force 'P', the oilers *Oligarch* and *Blue Ranger*. All ships quickly began topping up.

This high-speed fuelling was carried out all night without respite and by 0400 on Sunday 13th *Scylla*, *Milne*, *Martin*, *Marne*, *Meteor* and *Intrepid* sailed to rejoin the convoy. Visibility was good and as a result by 0855 they had been picked up by a Ju 88 and later this was joined by a He 111. The destroyer *Milne* loosened off a few rounds of 4.7-inch shells from her special A/A mounts and this aircraft vanished into the safety of the cloud banks.

They sped on to join PQ 18, now very much at bay in hostile waters apparently teeming with their enemy and with the skies full of watchers overhead. At 1130 Rear-Admiral Burnett received the *Faulknor*'s report of the two merchantmen being torpedoed and sunk. With this as an added spur course was altered to starboard and speed increased in order to affect as early a rendezvous as possible.

Just under three hours later the masts of PQ 18 came into sight off the *Scylla*'s port bow, steering 070° at a speed of seven and a half knots. The shadowing Ju 88 overhead was then joined by two others. If Rear-Admiral Burnett was glad to see the convoy then the sight of the *Scylla* and the five destroyers, bow waves creaming as they steered in to bring the screen up to full strength, was a much needed tonic to the men of the merchant vessels themselves.

Commodore Boddam-Whetham was to recall that moment with thankfulness later:

Nothing could have been more heartening when, at 1417, on September 13th, two ships having been torpedoed that morning and high and low level bombing [imminent], Rear Admiral (D) and Force 'B' were sighted.[3]

This elation was soon to receive a sharp knock however. As the *Scylla* and her companions steamed hard for the convoy the *Avenger* was observed from the cruiser's bridge to draw out of the convoy and fly off five of her Sea Hurricanes. Clearly the Luftwaffe was now about to take a hand in the proceedings.

IV

In fact the screen was still in the process of forming up at its maximum strength and the *Scylla* was heading for her place out ahead of the convoy when, at 1435, a large group of enemy aircraft was reported at a range of sixty-two miles. At 1450 one group of Sea Hurricanes was flown off to patrol in the direction of the contact and at 1503 some six separate groups were being reported by the radar.

A short time later, at 1525, the Sea Hurricanes were reporting that they were in contact with five Junkers Ju 88s which they chased into a cloud. They had expended all their ammunition in making feint attacks and no more fighters were immediately available to reinforce them.

Over the convoy itself at 1500 the first of these bombers began its attack and this continued intermittently for twenty-five minutes or so. Only about six Ju 88s broke through the defending fighters; the rest played a game of hide and seek in and out of the clouds. Of these six, each made individual bombing runs out of the cloud cover through convenient gaps, and the convoy replied at intervals whenever they could, without much success. It was a frustrating business and although some bombs were dropped right in among the convoy lanes no ship was actually hit.

To many of the watching seamen it seemed a tame event after they had keyed themselves up to expect something far worse.

The minesweeper *Gleaner* was attacked from out of the clouds by a solitary Ju 88 from astern but his bombs fell wide to the starboard and return fire from the minesweepers 20-mm Oerlikons was thought to have hit in reply. The *Exford* was near missed by two heavy bombs without result.

Ensign Rooker aboard the *Campfire* reported that:

> High waves [sic] of German bombers appeared dropping a number of bombs but causing no damage. There was no warning given before this attack occurred. Most of the merchant ships fired on this occasion, using machine-guns to large extent although the planes were out of range.[34]

Unfortunately this wild, undisciplined firing, which merely at best wasted ammunition, and at worse endangered the crews and gunners of nearby vessels, was to continue after this initial teething and not grow better. This lack of control was much commented upon later, although on first close sight of German aircraft it was understandable that the gunners would wish to hit back.

Lieutenant Blake Hughes of the *Patrick Henry* made a careful analysis of all these attacks in his report. Although the Admiralty press release later described this first air raid as 'high-level bombing', Hughes reasoned, quite correctly, it was not in fact so:

> I believe the attack would be more accurately described as medium, or low level, bombing because the planes flew just above an almost continuous layer of low dark grey cloud at some 2,000 to 3,000 feet altitude and dropped their bomb loads through gaps in the clouds.
>
> Two or three bombs were dropped simultaneously. One dud was observed. This type of bombing proved highly ineffectual in this attack. These first planes venturing over the convoy met terrific fire, particularly from the merchant ships 20-mm guns.[35]

The *Esek Hopkins* had a stick of bombs drop some 500 yards off the starboard beam but that was all.

Again, as in the case of anti-submarine operations, a prearranged fighting plan had been worked out for the Fighting Destroyer Escort during air attacks, although the emphasis had been placed on true dive bombing or torpedo attack at low level. Certainly third degree HA readiness was at all times maintained and, on the *Scylla* hoisting a red flag, first degree readiness against bombing was to be assumed.

The destroyer screen was carefully arranged to give what was hopefully expressed as 'maximum protection' against torpedo bomber and dive bomber attack. Again a code word was issued, PACK, on receipt of which all the destroyers were to close up against dive bombing. However dive bombing as such did not take place, rather a general kind of shallow bombing for which there was little time to prepare a standard defence as the aircraft appeared suddenly out of the holes in the cloud.

To maintain an umbrella barrage over the ships of the convoy those destroyers left on the outer screen were to lay down fire in a fixed pattern, those of the port screen over the left wing of the convoy, those to starboard over the right wing and those stationed in the van over the centre of the merchant ships. This umbrella of flak was to be fired at 20° elevation only and with a fuse setting to plan range. Economy of ammunition and restraint were emphasised.

Against the threat of torpedo bombing it was admitted that it was unlikely for the convoy to receive anything but a late visual warning, for low flying attacks of this nature wave-hopped *under* the radar screens. Therefore the destroyers on the screen were instructed to give instant warning at once by immediately opening fire and by broadcasting an alarm report. Particular vigilance against dusk attacks by torpedo bombers was always stressed, this being the best time for a surprise attack of this nature. A blind barrage was to be laid down in the event of this happening with the aircraft being merged with the dusk horizon and smoke was to be laid by the destroyers. An additional warning against such an attack was for the destroyers to flick their fighting lights on and off should they sight torpedo aircraft at dusk.

Thus every provision was allowed for and each ship was prepared for the worst the Germans could do. It had been proven quite clearly earlier in the war on repeated occasions however, that anti-aircraft firepower alone was not always enough to stop an enemy air attack if it was determinedly led and rigidly driven home. Few aircrews had the training and the courage to do this and the ever increasing anti-aircraft weaponry becoming available to warships and merchantmen was making the easy sinkings of warships a thing of the past. It was known that the Germans had increased their forces in Norway by the provision of extra torpedo bombers, but the precise numbers, and, more important, their calibre and skill, were of course unknown factors, the few examples known to date being of too small a nature to draw firm conclusions from.

Because the Germans had not been able to mount saturation air shadowing until the 12th and no large scale attack had developed up to that time the gunners on warship and merchantmen alike were all suffering from lack of practice. It always took several sessions of hard firing to knock even a proficient gun's crew back into form after a lay-off from actual action. PQ 18's gunners were not to get this vital period. Furthermore a large proportion of the gunners were far from experienced. Certainly none of the merchantmen had been subjected to a really heavy air attack directed at them. Of the escorts the Western Approaches vessels were similarly more concerned with the problems of anti-submarine defence than air attack out in the wastes of the North Atlantic.

The most experienced guns' crews were those aboard the fleet destroyers for even the *Scylla* was a brand new ship and had not yet fired guns in anger, albeit mounting a powerful battery on paper. The 8th and 17th flotillas had had mainly Arctic and North Atlantic experience in recent months, with not much air attack. The 3rd flotilla were the most powerful vessels by far in the convoy, but again had served mainly with the Home Fleet. The 6th flotilla therefore remained the most recently blooded unit for they had recently returned from the Mediterranean and Operation *Pedestal*, the August convoy to Malta. This convoy had been subjected to the heaviest air attacks ever mounted against British merchant ships and had suffered heavy losses. Certainly the skippers of *Ashanti*, *Eskimo* and *Tartar* were under no illusions of what a real air attack would be like, and Richard Onslow later recalled how he had pulled strings to stuff every available oerlikon he could aboard his *Ashanti*, including one right aft among the depth charge throwers.

This was the state of PQ 18's defences against the Luftwaffe.

At 1540 *Avenger*'s radar reported a group of aircraft were approaching the convoy at high speed. Aboard the *Scylla* out ahead of the convoy Robert Hughes was listening to the radar reports as they were passed through to his Director which controlled the cruisers main armament.

The voice in the headset spoke again.
'Director, there's a twenty-five plus echo in the east coming in fast!'
'What?' I faltered incredulously.
'Twenty-five plus!' said the voice clearly and slowly.
I spoke to Mead.
'Train right, about Green One-oh to Green Two-oh, and scan. There's a big gang coming in from about there!'

Mead trained slowly right, and down below the voice of Number
One came clearly to us over the battle commentary.

'We have now joined the convoy, and are leading one of the
columns. The escort are now in their places, and the *Avenger* is
on the port column. Radar have reported a twenty-five plus echo
headed towards us, and this will be a serious attack.'

'Aircraft!' The word came up to us shrilly, and we saw them at
the same time.*

* *Through the Waters*, William Kimber, 1956.

# Chapter Three

# The Golden Comb

## I

The convoy was now about to face its most severe test. It was known that the Luftwaffe had been steadily building up the strength of its torpedo bomber force in Norway. What was not expected was the strength that was available to the Germans at this time. It was not thought to be high for it had not been until early the previous year that the Luftwaffe had started to take a serious interest in the air-launched torpedo at all. The Royal Air Force had, through its control of the Fleet Air Arm in the inter-war years, some twenty years' experience in torpedo bombing techniques, and yet they had only been able to build up a very small force by 1942 (three squadrons of Beauforts in the Mediterranean and four Hampden squadrons at home). It was not therefore thought very likely that the Luftwaffe could mount more than a small scale attack at this time, similar to those thrown against PQ 16. This, however, was far from the case.

Ever since 1926 German torpedo development had been the sole responsibility of the Navy, and, with the expansion of all forces on the Fuehrer's assumption of power, the Kriegsmarine had purchased the patents of the Horten naval torpedo from Norway. Five years later greater harmony had been reached with the Italians, who were pioneers in modern torpedo bombing ideas in the 1930s, and this led to the acquisition of the White-head Fiume patents. Trials held by the embryo Naval Air Squadrons, utilising Heinkel He 59 and He 115 floatplanes, were far from encouraging. In 1939, for example, these trials resulted in a forty-nine per cent failure rate, due to depth control and fusing problems and the normal difficulties of launching torpedoes from aircraft, the finding of the most suitable height, speed and deflection for such attacks.

Thus it was that the German Navy's floatplane squadrons, of

which there were only two in operation during the early years of the war, were not a powerful instrument of air/sea warfare like the British Fleet Air Arm or the Italian *Aerosilurante* units at that time. Indeed shortages of torpedoes and the small size of the force meant that only small and inconsequential results had been achieved. The dispute between the Luftwaffe and the Navy reached absurd levels. For example the Navy's He 115 float plane units were designated 'general purpose' squadrons. Although they were legitimate torpedo-carrying aircraft they were, from the strict Luftwaffe viewpoint, for reconnaissance purposes only, for all striking power was to be reserved solely for the Luftwaffe itself.

In 1939 the Luftwaffe Coastal Air Force Command was abolished and the Luftwaffe officer Geisler was attached to the Navy Command with control over all the coastal air (*Seefliegerstaffeln*) units. By 1941 the Luftwaffe could contrast the British successes of Taranto and the heavy losses suffered by both sides in the Mediterranean at the hands of the torpedo bomber, with the almost total failure of orthodox bombing methods when used against shipping. Only the Junkers Ju 87 *Stuka* units had made any impression against warships because of their dive bombing accuracy, but their range was limited and they could make little impact outside coastal waters. Interest was therefore aroused in the use of the aerial torpedo by the Luftwaffe but this interest was, in turn, stoutly opposed by the Navy. According to the files of Milch, data on aerial torpedo development practice, which had been built up over the preceding years by the Navy, was deliberately withheld from the *Technisches Amt* (the Technical Department of the Luftwaffe), as also were approaches to private firms for collaboration and independent testing and trials.

Direct requests to take over all aerial torpedo development was turned down absolutely by the Kriegsmarine. Meanwhile increasing casualties were being taken by the two specialised anti-shipping bomber groups, *Geschwader*, KG 26 and KG 30, in the face of improved anti-aircraft defences and so the Air Force started to set up, despite the lack of assistance from the Navy, its own torpedo bombing trials school. This was established at Grossenbrode on the Baltic coast.

The almost incredible rivalry between these two arms of the

German forces had, by the end of 1940, resulted in Goering having, on 26th November, the Navy's own modest aerial torpedo operations halted, while production of the standard 1,686 pound LTF-5b air torpedo was, for a time, suspended as well, with the result that by 27th November the Quartermaster General's office reported that only 132 remained for operational use.

Exhaustive trials at Grossenbrode had meantime shown that the twin-engined Heinkel He 111H was a most suitable vehicle with which to launch aerial torpedoes and the Luftwaffe was eager to put them to a practical test. Thus was born the plan to attack Admiral Cunningham's Mediterranean Fleet in Alexandria harbour. In the autumn of 1941 therefore were despatched some He 111s to Eleusis airfield near Athens to carry this attack out. However the operation had to be abandoned. This was due to the intervention of Grand Admiral Raeder, head of the Kriegsmarine. He had a personal interview with the Fuehrer in the autumn of 1941 when he pointed out that by pressing ahead with their own schemes the Luftwaffe had caused the Navy's air operations against British coastal shipping to be broken off. He also indicated that Goering's proposed operation was unsound, although the Italians had attempted it.

Hitler therefore ordered an investigation of the whole affair and the Technical Department concluded that aerial torpedoes dropped in the harbour at Alexandria would probably merely dive to the sea bed from the proposed dropping height of one hundred feet. This verdict, coupled with the lack of torpedoes and the non-arrival of warheads in Greece, therefore saw the complete abandonment of the proposed attack. Moreover this led Admiral Kurt Fricke to demand both that the Navy's coastal operations should be resumed and, further, that they be equipped with the modern He 111s!

Goering was duly informed of this and within a short time the Luftwaffe was demanding in reply that they should take over the aerial torpedo programme in both Germany and Italy. Further that it should open more experimental bases, incorporate all naval personnel already engaged in such work and that a special commissioner be appointed to supervise all aerial torpedo development, supply, training and operations.

This was promptly agreed to and Generalmajor Harlinghausen,

who had served in the Navy from 1923 to 1933, and had conducted anti-shipping operations in command of *Fliegerkorps X*, was appointed Inspector of Aircraft Torpedoes in January 1942. At the same time he was appointed OC of *KG 26*, the 'Lion' *Geschwader*, which was the first unit selected for conversion of torpedo bombing.

The whole project was enthusiastically backed by Goering and Harlinghausen set about the formation and rapid enlargement of his force with great zest. Not all the Luftwaffe was converted to the idea of torpedo bombing however, despite the outstanding example of the Japanese Fleet Air Arm at this time during the opening phase of the Pacific War. Oberst Koller, Chief of Staff of *Luftflotte III*, for example, voiced the common viewpoint of Air Force officers of both sides during the war when he asked why it was necessary to drop a missile in the shape of a torpedo into the sea in front of a ship when a bomb could be dropped directly on to it. A similar query was raised by an RAF officer who could not see the point of carrying a torpedo into action in a 300 mph aircraft and then releasing it to cover the last part of its journey at 50 mph. Both men of course ignored completely the effect of a torpedo punching a hole below the waterline of a ship and the wasted effect of the small and inaccurately aimed bombs used at that period on a ship's upperworks.

Despite such comments the ultimate Luftwaffe plans envisaged a total torpedo bomber strength of 230 aircraft, all by conversions from existing bomber units. Also the Luftwaffe torpedo bombing school was moved from the now iced-in base at Grossenbrode to Grosseto on the west coast of Italy, where training could continue under more favourable conditions. Another valid reason for this move was that Grosseto was near to the Italian naval base of Leghorn and therefore close liaison could be kept with the new developments of long established *Aerosilurante* units of the Regia Aeronautica. Here was established *Kampschulgeschwader* 2 (*KSG* 2), under the command of Oberstleutnant Stockmann, and other experienced anti-shipping pilots, with Major Werner Klumper as chief instructor.

Extensive tests were carried out against the target vessel *Citta di Genova* which showed that low level attacks under the radar screens and from two separate directions would ensure minimum casualties. Tests took place with all types of standard Luftwaffe bombers, but it was the Heinkel 111, already well proven, which was the first to be generally adopted for the task as the He 111H-6.

With a crew of four this aircraft had a wingspan of 74 feet 11½ inches, a length of 54 feet 5½ inches, a height of 13 feet 9 inches and had a wing area of 942,917 square feet. It was powered by two Junkers *Jumo* 211F-2 twelve-cylinder, liquid-cooled engines of 1,060 hp giving a maximum speed of 258 mph at 16,400 feet. The service ceiling was 25,500 feet and range was some 760 miles when armed with two of the standard naval torpedoes mounted externally, although this was later increased.

The technique as developed at Grosseto was for the aircraft to approach the target at a height of about 40 to 50 metres and for the release to be at a range of at least 600 metres from the target. Against slow moving merchant ships the torpedoes would have a pre-set 'angle of lead' to compensate for a speed of ten knots, with the final adjustment being made in the last minutes of the approach. The torpedoes were released by the aircraft mechanic on instructions from the observer. This system caused a time lag which was a slight disadvantage as conditions might change in the brief interval.

In order to release at the correct moment the Heinkel did not have sufficient time to turn away before reaching the target. Therefore, after release, the aircraft was taken down to sea level and turned only after flying past the bow or stern of the ship under attack. This was the point of extreme vulnerability for the torpedo bomber, and it was obvious that if a diversionary attack could be made by dive bombing to draw away some of the anti-aircraft fire the bombers would have a greater chance of survival.

The first unit to be converted was the first *Staffel* of twelve aircraft of *I/KG* 26 whose aircrew were withdrawn in batches from north Norway to undergo the three-week torpedo course at Grosseto during the spring of 1942. By the end of April the initial twelve crews were ready and were transferred back to the specially constructed airfields of Banak, near the north coast at North Cape, and Bardufoss, south of Tromso, both units being connected by teleprinter link with headquarters of Luftflotte 5 at Oslo. *I/KG* 26 participated in attacks against convoy PQ 16 during the period 25th to 30th May and had sunk one of the seven ships the British lost from that operation.

By June 1942 *I/KG 26*, led by Oberstleutnant Hermann Busch, was at a strength of forty-two Heinkels and *III/KG 26* was at Grosseto training with Junkers Ju 88A-17s which had a higher operational speed than the He 111. The twin-engined bomber was an adaptation of the standard Ju 88A-4 and was powered by two Junkers *Jumo* 211J-1 twelve-cylinder, liquid-cooled engines, developing 1,350 hp and giving a maximum speed of 270 mph at 17,500 feet with a range of 650 miles fully laden. The inboard carriers under the wings were adapted to take two of the standard naval torpedoes.

The lessons learnt from PQ 16 were to form the basis of revised tactics when sufficient torpedo bombers became available. This was the *Goldene Zange* (Golden Comb) operation whereby combined dive and torpedo bombing attacks were to take place in conditions of half light, with the torpedo bombers approaching in wide line abreast and launching all their torpedoes simultaneously against the solid bulk of the convoy's ships silhouetted against the lighter sky.

*I/KG 26* accordingly went into action against PQ 17 on 4th July but co-ordination was faulty and they lost two aircraft in the attack while scoring hits on only two of the convoy.

By the time PQ 18 sailed *I/KG 26* had been reinforced by *III/KG 26* with their thirty-five Ju 88s which had been operating from Rennes in France, and so Luftflotte 5, under Generaloberst Hans-Jurgen Stumpff, could deploy a total of ninety-two torpedo bombers.

As has been frequently suggested this decision was brought about by the incorrect belief that it was the attacks of the Luftwaffe which had caused the break up of PQ 17 instead of the reported sailing of the *Tirpitz* and her battle group, which led to great confidence in the Luftwaffe units and in particular of Goering himself. The news that PQ 18 was escorted by an aircraft carrier had determined that this vessel was to be initially the major target.

As has been suggested frequently this decision was brought about by Reichsmarschall Goering's obsession with the fact that 'his' Luftwaffe had never sunk a British carrier, and on this occasion he was determined to do so. Certainly the much publicised bombing attack by *KG 30* on the *Ark Royal* early in the war, and the overplaying of the claim to have sunk her, had rebounded upon Goering when it was subsequently proven to be false. And certainly also the Luftwaffe had not succeeded in destroying any carrier in all the air/sea fighting up to that time, although the Stukas had on three occasions in the Mediterranean come very close to it with their highly punishing attacks on *Illustrious* in January 1941, *Formidable* in May 1941 and *Indomitable* in August 1942. Therefore to sink the little *Avenger* would certainly have been a long sought after feather in Goering's cap.*

In fact the Reichsmarschall issued a stirring directive to his aircrews urging, 'The attack against the aircraft carrier must be so violent that this threat is removed.'

This directive is quoted in the Operational Report of Luftflotte 5, apparently in an attempt to justify this course of action, for it is clear that the Kriegsmarine did not approve of throwing everything at the *Avenger*; in their opinion the only vital targets as far as the war effort was concerned were the merchant vessels with their cargoes of bombs, tanks and ammunition for the Eastern Front. Preventing the propping up of the faltering Soviet giant was a more worthwhile objective in their view than the prestige of sinking one small and ancient aircraft carrier. (Remember that the *Avenger* was thought to be the *Argus*.)

However it cannot be denied that this early elimination of the carrier would facilitate the later destruction of the merchantmen as Goering, in fairness, fully appreciated.

Only when this succeeds can we combine violent bombing and violent torpedo attacks to finish off the rest of the formation.[49]

However desirable this was it was still a side issue for it was obvious that the new factor presented by the appearance of an aircraft carrier on the Arctic convoy route invalidated the main lessons absorbed so far. All training had concentrated on attacking low in the face of anti-aircraft fire only. To have single-engined fighters to contend with in addition to this hazard, was

* Alas for the Reichsmarschall, this cherished ambition was never to be achieved. Particularly unpalatable for him was the fact that the weapons he scorned most, the capital ships of the Kriegsmarine, were themselves more successful, for they had sunk the *Glorious* off Norway in 1940, while the U-Boats sank the *Courageous*, *Ark Royal*, *Audacity* and *Eagle* as well as the battleships *Royal Oak* and *Barham*. The *Aerosilurante* of his despised ally had also claimed the sinking of *Eagle* and was widely believed – this claim, although untrue, must have been additionally galling to Goering at this time, while his other ally's Fleet Air Arm had quickly and simply sunk five American battleships, two British capital ships and the carrier *Hermes*, which added to his feeling of frustration.

an added complication and one which very little could be done about. The only fighter aircraft available to Stumpff's Luftflotte were the high performance Me 109Gs of JG 5 and although these aircraft were far superior to anything flown by the Fleet Air Arm, they did not have the range to accompany the bombers in their attacks out in the Barents Sea. The only solution then was for the carrier to be singled out as the first target and given absolute priority. Once she was despatched the attacking formations could concentrate on the trained task of eliminating the mercantile vessels.

Again, in order to eliminate the carrier quickly, it was considered essential that convoy and escort be surprised before all the fighter aircraft could be launched, or, alternately, that these fighters if already in the air, be drawn away from the vulnerable torpedo bombers. This task had therefore been entrusted to the dive bombing Ju 88s of *KG* 30 and, as we have seen, had proved only too successful.

At Bardufoss airfield the new commander of *I/KG* 26 attended the final briefing of his aircrew. They were among the most experienced of the Luftwaffe's torpedo bomber men and many had attacked PQ 17. Major Werner Klumper had only recently joined the unit to replace Hauptmann Bernot Eicke, commander of *III/KG* 26 who, as senior *Staffel* commander had earlier acted as the temporary *Gruppen* commander. Major Klumper was equally experienced however for he had been the chief instructor of the *KSG* at Grosseto.

The crews were told of the composition of the convoy, its escort, speed and approximate course. They were also told the fact that it was being reinforced by a 'carrier and six destroyers'. They were reminded of the Army's great achievements in the conquest of the Caucasus and the push to Stalingrad and how a victory against the Allied convoy would mean easier conditions at the front-line for their comrades.

The attacking force was to strike at the convoy that afternoon, twenty-eight He 111 torpedo bombers in two waves immediately after *III/KG* 30 had made its diversionary attack with twenty Ju 88 dive bombers, and they were to be reinforced for this major assault by the eighteen Ju 88 torpedo bombers of *III/KG* 26 commanded by Hauptmann Klaus Nocken from Banak airfield near Hammerfest with seventeen Ju 88s of *I/KG* 30 from the same base. A special effort was called for to eliminate the carrier for the reasons we have discussed. When the torpedo bombers were within a half hour's flying time of the target they were to be met by one of the shadowing Ju 88s who would then lead them straight to it to help in the element of surprise.

It was late in the afternoon when the Heinkels took off from Bardufoss and flew down Malangerfiord and over the lonely Lofoten Islands to form up over the sea before the rendezvous with Nocken's force. The attack was due to hit PQ 18 some 400 miles or so from their bases and the Heinkels and Junkers flew at an economical speed to conserve fuel. At low level they thundered north-west across the icy wave-crests toward the distant convoy for two hours. The cloud base was reported at 2,450 feet with light rain and drizzle which soon reduced visibility down to a mere six miles.

Little wonder then that on their outward track Major Klumper's force missed both the convoy and the guiding aircraft. Almost at their extreme endurance for the outward leg the formation turned east and fortunately for them soon sighted the solid phalanx of PQ 18 below them. Despite determined efforts to locate the carrier, however, she was not spotted. Furthermore the lack of British fighters over the convoy was noted, which led some to assume that the earlier precise intelligence reports had been in error. By hunting for *Avenger* the aircraft were wasting time and the flak from the outer destroyer screen was becoming intense. Klumper began to climb to 150 feet to avoid the worst effects of this, and in a single line abreast the 'Golden Comb' pressed in towards the starboard side of the startled convoy. The time was 1527.

II

It was with what has been described as 'undisguised awe' that the men aboard the convoy and escorts saw the forty-four aircraft lift up over the world's rim and deploy towards them. Rear-Admiral Boddam-Whetham, the convoy commodore, graphically described them as 'like a huge flight of nightmare locust'. Sub-Lieutenant Robert Hughes, a former school teacher, was now the Gunnery Control Officer aboard the cruiser *Scylla* out ahead of the plodding convoy, and he was at his action station in the Blue, after, director. He was to recall that moment equally vividly many years later.

> They rose up on the horizon, black and repulsive, and they extended far on either side of our view. The director was hushed. 'Open fire when in range,' said the voice in the headset. 'Hell!' breathed Cornish, 'Just look at that, just look at them!' 'One, two, three, four, five . . . six, nine . . . ' counted Cornish. My tongue was paralysed, and my stomach felt sick.*

Hughes described the torpedo bombers in his sights as 'rising and falling for some reason, like porpoises at sea'. He went on, 'Still they kept in rigid line abreast across the horizon, still they looked like some strange things from another world.'

There was a flash of flame as, in quick succession, the destroyers on the starboard outer screen and then the inner line of warships and the merchantmen themselves opened fire with every weapon which would bear, from 4.7-inch to 20-mm oerlikon, 2-pdr pom-pom and light machine guns. The fire from such a large screen was intense, and low flying aircraft approaching the ships broadsides without flinching had long been acknowledged as the favourite target for warship guns. The gunners on the starboard screen were given a 'nil deflection' shoot and the torpedo bombers flew at a low enough altitude for even the destroyers' main armaments of low-angled 4.7-inch guns, which could only elevate to forty degrees in most of these vessels, to join in the barrage.

As usual then almost every ship engaged was subsequently to make claims for numerous hits and 'kills'. The official British Naval Historian, Captain S. W. Roskill, states that five German bombers were destroyed in this attack, but others in their accounts are not so restrained as this. Very different descriptions exist as to the carnage inflicted on the attacking aircraft during this assault.

Captain Richard Hocken of the American Liberty ship *William Moultrie* was awarded the Merchant Marine Distinguished Service Medal for this convoy and his citation included the following passage:

> During the first attack on the convoy the *William Moultrie*

* *Through the Waters*, William Kimber, 1956.

distinguished herself by shooting down three torpedo planes and assisting in the destruction of six more.[64]

Other United States vessels were equally prolific in their massacre of the German aircraft taking part in this raid. For example the Armed Guard officer, Lieutenant R. M. Billings aboard the *Nathaniel Greene* was to write:

A swarm of torpedo planes were sighted near the water in front of the convoy on the starboard side . . . the planes circled and came directly at us, and we opened fire with everything we had . . . one plane crossing our bow received a direct hit from our three-inch gun and crashed in the water. Two more planes were shot down by our machine gun fire as they went down the port side and another plane was shot down on the starboard side. The planes were so close you couldn't miss with a machine gun.[33]

The *Virginia Dare*, 'was on her maiden voyage, yet her green crew was credited with the shooting down or assisting in the destruction of seven bombers'. Robert Hughes remembered over the years the effects of the *Scylla*'s opening salvoes:

Far over the water the first eight [shells] burst in front of the right hand plane, but still she came on, with the shells bursting in front of her. Suddenly she rocked sideways, and black smoke poured from her. She gave a sudden queer heave to starboard, as her companion on the right came up in one of the queer porpoise leaps, and the two planes locked together in a tangle and hit the water below in a welter of spray.*

With upward of eighteen warships and merchant vessels firing at these aircraft with a wide variety of weapons it is remarkable how each gunner, each ship, was positive that it was *their* shell from all the many thousand bursting around the oncoming bombers that had hit. Which makes all the more pronounced the postwar opinion of the German historian Cajus Bekker who, with full access to German records, claims quite adamantly, that not one single aircraft of Major Klumper's *Gruppe* was lost, although he fully admits that every one was hit and damaged to some degree, and six were so severely damaged that they were unable to take part in further operations against this convoy.

These aircraft, he indicates, were forced to jettison their

---

* *Through the Waters*, William Kimber, 1956.

torpedoes prematurely. The greater bulk of the torpedo bombers however pushed on in over the outer destroyer screen and in towards the convoy itself whose flank lay invitingly open. Most of the German pilots released at the same time at about one thousand yards range and some seventy torpedoes sped at fifty knots towards the wallowing freighters.

Why were the German airmen presented with such an open target as that indicated by the long columns of slow moving merchantmen steaming steadily ahead without deviation from their course? Their inertia would seem inexplicable until it is remembered that the convoy contained a very high proportion of American and Russian vessels and the former especially had, in their attitude towards authority and waging war under British orders, been notable in their lack of enthusiasm. For example Commodore Boddam-Whetham commented in his report that:

The Americans in particular pay but scant attention to signals, know little of the importance of good station keeping and do not as yet know anything about convoy work.[3]

The Commodore later recorded his orders to the convoy at this time. When, at 1527, the first German torpedo bombers had been sighted ahead of the convoy and, almost immediately afterwards the second, and much larger, formation had been seen approaching to starboard, the whole oncoming mass of aircraft had, in Boddam-Whetham's judgement, spread from ahead round to the starboard side of the convoy and on to the convoy's quarter. He judged, perfectly correctly, that the densest mass was coming in on the bow and therefore ordered an immediate alteration in course by turning forty-five degrees towards the enemy. This was done by his pre-arranged special procedure.

Commodore Boddam-Whetham's emergency turn procedure differed from the accepted method of combating such attacks and had in fact been revised by him to counter just such a situation. The ordinary procedure for emergency turns he did not consider swift enough to avoid torpedo attack from either the air or by surface craft and was more designed to combat submarine attack. The procedure was therefore altered and a full description of the new method was given to all ships' masters in Convoy PQ 18 *prior* to sailing.

In detail the new method to be adopted was that, on the

approach of surface craft or aircraft intent on massed torpedo assault, the usual fifteen-second warning blasts were to be sounded by the Commodore's flagship and repeated by the column leaders. It was stressed that this warning would not be repeated while the enemy were in sight but that, during this period, actual alteration of forty-five degrees either way would be executed by the hoisting of flags 'E' or 'I'. The actual hoisting of these flags was to be preceded by a five-second blast to warn ships that an important signal was about to be made. The executive was the usual rule-of-the-road signal of one or two blasts and the hauling down of the flag 'E' or 'I'.

The Commodore stressed the vital importance of a continuous and intent look-out being maintained upon the Commodore's ship for these flags and that the turns to be made instantly with the executive. Because the fifteen-second blast, with its attendant repetition and noise, would take far too long and, if the expected torpedoes were to be avoided, it was essential that the convoy should turn immediately the Commodore judged the attack was definitely taking place and the most likely path of the torpedoes had been calculated. In order to make such a move effective avoiding action had to be taken by all the ships turning together at the last possible moment.

What the Commodore's plan could not allow for was the fact that, whereas the warships of a fleet at sea are highly trained to make such a turn and could be relied upon to carry it out promptly, the crews of the merchant ships had no such training. In time of peace there was no more independent breed of men than the Masters of merchant vessels and each liked the minimum interference with the command of his ship and the maximum sea-room in which to operate her. Sailing in convoy at all was something directly contrary to their natures.

By September 1942, three years of all-out war had taught the value of obedience to orders to the British skippers. They were far finer seamen anyway to those of the other Allies but had the added edge of wartime experience and example to back their instinctive competence. However the Soviet and United States mariners, the latter grossly overpaid in comparison with their British brethren, had only fifteen and ten months respective experience of wartime conditions, and for many of the Americans this was their first real wartime convoy save for the passage of the North Atlantic. To expect such untried crews to face, with the same skill and precision as their British counterparts, the heaviest aerial torpedo attack yet mounted against a convoy of merchant ships in Arctic waters was to ask too much. And yet rigid observance by all ships of Commodore Boddam-Whetham's command might have saved so many lives.

As the Commodore was himself to record:

> It is, of course, impossible to say what might have happened had all the ships obeyed my signal promptly, but the fact remains that the 9th and 10th columns, either did not turn, or were far too slow. In consequence, with the exception of the *Mary Luckenbach*, they were all sunk.[3]

Captain McLeod, the Vice-Commodore in the *Dan-y-Bryn* was of the opinion that Number 10 column in fact started to carry out a wheel instead of turning together and this is why they failed to avoid any torpedoes, while *Empire Stevenson* did not turn at all, and nor, as far as he could make out, did any of her column, Number 9. In a similar manner, Lieutenant Blake Hughes, USN, the commander of the *Patrick Henry*'s Armed Guard, also backed up the general opinion on the cause of this disaster. In his summary of the action he stated that the reasons for the success of this German attack was partially due to the fact that:

> Some ships failed to make their emergency turns with necessary promptness.[35]

This was not however the only reason he listed and we shall return to his very interesting comments later. The Commander of the Through Close Escort, Commander A. B. Russell of the *Malcolm*, reached almost identical conclusions to those expressed here. He was to write that he felt 'most strongly' that the number of ships in the convoy was too great. If all the ships had been British, and accustomed to convoy work, then the size of the convoy might have been acceptable. However in Commander Russell's very experienced eyes, when such a large convoy consisted of American, Panamanian, Russian and British ships, then the station-keeping and communications problems became acute. Commander Russell had just returned from Operation *Pedestal* in the Mediterranean where the convoy had consisted of twelve ships only, all of high speed and with an enormous escort, and the contrast might have influenced his opinions somewhat. None the less his points are valid and made independently of the Commodore, which makes their identical conclusions all the more influential.

Commodore Russell continued by describing the great torpedo attack:

> As an instance, when the large torpedo bomber attack at 1530/13 developed, the Commodore made an Emergency Turn to Port. This signal was obeyed by the convoy with the exception of Columns 9 and 10, who held on the original course. Had these two columns carried out the Emergency turn their losses from the torpedo-bombers might well have been much smaller.[27]

Lieutenant-Commander J. P. Stewart, DSC, RNR, of the *Bryony* also emphasised that:

> Signalling in some of the ships (not British) was very poor, and very often no attention was paid to flag signals, especially Emergency Turns.[19]

In a letter written to Rear-Admiral Bob Burnett, while the convoy was still forging on under attack, on 15th September, Commodore Boddam-Whetham unburdened himself of his nagging, and unjustified, self-doubts about the crucial order he gave at 1530. He was already feeling the enormous strain of command that was to bring him down soon after and began his letter by stating:

> You will agree I think that it is on the cards that I won't get home, so am writing this to suggest a few things which you may be willing to bring to My Lords' notice.[56]

On the question of the Emergency Turn order he was in some agony of spirit.

> I think I was right in making my own orders for emergency turns and I think that might be brought up if you agree. My turning or not turning may have been the cause of the loss of the ships sunk but on the other hand it may have been the means of saving far more. However, perhaps the wish is father to the thoughts and I may be quite wrong.[56]

He added later that the outstanding impression made upon him during the battle thus far included the complete disintegration of the *Empire Stevenson* and the *Mary Luckenbach*, 'a really terrible and awe-inspiring sight' and his first view of the big torpedo bomber attack.

> The latter really did give me cold feet I must say and I thought we'd lose far more. They looked to me like a huge flight of nightmare locusts coming over the horizon![56]

Out in front of the convoy, and fully engaged as he was, it would appear that, despite this letter, or perhaps through a faulty interpretation of it, Bob Burnett was under the misapprehension that no emergency turn order had been made. This is inexplicable, but, none the less, Rear-Admiral (D)'s report, dated 29th September, included the following point on this issue:

> The individual handling of the ships of the covering force and the screen, as far as I had time to observe, was admirable; the Commodore, to my mind perfectly correctly, *made no emergency turn;** such a manoeuvre would have only thrown the convoy into confusion and would not have reduced casualties; indeed, it quite probably would have increased them.[2]

This remark is not commented upon in the report despite the fact that it is surely incorrect, certainly in fact if not in conclusion, and remains a riddle. Perhaps 'Uncle Bob' was unaware at the time that an emergency turn had in fact been ordered, or even carried out; perhaps he could, during the action, only notice the movements of Columns 9 and 10 and had therefore from their strict station keeping in original formation deduced that no order to turn had been issued, and had therefore misunderstood Boddam-Whetham's missive of the 15th, but was clearly on record in a score or more ships that the order to turn *had* in fact been given.

Whatever the reason for the non-compliance of the two starboard columns they were to pay terribly and in abundance in consequence.

By the time this moment of decision had passed the escort vessels were moving out to engage the enemy in a desperate attempt to head them off, but in one notable field the escort defence had been caught napping. There were no fighter aircraft in position to distract the oncoming hordes. They had only the barrage of the leading and starboard escorts to face as they made their final deployment.

* Author's italics.

Again Blake Hughes aboard the *Patrick Henry* made an on-the-spot assessment.

> It is my impression that this was the only time when the planes were off a little too late to fully engage the Heinkels before they had become dangerous to the convoy. This impression may be erroneous, however.[35]

Blake later amplified his initial impressions thus :

> To some extent the aircraft carrier appeared to have been caught off stride. Some planes had returned for refuelling a short time previous to sighting of torpedo plane and were not ready. Those that were flown off may have been flown off few seconds too late for maximum effectiveness. In all other attacks fighters were off in ample time.[35]

Perfect timing was, of course, the most important factor in carrier defence work as Blake pointed out, and he considered that the 'somewhat less than perfect' timing in this attack was the largest single factor in the German success. In these appreciations Lieutenant Hughes had the rueful support of Commander A. P. Colthurst of the *Avenger* herself, who was later to recall :

> At the end of this unfortunate day I realised that my operation of the ship and her fighters had been very wrong. At the start of it I had not realised the heavy scale of the attack to which the convoy would be subjected, nor the duration of the attack. I did not appreciate the hopelessness of sending even four Sea Hurricanes to attack the heavily armed enemy shadowers. We had not learnt to differentiate between small groups of shadowers and striking forces on the RDF screen.[16]

With the Sea Huricanes re-arming on deck there was nothing *Avenger* could do except join in the general barrage when possible and keep on the disengaged side of the convoy. The time was 1530.

### III

The attack now broke over the convoy in full fury. Such was the scale of the attack that only the individual reports of each limited viewpoint can describe the impression of the desperation of the defence, the bravery of the German aircrews and the ghastly carnage inflicted in a few brief minutes upon the heavily laden merchantmen. Rear-Admiral Burnett set the final scene as the aircraft closed. By this time *Scylla* had moved out ahead of the convoy and was zig-zagging at high speed inside the screen. Intense fire was opened by all ships with both long- and short-range weapons and the torpedo bombers split into two groups and passed down either side of *Scylla*, the larger portion passing to starboard.

Again Blake Hughes:

> Some torpedo planes dropped torpedoes from 500 to 1200 yards outside of convoy. Others, with suicidal daring, flew in amongst the ships dropping their torpedoes at very close range.[35]

The torpedoes themselves he described as between six to eight feet long and 12 to 15 inches in diameter. They travelled, he underestimated, at between fifteen and twenty-five knots. He could not decide whether the torpedoes travelled in a straight line or a curve but in the attacks he observed the aircraft appeared to head directly at the target when dropping torpedoes. Ensign Daniel J. Rooker aboard the *Campfire* was busy directing his gun crews but noted that the German planes were met by a heavy barrage some three miles from the convoy, and they thereupon fanned out striking the ships in three different thrusts. A number of torpedoes were dropped at 1500 yards range to starboard, from dead ahead also but that many ships on the port (disengaged) side of the convoy joined in the barrage with wild firing, 'many of their shells landing on our decks!'

He admitted that in this first attack that his men too, although barely within range, wasted ammunition by firing too soon. With a poor anti-aircraft armament, consisting only of two .5 machine-guns and two 20-mm Oerlikons, with four .303 machine-guns, the *Campfire*, he stated, was forced to wait until the bombers had closed to within under 1,000 yards before they could join in with any effect. The machine-guns were useless he reported but a cryptic note in the margin of his report states that the *Campfire* was assigned to PQ 18 in the UK and was not therefore armed up to US standards for other than an Atlantic crossing.

Aboard the *Exford* Coxswain John H. Currant was recording events as they happened:

Five [ships] have been hit, men are abandoning their ships, many are drifting by us. One ship blew up as soon as it was hit, others are burning whilst others are slowly sinking.[30]

The unfortunate ship which blew up was the *Empire Stevenson*. Ensign John Landers Laird of the *Virginia Dare* graphically reported her abrupt passing:

Ship 91 was suddenly enveloped in a tower of flame and smoke, and, when that subsided, there was nothing there but an oily slick on the water.[36]

The *Virginia Dare* was better armed than the *Campfire* and made a notable contribution to the battle over the convoy that day and later. They opened fire with every gun and Seaman George Goddard raked one plane with 20-mm shells and, as it disappeared into the clouds, a wing fell into the sea. Shortly after another bomber came in on their starboard bow. Heavily engaged by all guns which would bear, it dropped two bombs near the ship and straffed her decks. As he continued past at close range the guns continued to fire and this aircraft went into the sea about half a mile astern of the *Dare*.

*Empire Stevenson*'s funeral pyre made a deep impression on all who witnessed it. Blake Hughes recorded that the unfortunate vessel was 'pulverised in a tremendous explosion that left no trace of her', while Daniel Rooker recalled how she 'completely disappeared in flames'.

Many vessels had very narrow shaves indeed; the *Dan-y-Bryn*, for example, reported no less than six torpedoes running more or less parallel to her after she had completed her 45-degree turn. In addition to the *Empire Stevenson* some seven other merchantmen fell victims to this attack though none, fortunately, suffered her ghastly fate. This fact seemed to disappoint our Soviet ally whose contribution to the defence of this convoy had to date been nil. Far from expressing sorrow at the carnage inflicted, Admiral Arseni Golovko was sneeringly recording:

In addition the only one of the first ten to sink at once was the *Stalingrad*. The remaining nine, flying allied flags, remained afloat and were finished off by the escorts.

He added with even more callousness:

> Evidently it causes them no great heart-ache to complete the
> destruction of vessels loaded with cargoes for us![*]

For such men the crew of the *Empire Stevenson* were sacrificed.
What really happened was that the Soviet *Sukhona* was hit and
abandoned as was the Panamanian vessel *Afrikander*. The *John
Penn* was hit by two torpedoes. The first struck her starboard
amidships and the second hit the starboard bow almost simultaneously. Three men were killed in the engine room and the
ship began to settle rapidly. The engines were stopped and
the crew abandoned ship in an orderly manner in the lifeboats
and were immediately picked up by the escorts and rescue ships.
The three little motor minesweepers gave invaluable aid during
such rescue operations. There was no question of saving the ship
with two torpedo holes in her hull and she was sent to the
bottom with gunfire.

The *John Penn* had been a 7,200-tonner owned and operated
by the US Maritime Commission and went to the bottom with
her cargo of general Lease-Lend equipment and tanks, sinking by
the head in position 76° 00′ N, 10° 15′ E.

The *Empire Beaumont* was hit and set on fire, her crew
abandoning ship in the lifeboats. The minesweeper *Sharpshooter*
was ordered to stand by her and picked up 35 survivors from one
boat while the rest were rescued by the *Copeland*.

The *Macbeth* was attacked by a Heinkel 111 which approached
from the starboard bow about eighty feet high. The survivors
later stated that the German aircraft flew right into their
objective regardless of the anti-aircraft firepower and that their
own puny .5 machine-gun fire seemed to hit but just bounce off
the plane.

At a range of only some forty feet the bomber released two
torpedoes and then banked away unscathed. Both these torpedoes struck the vessel below the waterline, exploding on
contact and rendering her helpless. The crew abandoned ship
and the *Macbeth* was found sinking by the *Sharpshooter* soon
after. The crew had meanwhile been picked up by the trawler
*St Kenan*. The *Macbeth* sank with her cargo of foodstuffs, explosives and tanks 76° 05′ N, 10° 0′ E. She had been a 4,885-ton
Panamanian freighter operated by the US Maritime Commission.

The little *St Kenan* had already picked up survivors from the

[*] *With the Red Fleet*, Putman & Co., 1954.

*Oregonian*, a 4,862-ton freighter owned by American Hawaii Steamship Lines and working under charter to the Commission. She was lost a long way from the sunny Pacific route of her calling and with her went twenty-eight members of her crew of fifty-five. She was heavily laden with tanks, rails, steel, and food in addition to a deck cargo of aircraft and she never stood a chance.

The *Oregonian* was right at the main focal point of the attack, being the leading ship of the ill-fated starboard column and she was struck simultaneously by three torpedoes which almost blew in the entire starboard side of the ship, flooded the engine room, thus causing the ship to take on a heavy list. The lifeboats were lowered but the ship capsized almost immediately before many could get clear. It was all over in a few minutes.

Although quickly on the scene the *St Kenan*'s skipper, Lieutenant J. Mackay, reported that many of these unfortunate men were in a very bad way. Ten of them, on account of the oil and water they had swallowed and the temperature of the sea, were in a state of collapse for the following twenty-four hours. The conduct of *St Kenan*'s tiny crew was in the best traditions of the service. Although themselves exhausted by prolonged periods of action many of them gave up their bunks and hammocks to the Americans, while Mackay reported later that the hardship of feeding and sleeping so many survivors in such cramped quarters was cheerfully accepted.

The eighth ship to be lost in this attack was the American *Wacosta* with 7,098 tons of war supplies and a deck cargo of tanks. She was stationed immediately astern of the *Empire Stevenson* and when that vessel exploded with such violence the *Wacosta* received the full force of that colossal blast. This explosion was such that aboard the *Wacosta* steam valves, oil lines, instruments and other delicate mechanisms were fractured and the main engines were rendered useless. The freighter came to a halt and, as she did so, a Heinkel was seen approaching this stationary target at a height of about 100 feet. When an estimated thirty feet from the *Wacosta* the aircraft released a single torpedo. This missile was dropped so close to the vessel that it missed the hull and landed instead atop of No 2 hatch which it penetrated and exploded, blowing a large hole in the side of the ship which immediately began to settle by the bows. The Heinkel 111 flew over the stricken vessel completely unaffected by the hail of machine-gun bullets which bounced off its wings and body.

*Wacosta*'s crew abandoned ship and, remarkably, there were no casualties from this unique attack which must be the only case recorded of a torpedo sinking its target from *inside* the ship! All the crew were quickly picked up by escort vessels.

Above the convoy the air was rent with a thousand bursts of flak and criss-crossed with tracer as the German pilots penetrated right into the convoy lanes at low altitudes. Cross-fire from friendly ships proved almost as much a hazard as the enemy attacks and several merchant vessels were struck by the un-disciplined firing of vessels in adjacent columns. When an un-trained gunner has an aircraft in his sights it is hard for him to stop firing in the heat of battle, with his companions being blown up around him. The torpedo bombers were lower than the superstructures of the merchant ships in the convoy and consequently many ships had their upperworks riddled with light machine-gun fire and even cannon shells.

Despite post-war claims of heavy losses the German records show that they lost only five aircraft in this attack.

Major Klumper's *I/KG 26* from Bardufoss had been reduced from twenty-eight to twenty-six when two Heinkels aborted the mission at take-off due to engine defects. Of the twenty-six which took part in the attack four were shot down and eight damaged. The crews of two of the Heinkels which managed to ditch successfully took to their inflatable rubber rafts and eventually made landfall on the northern coast of Norway. The third was soon rescued by one of the indefatigable He 115s of *I/406* and whisked back to safety, while the crew of the fourth also escaped death for Lieutenant-Commander Hopmann brought *U-405* to the surface and rescued them. He later picked up the crew of one of *I/906*'s float planes including an air mechanic from his own home town.

Klumper's force claimed the destruction of four merchant ships for certain with hits scored on at least two others.

Hauptmann Klaus Nocken's *II/KG 26* took off from Banak at 1305 with his eighteen Ju 88 torpedo bombers reduced to seven-teen through engine failures. All seventeen attacked and, of these, four were badly damaged by flak and two by fighters.

One aircraft was lost from Nocken's force and was last heard of via poor radio broadcasts, trying to make Spitzbergen on one faltering engine. The six damaged machines were unserviceable for the rest of the operation.

The only Allied confirmations of these figures which can be relied upon are those listed by reliable witnesses aboard HM ships. If every merchant ship's claims of kills were to be taken seriously the Germans would have lost slightly more aircraft than they actually used in the attack, with many more damaged!

Commander A. D. H. Jay of the *Harrier*, the senior officer of the Sixth Minesweeping Flotilla, was stationed astern of the convoy from where he had a grandstand view but could only confirm that a single Heinkel 111, which had passed right through the convoy, crashed into the sea about three quarters of a mile from *Harrier*'s starboard beam. Similarly the *Achates*, which was stationed ahead and to the port, or disengaged, side of the convoy, confirmed that she had no opportunity in her position to engage any German aircraft during their approach but did engage two at 800 yards range as they were retiring, without a conclusive result. The corvette *Bluebell* was also on the port side of the convoy and she also had to be content with firing on a Ju 88 as it emerged from the convoy's ranks. Lieutenant Walker claimed that hits were scored on his target by his 20-mm Oerlikon guns and the aircraft flew away ahead of the convoy smoking and losing height.

The little *St Kenan* with her cargo of survivors was hastening to re-join the convoy at her best speed when she was attacked by a Ju 88 armed with bombs. This aircraft attacked in a shallow dive, attracted no doubt by a lone target away from the protective flak umbrella of the convoy. None the less the *St Kenan* conducted a vigorous defence with her puny armament and several hits with the Oerlikon caused Lieutenant Mackay to claim that the aircraft released her bombs prematurely and harmlessly. Smoke was seen to break from this aircraft but it was not seen to crash. *St Kenan*'s skipper therefore only claimed a 'possible'.

The powerful anti-aircraft armament of the *Ulster Queen* was not brought into play with any effect during this attack for her position in the convoy was astern and to port. Her captain, Captain C. K. Adams, reported sighting five Heinkel He 115 float planes after the main attack and assumed that they were employed on rescue duties as he saw them make no torpedo attacks.

The forty merchant ships of this convoy mustered between them a total of 167 20-mm Oerlikons, eleven 40-mm Bofors and seventeen 3-inch or 12-pdr guns as well as many smaller weapons, and for the first time ammunition supplies for the Oerlikons were on an adequate scale. It was therefore considered by the Director of the British Trade Division that the close-range barrage of the merchant ships themselves was a major factor in defeating this and other air attacks. However the fact that the merchant vessels had such fire-power is not conclusive that it was used to maximum effect, and, despite the fact that some fantastic claims were later made, in particular by the American vessels, there is considerable evidence to show that many gunners were completely untrained and unready.

The reports of the Armed Guard gunners were unanimous in the condemnation of the .303 and .5-inch machine-guns, and their installation and manning was universally decreed a complete waste of time, effort and manpower. Report after report bewails the fact that their bullets just bounced off the German aircraft.

Ensign Rooker voiced the opinion of all his United States Navy comrades:

Of the type of guns now installed aboard American merchant ships there are only three that are any use. The 3-inch, 50 cal., the 20mm Oerlikon and the 4-inch, 50 cal. this latter only being effective if supplied with shrapnel.[34]

The *Patrick Henry* observed five aircraft shot down but also thought that low cloud and restricted visibility during the action may have meant that more than this were destroyed. Blake Hughes also stated that many gunners, particularly on American merchant ships had never been in action before. Certainly none of his gunners had and this was the case on many other ships. Ensign Laird also thought that much fire was wasted when the planes were still out of range and, by the time the aircraft were upon them, the rate and volume of fire was considerably less. He added:

Some sort of training similar to the British DEMS courses

should be given to our gunners. Although my men did well, it was the first time they had ever fired these guns at a target! Actual combat is the best experience, but it seems a poor place to train men.[34]

One interesting observation was made by the crew of the *Kentucky*. They noted that during this attack, and subsequently, some aircraft trailed smoke from both engines; this was observed during several attacks and was assumed to be a misleading device by the enemy!

The Armed Guard commander of the *Nathaniel Green* described how:

One plane dropped two parachutes which we fired at. We hit one of the parachutes and it dropped into the sea without exploding. We could not accurately determine what was on the parachutes.[40]

It is not hard to guess and one wonders at the kind of publicity this incident would have been given had the unfortunate aircrew bailing out over a hostile convoy had been British or American!

Lieutenant-Commander Stewart of the *Bryony*, stationed astern with her submarine charges, also commented that there was a tendency for ships to reduce speed during air attack. In several cases it was observed that the rear merchant ships were nearly stationary. It was of course inevitable that considerable bunching should take place, especially when ships were being hit and stopped in line and those astern had to pass them. In particular the appalling devastation caused by the explosion of the *Empire Stevenson* made other skippers very reluctant to close up any gaps in case they shared the fate of the *Wacosta*. However such a dispersal of the convoy's lines, even during air attack, was dangerous.

There is every reason to believe that an effort was made to co-ordinate aerial and submarine attacks and some reports of submarines firing inside the convoy were made while the torpedo bomber assault was in full swing. John Currant of the *Exford* sighted a periscope on the starboard beam and opened fire on it. Commander Russell of the *Malcolm*, was quite certain that such an attempt at synchronisation was made, for at this time *Malcolm* sighted a periscope and Captain Russell was almost positive that the *Empire Beaumont* was sunk by this

U-boat and *not* by aerial torpedo for he thought he saw the torpedo hit her on her *port* side. Certainly it was recognised that during air attacks the anti-submarine efficiency of the screen was apt to deteriorate. The continuous underwater explosions of the bombs and the noise of gunfire made asdic operations very difficult indeed.

The periscope sighted was about one cable off *Malcolm*'s starboard quarter. There was only time for the destroyer to turn and drop a five-charge pattern set shallow. This attack was made by eye and no firm submarine contact was ever obtained.

Whether the unfortunate *Empire Beaumont* was actually sunk by air or underwater attack mattered little, for as the surviving German bombers winged their way swiftly into the distance surrounded by the last few isolated pock marks of long-range flak they left behind them a stricken convoy stunned by the speed and extent of their power. Columns nine and ten had ceased to exist and where minutes before had steamed eight proud ships there remained only pools of oil and debris, little clusters of men in the water and the acrid smell of charred and burnt flesh and steel.

The time was 1540.

IV

In thirteen minutes and at a cost of five machines destroyed the German torpedo bomber pilots had sunk eight ships and thereby inflicted the heaviest defeat ever recorded on a British convoy in a single attack by aircraft. The exchange rate of five bombers for eight freighters was completely unacceptable and it required no computer to calculate that another four attacks on this scale would mean the complete destruction of PQ 18.

The dramatic effectiveness of the 'Golden Comb' technique was quite shattering and more so when it is recalled that this was *not* the largest force of torpedo bombers that had been faced by the Royal Navy, even though close to it. Just the previous month, the *Pedestal* convoy to Malta had combated much larger formations. These Mediterranean attacks had been mounted by over one hundred aircraft of all types but had faced a stronger escort by far, including two aircraft carriers of the latest type.

In the face of such a daunting prospect a great deal of hasty rethinking had to be done by Admiral Burnett and his fellow commanders. It is to their credit that this ghastly carnage neither prevented them carrying on with the convoy nor blunted their capacity for seeking out and immediately adopting several reasonable counters to it.

The first lesson was absorbed by the *Avenger*. The hopelessness of sending out even four Sea Hurricanes against enemy shadowers which were heavily armed was digested with some bitterness. The armament of the Sea Hurricane, as had been expected, proved to be completely inadequate for dealing with the German aircraft they had encountered. Cannon were essential and machine-guns useless, the same lesson that had been absorbed by the anti-aircraft gunners. The actual performance of the Sea Hurricane at low altitude was also sadly lacking, in fact so inferior were the fighting qualities of this, the Royal Navy's front-line single-seater interceptor in 1942, that Commander Colthurst had to report that in his opinion these aircraft should never again be allowed to approach such aircraft as the Blohm and Voss BV 138 or the Focke Wulf 200 'Condor'. This gave the German reconnaissance squadrons complete freedom of action over British convoys. Nor were the Sea Hurricanes very effective against the standard bombers encountered. The Junkers Ju 88 and the Heinkel He 111.

These lessons had all been learnt before, by the RAF two years earlier during the Battle of Britain, by the RAF and the Fleet Air Arm a year before during the Battle for Greece and Crete and yet the Fleet Air Arm was still sent to battle with obsolete material against the cream of the Luftwaffe. Such was the astounding lack of understanding by the War Cabinet that the threatened merchant ships of PQ 18 were actually carrying in their cargoes Hurricanes of a much later type, Marks X or XI, while the Royal Navy was expected to defend them with the maritime equivalent of the Mark I!

Commander Colthurst quite rightly reported that had his fighter aircraft been fitted with cannon then a much larger proportion of those German aircraft reported as damaged would have certainly been destroyed. Treated in such a negligent manner by the Ministry of Supply the attitude of the young Fleet Air Arm pilots is all the more commendable. Although

Commander Colthurst recalled that 802 and 833 Squadrons had been demanding cannon wings in vain since joining the *Avenger*, he heard no actual word of complaint from any of these young men. He concluded that their very attitude was surely more deserving of action because of this, and emphasised their right to be given a modern weapon with which to fight.

With regard the tactics, which were so obviously at fault, the solution rested on the greater ability to differentiate between small groups of shadowers and striking forces picked up on the radar screens. Thus a standing air patrol had to be held over the convoy and fighters held armed and ready to be sent against only the major attacks rather than wasting their strength fruitlessly trying to chase away shadowers. Each squadron provided sections of fighters which could land for refuelling and re-arming and with intense effort on the part of the deck parties, be made ready for combat again.

Once this smooth flow was achieved then congestion aboard the *Avenger*'s tiny flight deck would be avoided and it would ensure that there were always some fighter sections ready to counter any large striking force. It was great credit to the small carrier's complement that this rotation was achieved throughout the next stage of the voyage.

As in the Fleet Air Arm the captains of the escorts were also reassessing their role.

Aboard the anti-aircraft ships *Alynbank* and *Ulster Queen* there was some dissatisfaction about their role in the torpedo bomber attack. Both ships bristled with close-range and long-range weapons but both had been made impotent in the face of this assault by the strict orders issued by Admiral Burnett that they should stay in their allotted positions astern and within the convoy's lines.

Both captains had expressed dissatisfaction with these allocations and, in response to the submarine threat, Admiral Burnett had in fact moved the *Alynbank* forward one column, although the *Ulster Queen* was given no such respite due to her superior speed and manoeuvrability. This was despite the fact that both captains had pointed out to him that in such positions their firepower against what was even then considered the greatest threat, low flying torpedo bombers, would be masked. Admiral Burnett's view, however, seemed to be concentrated on high altitude defence and positive orders were issued by him for the AA ships to stay in line.

However, Captain Adams of the *Ulster Queen* repeated the tactics of Nelson with regard to these orders once the lessons of the big assault had been digested on the bridge of the *Ulster Queen*. The new plan was that, when torpedo bombers were seen, the *Ulster Queen* would turn to meet them at full speed and employ all the excellent qualities of manoeuvring which the ship possessed. Also held in mind was the good effect on the morale of the ship's company by adopting an attacking rather than a static stance in the face of such attacks.

The Gunnery Control Officers were to estimate the ranges and would apply approximate fuse setting which they had previously memorised from 14,000 yards down to a short barrage, dropping their curtain of flak in 2,000 yard steps using eye shooting for control.

It was planned to put up this short barrage in ample time to counter any deliberate aimed runs at full blast until the torpedo bomber attack was expected. As soon as torpedoes were seen to drop, then, her deterrent value finished, the *Ulster Queen* would put about and return to her ordained station in readiness for high-level defence. All aboard looked forward to testing the new tactics.

The *Scylla* of course had already adopted such tactics for herself but in this first attack she had remained the only ship given this freedom. This is surprising for its value had been shown on two separate occasions recently against torpedo bombers. During the passage of PQ 17 the American destroyer *Wainwright* had steamed towards and met such an attack out from the convoy and her barrage fire had been the main instrument in breaking up the attack. During the *Pedestal* convoy the British destroyer *Pathfinder* had taken upon herself to assume the same role when attacked by eight Italian torpedo bombers and the effect had been equally gratifying.

One of the main reasons for the success of the 'Golden Comb', was the passive nature of the defence and it is evident that these two precedents either were not known, or not digested in the time available before the sailing of PQ 18. It has already been seen from the screening plans that the standard British method of closing up in the face of air attacks was still adopted. On the other hand it was noted that some of the destroyers, which had been fuelling and were therefore away from their positions, were, by reason of their being out towards the aircraft, able to contribute a greater measure to the aerial defence.

One of the American naval officers aboard the merchant ships emphasised the need for an outer screen in future convoys to break up such attacks. It may well have been the restricted fire-power of the British destroyers themselves that forced such tactics on them. Of the sixteen Home Fleet destroyers present, which were the front-line ships, only the four new vessels of the 3rd Flotilla mounted a dual-purpose gun which was fully enclosed in a weatherproof shield resembling a turret. These four destroyers had wisely been given places on the screen on the starboard bow and therefore their first-rate fire was invaluable. Each of these four destroyers, the *Milne*, *Marne*, *Martin* and *Meteor*, had three twin turrets of the new 4.7-inch Mark XI gun on the Mark XX mounting. These weapons only had a maximum elevation of 50-degrees, but this was an improvement on the 40-degrees which was the limit of the other destroyers' main armaments. The Mark XI fired a 62-lb shell and had a muzzle velocity of 2,543 ft/sec. They were semi-automatic weapons but, as the central ammunition hoist was fixed rather than swivelling, fire was restricted to about twelve rounds per minute. Even so it was an impressive weapon and when switched to barrage fire each 'M' boat could lay a ton of explosive a minute in the path of oncoming bombers. Unfortunately there were only four of them on this convoy. The other 'Fleet' destroyers had to make do with wartime adaptations which were far less effective.

Some of the 'O' class, four of the eight, were built to carry four or five old style 4-inch HA single mountings instead of four single 4.7-inch guns, but, of the four so adapted, only the *Opportune* was with PQ 18. The four big 'Tribals' had dropped their 'x' 4.7-inch twin mounting and replaced it with a twin 4-inch mounting, while the older destroyers of the 'I', 'F', and 'A' classes only had a single 3-inch HA gun mounted in place of a set of torpedo tubes for morale effect.

Among the smaller escorts the problems were even worse of course, for whereas the destroyers might contribute some long-range fire with their main armaments and had a few Oerlikons as well, the little ships like the corvettes and minesweepers only had a single useless 4-inch gun and lacked also the destroyers' speed with which to dodge. Restricted to fifteen knots in the main part and less well armed against aircraft than the merchant ships they were protecting, these little ships just had to passively suffer attack for the main part — although of course they fired back whenever possible but it was without much effect. Like the trawlers, they were there to help fill gaps in the anti-submarine screen, but in this role too the destroyers were supreme; the little corvettes, with their lack of speed, could not dart out to put the U-boats down and then re-join the convoy. They had no option but to endure it.

Still with new tactics and a determination to win through the Royal Navy escort prepared for the next assault.* However it was the Luftwaffe itself which really gave the convoy the respite it enjoyed the following days and made certain that the assault of 13th was not repeated. As they had previously failed to synchronise their air and surface attacks, so they now failed to concentrate their forces. Never again did the torpedo bombers converge on PQ 18 in such strength. The subsequent attacks were made in smaller numbers and this in itself helped the defence which was no longer swamped as it had been. Further, this error was compounded by the repeated instructions to try and sink the aircraft carrier, and more, of further instructions to go for the escorts, in particular the *Scylla* and *Ulster Queen*. By concentrating on such vessels, well able to take care of themselves and with the speed to avoid torpedoes, the Germans dissipated their subsequent attacks disastrously.

The first of these smaller attacks commenced at 1615. Admiral Burnett had congratulated his command and the convoy for their steadiness earlier, but admitted that he had heaved a sigh of relief when he learned that his vital and precious tankers had survived the fury of the first attack. While admitting that the loss of the two starboard columns was a heavy blow he was of the opinion that nothing would prevent a like number of attackers, 'gallantly led as they undoubtedly were', scoring many hits.

The second screen attack was something of an anti-climax.

---

* The only survivor from the starboard wing columns, *Mary Luckenbach*, was re-positioned in Column 8, astern of *Dany-y-Bryn* and ahead of *Virginia Dare*.

Nine torpedo bombers were seen on the starboard beam low down on the horizon. These were the float planes sighted earlier, the Heinkel 115s of the German Navy's 1/406 unit from Soerreisa. These slow aircraft obviously faced suicide if they attempted to adopt the tactics of the Heinkels and Junkers, instead they hovered round the convoy seeking an opening, a patch of low cloud or fog, anything to enable them to venture into range, drop their torpedoes and escape. Unfortunately for them there was no such cover this time and eventually they decided to take the bull by the horns and make a two-pronged approach. They approached from the starboard side of the convoy again, where they found the escorts particularly sensitive and as the first shells burst around them the German float planes split into two formations of six and three respectively.

The larger group tried to work their way round astern of the convoy, but here of course they found the two AA ships, and an already alert screen and the intense barrage made them launch their missiles at long range. Despite this two were hit by gunfire and thought to crash. The three aircraft that moved ahead of the convoy met the same scale of resistance and no hits were achieved, the float planes lumbering away defeated by such firepower. German records claim that none of these aircraft were lost.

Soon after this came yet another disappointing example of the needless self-sacrifice being made by the Fleet Air Arm pilots. Two sections of fighters had been flown off at 1645 to intercept one of the very persistent shadowers, which turned out to be one of the He 115s. All four Sea Hurricanes closed on this aircraft as it tried to escape but what should have been a massacre turned into a minor tragedy for the watching British and Allied seamen. Admiral Burnett reported later how:

It was a pathetic sight to see four Hurricanes each in turn making attacks on a retiring Heinkel floatplane only to see one being shot down and the creature still going on.[2]

Their puny machine-guns made no impression on the German machine which in turn shot down Lieutenant E. W. T. Taylor, the squadron commander of 802 Squadron, in flames. The destroyer *Onslow* was the nearest on the screen and 'Beaky' Armstrong took his ship out to the scene of the crash but

Lieutenant Taylor had sunk with the remains of his aircraft. His death proved the only loss the Fleet Air Arm suffered despite the scale of their commitment in the ensuing days. Credit is also due to the crew of the lumbering He 115 however, who fought off four single-seater interceptors with twice their speed and escaped unscathed.

During this period radar reports of small groups of aircraft operating between seven and twelve miles from the convoy were received but none were sighted, however at 1730 a more precise report was taken in of a large number of aircraft some fifteen miles ahead. Captain Scott-Moncrieff of the 8th Flotilla aboard the *Faulknor* had been stationed ahead of the convoy and had earlier reported that enemy aircraft had been apparently laying mines in front of the convoy.

Again the bait was taken and an emergency turn to port of seventy degrees was carried out by the convoy, normal course being resumed at 2015. No torpedo attack followed immediately but at 1751 *Faulknor* reported a floating mine to starboard while *Impulsive* fired upon what was thought to be a periscope.

At 2035 it was almost dark and the final torpedo bomber assault took place, twelve Heinkel 115s of *I/906* from Billefiord being reported approaching from the starboard quarter of the convoy. Two of these tried to close in at their best speed but they were once more frustrated by the alertness of the escort. The *Avenger*'s aircraft played no part in thwarting this attack for the guns of the starboard escorts proved quite capable.

Almost at once one of the aircraft was seen to catch fire. It flew on for about two minutes with the flames increasing their hold and then fell into the sea well astern of the convoy, the flames being instantly quenched in the dark, cold sea. A lonely death awaited these airmen with no apparent hope of salvation, but this crew was later rescued by *U-405*, although two died aboard her. Another He 115 was hit soon afterward and crashed into the sea alongside the *Onslow*. The remainder continued to hover in the vicinity of the convoy for a considerable time but did not attack. The radar screens did not finally clear until 2105 but no success attended their visit. A few Junkers Ju 88s made altitude attacks with bombs from time to time. They scored no hits once more but two heavy bombs fell into the sea within 150 yards of the port bow of the *Exford*.

The ship shook from stem to stern. We thought sure we were done for. We saw two torpedo planes burst into flames and crash. 2115 air raid over.[30]

So reported the *Exford*'s Armed Guard Commander. The wild firing of the merchant vessels continued and machine-guns from a 'friendly' ship slammed into the *Campfire* during this attack peppering the poop and rigging and wounding three USN gunners, Wohlers, Capobianco and Ostrander, the first two seriously.

Thus a day of tragedy both major and minor, ended on the same note. Taking stock, Admiral Burnett recalled it as a day of deep disappointment over the losses taken. In one of the vulnerable oilers a young officer sat and wrote in a steady hand.

'O Weak of Faith'
Now yesterday is dead
How dull was yesterday while it did live,
How sweet it was today,
For does not this day bring me nearer death,
And now I wait in dread,
For when I meet my judgment, can I thrive,
Or shall I fade away?
Fear mounts on fear with quick uncanny stealth.
The ice reflects a thousand darts of light
And still in fear I wait.
Surely, death must come to me tonight!
I lie with breath abate
Whilst Thor himself a 'hammers at my breast.
I start. Relax again
And think of the importance of my guest,
Yet still I wait, in vain.*

His ship was the *Atheltemplar*.

* Quoted in *Through the Waters*, Robert Hughes, William Kimber, 1956.

# Chapter Four

# The Phantom Fleet

I

If the massed torpedo-bomber attack came as the equivalent of a hard right hook against the convoy's jaw, and if the massing of the U-boats across its path constituted an equally deadly left cross, then the Germans had available to them what should have proved a decidedly final Sunday punch in the shape of the grim bulks of its heavy ships at anchor in the Norwegian fiords.

The lesson of PQ 17 had seemed so obvious to the British planners that they could not imagine that the Germans would not have drawn the same conclusion as them, which was that the mere threat of the intervention of the surface fleet had caused the destruction of the bulk of the convoy. As we have seen, the very presence of the 'Fighting Destroyer Escort' owed its origin to the vital need for the convoy to be ringed by a formidable torpedo defence against any such intervention.

There was every reason therefore for the British to expect that the German Navy, greatly encouraged by their effect on PQ 17, would take the next possible opportunity to strike hard with their big ships while their morale was high. Certainly a combined operation with all three arms, the large submarine force, the reinforced air component and the surface ships, with their tails up with further recent successes against Soviet shipping under their belt, would have presented the convoy with an almost unsurmountable task of defence. It is difficult to see how any such defence could have stood up to such a combination if delivered en masse.

Serious assessments were therefore made both of the strength of the German surface fleet in Norway, and the chances of its being committed to action against PQ 18. Certainly over the previous three years of sea warfare the results and handling of German warships had been poor. The post-war explanation for this had been, as with everything else that did not work correctly, laid at Hitler's door. His cramping instructions not to engage unless British units were hopelessly outnumbered and outgunned, his constant fears and concern about his big ships when at sea, his intervention into the handling and planning of surface ship operations, all these were certainly factors which weighed heavily on his Admirals' shoulders.

Hitler was a primarily land animal. He had been deeply impressed by the role of the Royal Navy in building up Britain's Empire and he saw the Kaiser's futile attempts to rival that long established seniority as completely useless and wasteful. He always maintained that he had no conflict with Britain or her Empire and that therefore there was no need for war again on that scale. His vision was a Europe dominated by Germany, in friendly co-existence with the British, using her world-wide influence and stability as a bulwark against the East and West. Little wonder then that when he was forced to face British sea power he was overconcerned with the fate of his own modern but tiny fleet.

Hitler's attitude and orders, however, cannot be held as the only excuse for Germany's lamentable naval record during the Second World War. Their individual ships were far better vessels than their British counterparts in almost every way. German battleships and cruisers were larger by about one third, more heavily armoured, faster and better protected against air attack. Their light forces, the destroyers and E-boats, were superior types to their British equivalents. But time after time lack of aggressive spirit seemed to permeate the handling of these vessels in battle. The battles of Narvik, the feeble handling of the *Graf Spee* and the operations of the *Scharnhorst* and *Gneisenau* in the North Atlantic during 1941, are all good examples of the timidness and half-heartedness of all their surface ship actions.

Against this must be set some undoubted strategic successes. The sinking of the *Hood* and the Channel Dash are two of the most well known. Here German efficiency and boldness had brought them victory in the face of overwhelming odds. Hitler's conviction that the British could not respond to sudden and audacious moves was proved to the hilt by his successful invasion of Norway, the passage of the battle cruisers through the Channel and other incidents.

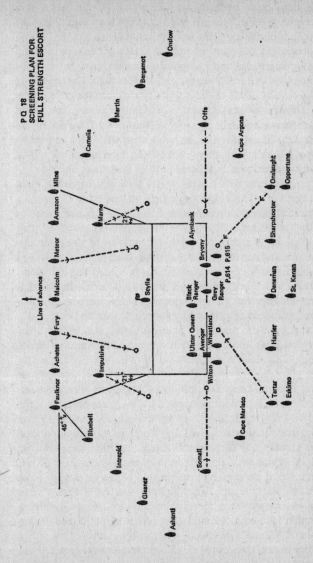

PQ 18
SCREENING PLAN FOR
FULL STRENGTH ESCORT

when air attack due close to new position

So their poor performance overall could not be a sure guarantee that the Germans would not use their big ships, even in the face of the large destroyer escort of PQ 18.

Accordingly the plans to fight the convoy through included highly complicated and powerful moves designed to reinforce the Royal Navy's surface escorts with other help. The pre-sailing intelligence available to the Admiralty was that the great battleship *Tirpitz*, the pocket battleship *Admiral Scheer*, the heavy cruiser *Hipper*, the light cruiser *Köln*, with seven large destroyers of the *Narvik* and *Maas* classes, were all available for operations in North Norway. All these ships were powerful vessels which could, type for type, outmatch all their British opponents.

The *Tirpitz* displaced some 42,000 tons and carried a main armament of eight 15-inch guns against the *King George V*'s 35,000 tons and ten 14-inch guns. In addition she was far more heavily protected. The *Scheer* displaced 14,000 tons and mounted six 11-inch guns, while *Hipper* was of the same displacement and carried eight 8-inch guns; both easily outmatched the British heavy cruiser cover. *Köln* was a small ship and older, but her 5.9-inch guns outranged the *Scylla*'s 4.5's. The German destroyers also had 5.9 and 5-inch guns for their main armaments, and could thus in theory dictate the action.

It was with the possibility of these vessels descending upon the convoy that Admiral Tovey had prepared his various lines of defence.

His plan differed from that used on previous convoys in several important respects. Instead of relying on a heavy covering force with a carrier in company and a cruiser covering force Admiral Tovey radically recast his dispositions. As PQ 17 had shown that the Germans were now prepared to take the risk of making sorties out despite such forces, and that their selected point of attack was almost certainly the eastern part of the Barents Sea, it became the first essential of the defence to meet this threat in this area. The 'Fighting Destroyer Escort' was therefore, as we have seen, primarily intended to give this protection although it could also prove a useful and heavy additional AA and A/S defence while in company.

Under overall command of Rear-Admiral Burnett in the *Scylla* the sixteen 'Fleet' destroyers were drawn from four flotillas. They were divided into two groups. Group 'A' consisted of the

6th and 17th Destroyer Flotillas, Group 'B' of the 3rd and 8th Destroyer Flotillas. This is best shown in diagram form thus:

*Scylla* (flying flag of Rear-Admiral(D))

Group 'A' (17th D.F.) *Onslow, Offa, Onslaught, Opportune.*
      (6th D.F.) *Ashanti, Somali, Eskimo, Tartar.*
Group 'B' (3rd D.F.) *Milne, Meteor, Martin, Marne.*
      (8th D.F.) *Faulknor, Fury, Intrepid, Impulsive.*

Rear-Admiral Burnett's plans in the event of surface attack materialising were comprehensive: the sixteen destroyers would form into eight temporary divisions from the 2nd September to allow for its implementation. Again in diagram form this was as follows:

*5th Division: Milne, Meteor.*     *6th Division: Martin, Marne.*
*15th Division: Faulknor, Fury.*    *16th Division: Intrepid, Impulsive.*
*33rd Division: Onslow, Offa.*     *34th Division: Onslaught, Opportune.*
*11th Division: Ashanti, Somali.*    *12th Division: Tartar, Eskimo.*

As soon as surface action appeared likely, Rear-Admiral Burnett was to order these forces to concentrate on their Captains (D) in their respective flotilla leaders by use of the code word *STRIKE*. On receipt of this order the screen would immediately adopt the prearranged formation as follows: The *Faulknor* (Captain (D) 8th flotilla) and the *Milne* (Captain (D) 3rd flotilla) would move outward from their respective positions ahead, to port and starboard, of the screen and once clear their divisions would form on them. The *Ashanti* (Captain (D) 6th flotilla) and the *Onslow* (Captain (D) 17th flotilla), would remain in their positions on the wings of screen, to port and starboard, while their divisions also formed on them. (See Diagram p. 97.)

The remaining escorts would reform the screen as previously arranged by Commander Russell of the *Malcolm*. As the enemy surface attack developed the nearest flotilla to the bearing given by Rear-Admiral Burnett would go out and make smoke and the next flotilla nearest to the bearing would form up to attack under cover of this screen, the remaining flotilla coming across to support.

Should the attack develop from two sides the nearest flotilla to each bearing would make smoke and the remaining two flotillas would form up for the attack. In this case it was accepted that there would be no supporting flotilla unless it was found necessary to employ the three destroyers of the close escort to carry out an attack. These, the *Malcolm*, *Achates* and *Amazon*, still carried four torpedo tubes each and so could contribute. The two little 'Hunts' protecting the *Avenger*, however, carried no torpedo tubes and would have only been able to carry out dummy attacks.

Meanwhile the convoy would have been turned away from the line of attack and the through escorts would be laying smoke to cover their withdrawal. Thus any German heavy units forcing their way in through the smoke would face a potential threat of a maximum torpedo launching of 76 torpedoes backed up by a mixture of 4.7, 4.5 and 4-inch guns only. It was slim barrier but one that had worked in similar circumstances before, and certainly no previous Russian convoy had been so well protected.

They were not called upon, and their story is the story of the convoy and its passage. But even though these vessels represented the front line defence of the convoy, they were by no means the sole surface ship force which the Royal Navy deployed in this operation.

The battle fleet was moved up to Akureyri in Iceland, which they employed as an advance base for the entire period of operations. Under the command of the second-in-command Home Fleet, Vice-Admiral Sir Bruce Fraser, it consisted of the battleships *Anson* (flag) and *Duke of York*, the light cruiser *Jamaica*, with what destroyer escorts they could find. The third modern battleship, *King George V*, was unfortunately not available, for Admiral Tovey decided to retain her at Scapa Flow. From this stationary giant the commander of the Home Fleet conducted the operations and was at the same time in direct contact with the Admiralty by telephone. It is convenient here to trace the movements of this force during the whole passage of the convoy for its role was preventive rather than active.

The first period of operations from Akureyri commenced on the morning of Thursday 10th when the two battleships and the *Jamaica* arrived escorted by the destroyers *Keppel*, *Campbell* and *Mackay* under the command of 'Jackie' Broome in the former. The *Bulldog* and *Venomous*, which had helped screen them up from Scapa, had already been detached to Hvalfiord for duty with the 18th Cruiser Squadron whose movements we will return to shortly.

At Akureyri they found the destroyers *Montrose* and *Bramham*. With the heavy ships in this somewhat exposed anchorage anti-submarine patrols were established by the destroyers and some trawlers that were on hand. Northrop aircraft from the Akureyri base also kept watch and US Army fighters in batches of four maintained a constant umbrella overhead from the Melgerdi Air Station.

Vice-Admiral Fraser took his force to sea during the afternoon of the 11th on its first sortie, screened by *Keppel*, *Montrose*, *Campbell* and *Bramham*, with the intention of proceeding to a position approximately one hundred miles east of Jan Mayen Island, which was almost the limit of the destroyers' endurance. This was done and the fleet was sighted by two Blohm and Voss flying boats early the following day. These made off when an escorting Catalina appeared as A/S escort. When they had gone Vice-Admiral Fraser altered course north-west and passed to the westward of Jan Mayen Island which kept him as close to the convoy as his fuel situation would allow, while at the same time throwing the German aircraft off the scent before he returned to Iceland.

Admiral Fraser considered that now that he had been sighted steering north-east a subsequent disappearance would perform a vital deterrent effect and the farthest on position reached by the squadron was some sixty miles north of Jan Mayen Island. On Monday 14th the battle fleet returned to Iceland after encountering thick fog. Here Admiral Fraser felt uneasy for in his opinion the anti-submarine defences were far from adequate and therefore he felt safer at sea.

Accordingly on Saturday 19th the two battleships and the cruiser put to sea at dawn once more escorted by *Keppel*, *Montrose*, *Broke*, *Campbell* and *Mackay* (all veteran flotilla leaders incidentally) to cover the homeward passage of QP 14.

During the 20th the force again steered north-east through patchy fog until that evening when it turned south-west on learning that QP 14 was ahead of its schedule. Next morning reports seemed to indicate that U-boats were present off Akureyri lying in wait for the big ships return. Accordingly therefore Admiral Fraser decided to return instead to Hvalfiord and to pass through the Denmark Strait north of any possible minefields. Although he realised that the presence of icebergs would be rather an unpleasant hazard this was thought to be more acceptable than crossing an unknown minefield, As Admiral Fraser later recalled:

> Indeed it was an unpleasant night. A north-easterly gale sprang up. Numerous icebergs were sighted by RDF (radar) in time to take avoiding action but on at least one occasion, course had to be altered without previous warning to avoid a large fragment of pack ice, other were smaller and low in the water being difficult to detect except visually.[1]

Reading between the lines it would appear to have been quite an eventful passage, and if the battleships found the icebergs hazardous the destroyers, with their paper-thin hulls, must have been even more keenly on their toes during this period.

No harm was done however and the force arrived at Hvalfiord the next evening thus completing its contribution to the safe passage of the convoys. Admiral Fraser was of the opinion that after having been sighted earlier the purpose of these sorties had been achieved.

The cruiser covering force was also at sea during this period but their operations were complicated by two factors. Firstly in Admiral Tovey's opinion the risk of sending these heavy cruisers to the east of Bear Island where they were exposed to air and sea attack was not a justified one. Secondly there was the complication of the necessity of landing stores at Spitzbergen (Operation *Gearbox II*). It was planned to do this while the German aircraft were being kept busy by the main convoy operation so cruiser cover was only provided for the passage of QP 14 west of Bear Island.

The cruiser force consisted of the heavy cruisers *Norfolk* (flying the flag of Vice-Admiral S. S. Bonham-Carter), *Suffolk*, *London* and *Cumberland*, the light cruiser *Sheffield* and the destroyers *Bulldog*, *Eclipse* and *Venomous*, to which was added the *Amazon* when she got back to Iceland after her earlier adventures.

Of this force the *Cumberland*, *Sheffield* and *Eclipse* were to be detached and were to carry out the supply mission by landing their cargoes at Barentsburg. In fact this operation was very smoothly carried out and Admiral Tovey later paid tribute to the speed and efficiency with which a large quantity of stores was put ashore.

Thus did the larger warships of the Royal Navy fulfil their age-old role of quiet support. Unsung and sometimes abused, the big ships went about their business and under their comforting, though not obvious, shadow, the convoys fought their own personal wars. But just as active in defence of PQ 18 was that other arm of the 'Silent Service', the submariners, equally unseen and quietly, were playing their part in the complicated web that was woven around the forty merchant ships and their crews.

## II

Submarines meant Max Horton. To many people in the service Max Horton *was* the submarine service; certainly he was one of the greatest submariners of all time and his exploits during the First World War were legendary. It was with great satisfaction that he had received his appointment early in 1940 to the post of Vice-Admiral Submarines and he soon applied his boundless energy, coupled with his unique knowledge, experience and feeling, to the demanding job and soon made himself felt.

The post was usually held by a Rear-Admiral as the First Sea Lord Dudley Pound had mentioned at the time. Horton's reply had been typical of the man. 'I don't care a damn about the seniority as long as I have a free hand!'

And this he had been given. One of the first moves was to take his headquarters from the fastness of Aberdour in Fife down to London. He felt very strongly that the full co-operation of the Naval Staff and the Coastal Command of the Royal Air Force was absolutely essential to submarine operations. On the other hand he did not wish to be sucked into the labyrinth of the Admiralty itself as this would inevitably compromise the free hand he had just gained for himself. Horton's compromise was to move the Submarine headquarters to Swiss Cottage where he took over three floors of Northways, a smart block of flats. This position was ideally situated mid-way between the Admiralty in the centre of London and Coastal Command headquarters just on the edge of town at Northwood. Horton could thus liaise very closely with both.

Max Horton had laid his plans well but as usual his resources were slender. Every available operational submarine in the Home flotillas, the 3rd, 5th and 9th Submarine Flotillas, were detailed for operations in connection with the safe passage of PQ 18.* Even so the total number available to him was only eleven boats and these included the *Shakespeare*, a brand-new vessel carrying out her very first patrol after building, and two others, the *Unique* and *Unrivalled*, who were carrying out working-up patrols after extensive refits and repairs.

These few boats were allocated as follows:

Convoy Escort Force: *P.614, P.615.*
Covering Force: *Shakespeare, Unique, Unrivalled.*
Patrol Force: *Tribune, Tigris, Sturgeon, Unshaken* and *Uredd.*
Minelayer: *Rubis.*

Thus of the eleven boats two were from allied navies, the Norwegian *Uredd* was a British 'U' class boat commanded by Lieutenant R. O. Roren, Royal Norwegian Navy, while the *Rubis* was a Free French boat commanded by Captain de Corvette H. Rousselot, DSC. The *Rubis* had been based at Dundee carrying out minelaying operations under British control when the French collapsed in June 1940. A direct appeal from Admiral Horton had resulted in her joining the Free French forces to continue the fight, one of only a dozen which did so.

For the rest the nine British boats were from three different classes. The 'T' boats were the most suitable for northern waters being larger than the 'U's. Displacing 1,090 tons on the surface the 'T' class submarines carried a single 4-inch gun and eleven 21-inch torpedo tubes. They had a complement of 59 and an underwater maximum speed of only nine knots. The 'U' class were designed for coastal work and had won great fame in the Mediterranean theatre. Displacing a mere 540 tons, they had a crew of 31 and were armed with a single 3-inch gun and four 21-inch torpedo tubes. Their maximum speed submerged was also nine knots. These slow speeds must be remembered by those attuned to today's high speed submarines; in 1942 the submarine was not much advanced over the boats of the First World War and their performance was very limited.

The *P.614* and *P.615* were unique vessels in that they were not a British class of submarine at all but were building in the Barrow yards of Vickers Armstrong for the Turkish Navy when war

* See map pages 116–17.

broke out. They were therefore taken over by the Royal Navy and added to the fleet where they performed a useful service on the Arctic convoys before being relegated to training duties at Freetown later in the war. They never received names. At this period it was not Admiralty policy to name submarines which were identified only by their pendant numbers. This did not lend itself to pride in their ships by the crews and Winston Churchill ordered that in future all submarines should be named. This in fact was done later in the year but many boats by then had been lost without names. During this operation the *Unshaken*, *Unrivalled* and *Shakespeare* had not yet received their names but for the purpose of identification these are used throughout this book.

As we have seen the Convoy Escort Force joined PQ 18 north of Iceland and its orders were to act in this role to the vicinity of the White Sea and thence proceed direct to Polyarno Naval Base. In the event however it was later found possible for these two boats to cross over the QP 14 and escort them for a larger part of their journey to Iceland.

The Covering Force was intended to provide warning and cover in wide zones between the north of Norway and the route of the two convoys. It was fully appreciated that though this force was small it could probably be reinforced by the submarines of the patrol forces once the German ships had moved north from Narvik.

The intention of the Patrol Force was to attack these heavy units as they proceeded up from the Narvik area to their operational bases in the north. The minelaying submarine *Rubis* was unfortunately not available until later in the operation and it was therefore decided to place her on patrol off the Lofoten Islands from where she could carry out a minelaying mission across the path of the German heavy ships when they returned to Narvik after the operation. Although this looked like a case of closing the stable door atfer the horse had bolted at least such a mission would contribute something to the final score sheet if successful.

The Covering Zones were each of about fifteen miles wide and twenty miles deep and were established between positions 73 degrees north, 16 degrees east, 73 degrees north, 26 degrees east and 72 degrees north and 36 degrees east as shown on the map on pages 116–17. The intention was to establish a line of submarines in these zones and to move them so as to cover the convoys against any break out by the German battlefleet from the Altenfiord area.

In appreciation of the Germans' most likely movements, drawing on previous experience and the limitations of the Norwegian coastline, it was thought that the heavy ships would leave Narvik and proceed down Vestfiord, by Gimsostrommen through the Lofoten Islands and thence to the north-westward or else via Gavlfiord to re-enter the Leads at Malagenfiord or Haajfiord. The *Scheer* had recently been sighted in this area after her successful sortie into the White Sea. A third alternative considered was that the German ships, after leaving Narvik, would keep clear of all dangerous coastal waters and re-enter the Leads in the vicinity of Fugloysund.

It was thought that the deep draught of the *Tirpitz* would prevent her from using Tjeldsundet and Andfiord but the pocket battleship and the cruisers could certainly do so and this had to be taken into account during planning. Zones K 150 and K 154 were therefore established as indicated. K 150 was to cover the exit from Gimsostrommen to the north-west. K 151 and K 152 would cover the exit from Gavlfiord while K 153 and K 154 would cover the exit from Andfiord and allow the interception of units moving coastwise from the vicinity of Andoy.

The patrol positions were therefore selected in each patrol zone through which it was expected that the German big ships would move and alternative patrol positions were selected to cover the entrance to the Leads. These were so established that they would give any submarine forced to leave their patrol zones by enemy action a still reasonable chance of intercepting their quarry further northward.

The *Tribune* was allocated K 150, *Tigris*-151, *Sturgeon*-153, *Unshaken*-154 and *Uredd*-155. In the event however the *Sturgeon* broke down before reaching her patrol zone and returned to Lerwick as she was unable to dive. *Tigris* was therefore allocated K 152 and K 153. With the covering zones as indicated, the *Unrivalled*, *Unique* and *Shakespeare* were given K 61, K 62 and K 63 as being the least worked-up submarines, and the line was subsequently extended by the four submarines from the patrol zones.

To these boats Admiral Horton issued the orders that their targets in the patrol zones were 'Cruisers and above'. Those submarines on passage to or in the covering zones were given the same objectives and could report enemy vessels and U-boats, but all submarines were instructed to hold in reserve one full salvo of torpedoes for the heavy ships.

These were the plans; let us follow them through and judge how accurately Vice-Admiral Submarines had assessed the probable German movements.

On the 2nd September the *Tribune*, *Tigris*, *Sturgeon*, *Unshaken* and *Uredd* had sailed from Lerwick in the Shetlands to take up their positions. The following day the *Sturgeon* sighted a U-boat at seven miles range but was unable to close for an attack. It was not known whether she herself had been sighted. Also on the 3rd the *Tribune* was heavily machine-gunned by a Blenheim aircraft while sailing on the surface in a total bombing restriction area, apparently a far from uncommon experience at the hands of the Royal Air Force. It was three days after this that the *Sturgeon* developed defects in her after hydroplanes which rendered her incapable of diving and she was forced to return. The slender line of submarines was thus one less even before the operation had begun.

On the 7th the *Unique*, *Shakespeare* and *Unrivalled* also left Lerwick for their zones, at the same time the patrol force was entering their respective zones. Here they spent three days on watch and finally, on the 10th September at 0345, they were rewarded with a firm sighting.

As usual the first signs of a sortie by the German battlefleet was heavy minesweeping activity along the vital stretches of the route north. The *Tigris* (Lieutenant-Commander G. R. Colvin) sighted two minesweepers entering Gavlfiord steering south and three hours later the *Unshaken* (Lieutenant C. E. Oxborrow, DSO) sighted another pair sweeping to the northeast off Andoy Point. The position was made absolutely certain by the similar spotting by the *Tribune* (Lieutenant M. C. R. Lumby) of a further two minesweepers steering south into Gimsostrommen.

If there were any lingering doubts that the German big ships were out they were removed at 1037 when Lieutenant Lumby sighted through his periscope the foretops and funnels of heavy units proceeding from the entrance of Gimsostrommen towards

Gavlfiord. The force passed *Tribune* at speed and Lumby thought that one of the vessels was the *Tirpitz*. Cursing his impotence the British skipper could do little to hinder their swift passage for the sighting was made at a range of 20,000 yards and there was no possibility of carrying out an attack. The stately squadron swept past on the distant horizon and vanished. At 1158 Lumby brought the *Tribune* to the surface and broadcast an enemy report but received no acknowledgement. She repeated this report again that afternoon again without a reply. In fact both her messages had got through to Flag Officer Submarines but too late for him to act on them. He could only trust to his previous dispositions and good fortune.

The *Tigris* was the next submarine to sight the German ships. At 1340 Lieutenant-Commander Colvin caught a glimpse of the fore top of a German heavy ship leaving Gavlfiord at a range of about nine miles. The weather was fine and sunny and the sea was a glassy calm with a low westerly swell. Visibility was very good. These were not the ideal conditions for an attack by a lone submarine against a fast, heavily escorted battlefleet but none the less Colvin commenced his attack.

After a few minutes he made a further observation of his target and Colvin could now see and confirm that the force consisted of three heavy ships accompanied by destroyers. Colvin's sightings he thought were the *Tirpitz* herself, the *Hipper* and *Köln* but in fact he was mistaken; the *Tirpitz* had not moved from Narvik, and the largest vessel was in fact the *Scheer*. In addition to the destroyer escort Colvin now made out a Heinkel He 115 carrying out a search ahead of the German squadron and this caused him to be very cautious in the use of his periscope.

By 1350 the *Tigris* had worked her way into a position some ten degrees on the port bow of the centre ship of the formation which was observed to be steering in line abreast in open order. The light cruiser *Köln was* to seaward, the *Tirpitz* (in fact the *Hipper*), and the *Hipper* (the *Scheer*), on the landward side. Colvin estimated that the escorting screen comprised about six destroyers which were deployed both ahead and on the seaward side only of the heavy ships. The German destroyers were proceeding at very high speed and zig-zagging under continuous helm.

Thus, eleven minutes after her initial sighting, the *Tigris* found herself ten degrees on the bow of the port wing ship, the *Köln*, at a range of about six miles. The British submarine was herself steering northward roughly parallel to the enemy's line of advance and retiring from them. As was later pointed out, submarines rarely find themselves placed in such a favourable position in time of war.

However conditions otherwise were about the most difficult possible from a submarine's point of view with the flat calm sea, the squadron moving at very high speed and an effective and mobile force with air cover as well. The German squadron had used the advantage offered by the shoal water to the eastward and could thus deploy the whole of his screen on the exposed side. Such a screen is most disconcerting at any time and doubly so in flat calm weather when observations through the periscope must be kept to the barest minimum if the submarine is not to be sighted.

Lieutenant-Commander Colvin appreciated that the enemy might commence to zigzag or alternately make a bold navigational alteration of course to the westward to gain deep water so he therefore maintained his northerly course which placed him about 1,500 yards off track. He wanted to fire after the screen had passed *Tigris* and Colvin also thought that there would be less chance of the torpedo tracks being sighted if they were fired from abaft the beam. He therefore decided to turn in and fire on a comparatively broad track, 110 degrees, at the appropriate moment.

The choice of a broad track angle, especially against a high speed target, was later said to have one very great disadvantage which overrode all other considerations and this was the fact that such an attack allowed for no last-minute margin for adjustment. The target was proceeding at twenty-five knots plus at a range of 1,500 yards and was thus changing its bearing at an average of thirty degrees per minute or half a degree per second. It was therefore almost impossible to regain the Director Angle once it had been missed. All depended therefore on Colvin and the *Tigris* having an uninterrupted shot at the vital moment. But this was not to be.

By 1351 the port wing ship appeared to alter slightly to starboard as viewed from *Tigris* and the He 115 was almost overhead the British submarine. Colvin therefore took his boat down to forty feet returning to periscope depth three minutes later. The He 115 had gone on by and was not seen again.

Colvin quickly estimated his position as some 500 yards from the *Köln* and about 4,000 yards from *Tirpitz* (*Scheer*). He decided to fire a dispersal salvo of ten torpedoes at the bigger target, and, as it appeared that some of his torpedoes might run under the other two ships of smaller draught, he reduced the depth settings of the internal torpedoes from thirty-four feet to twenty-four feet. Colvin put the German squadron's speed at twenty-eight knots and ordered a firing interval of five seconds.

The vital seconds began to tick away, Colvin concentrated on his target taking quick glimpses which confirmed his attack. At 1400 he turned to attack altering course to 080 degrees to give a track angle of 110 degrees. As the *Tigris* turned one of the screening destroyers went past at a distance of about three cables to the eastward. Her bow wave was piled high and her wash was thrown up above the level of her quarterdeck showing that she was steaming flat out.

The attack was timed at 1406. Two minutes to firing and with a few degrees still to go on Colvin's course there still remained two destroyers yet to pass over *Tigris*. Colvin himself takes up the story.

The nearest was close, but although they were weaving constantly I thought that I was inside the screen. At 1405½ the submarine had just steadied on her firing course when the Asdic Operator reported very loud HE on the starboard quarter; this was the first of the two destroyers about five cables distant and swinging under helm towards me; I kept her under observation using an inch or two of periscope for a few seconds at a time and she kept swinging until I was fine on her port bow when she passed down my starboard side about fifty yards distant. When the destroyer had cleared my bow, I found I had missed the DA by between five and ten degrees; this was at 1406½.[9]

The *Tigris* frantically altered course to port in a vain attempt to retain a DA and as she did so the last destroyer of the screen passed ahead about two cables distant with the noise of an express train. Once this escort had crashed past Colvin was able to use his periscope more freely. At 1414½ the *Tigris* commenced firing a salvo of individually aimed torpedoes, but the range as Colvin himself admitted, was clearly excessive and after he had fired two torpedoes with a point of aim amidships, three more were fired spread well ahead to compensate for the tail-off of speed at long ranges; he then ceased firing as the range was by this time well outside the capacity of his torpedoes. The estimated range was about 7,000 yards and the enemy speed twenty-eight knots. The five Mark VIII torpedoes with CCR Pistols had a speed of forty-six knots and were set to seventeen and twenty-four feet depths. There were no hits.

In such a way could the patient and unrewarded searching of months be missed by a few fleeting seconds which would never recur. As the Admiral later concluded in his report;

> A glimpse of this destroyer through the periscope revealed that she was swinging towards *Tigris* and in watching her until she passed him, the Commanding Officer's attention was diverted from his targets at a most crucial time. When he next sighted his target, his chance of firing had passed. Had *Tigris* been steady on his firing course for even one or two minutes he must have appreciated the rate of change of bearing, but he denied himself this chance and failed to realise that by concentrating his attention on the destroyer he was throwing away his chance of a successful attack.[9]

However it was admitted that the physical obstruction tactics employed by the German destroyers during this operation were a new factor in submarine operations as was the very intelligent use of shoal water. It was further admitted that wartime conditions had precluded sufficient practice of attacks against high speed heavy ships screened by destroyers and British submarine officers had to be content with attacks on slow and small targets occasionally screened. It was only on rare occasions that attacks on single destroyers moving at comparatively high speeds had been possible. Attacks on slow targets do not train Command Officers to appreciate and think quickly in rapidly changing situations and this was of course yet another inevitable outcome of the general shortage of ships and training facilities under which all British naval operations were labouring, and indeed always laboured in time of war following a long period of retrenchment.

The disappointed Colvin brought *Tigris* to the surface at 1502 and made an enemy sighting report which was picked up by FOS thirty-two minutes later at Swiss Cottage. What other flags remained on the chart between the German big ships and Altenfiord? In truth only two, and these had already been bypassed by the speeding German units.

The *Unshaken* had already heard, at 1415, the explosions which resulted from the *Tigris's* torpedoes exploding at the ends of their runs and five minutes later she sighted the same aircraft that had been sweeping ahead of the German squadron. At 1448 the hydroplanes picked up noises from the direction of the west coast of Andoy moving slowly eastward, and at 1504 Lieutenant Oxborrow sighted masts. Nine minutes later he too had the heart-lifting sight of the fighting tops of the three German ships lifting over the horizon nine miles away.

The hydrophone effects disappeared and Oxborrow estimated from his plot that the big ships had rounded Andoy and gone into Andfiord but this was not the case. However Oxborrow considered that as he and *Uredd* were both in such an excellent position to intercept the enemy when they re-emerged from Andfiord he would not break W/T silence and give herself and her consort away. *Unshaken* therefore lay siege to an empty burrow.

Meanwhile the *Uredd* (Lieutenant R. O. Roren, Royal Norwegian Navy), which was on the west side of the Andfiord entrance, had sighted the German squadron eleven miles to the north of him. Roren identified the ships as the *Hipper* or *Tirpitz* leading the *Scheer*, and at 1557 she lost sight of them on a bearing of forty-six degrees.

The sightings of *Unshaken* and *Uredd* when placed together on the chart became completely irreconcilable, and either the *Unshaken* was far further to the north than she thought or the *Uredd* was seven or eight miles further south. A full and careful investigation into the statements made by both Oxborrow and Roren however failed to produce any firm answer to this mystery. In any case the main thing was that the German ships had now passed safely through all the patrol zones and were certain to reach Altenfiord unscathed. From here they were in position to sortie against the convoys.

*Uredd* surfaced and transmitted a report that three enemy main units had entered Malangenfiord at 1630 but as this was broadcast on the mast aerial only it was not received. Back at Northways the position was now far from clear. Only *Tribune's* and *Tigris*'s reports had been picked up at 1708 and it was uncertain which German vessels were in fact at sea, although both reports categorically included a single battleship. It appeared therefore that at least one battleship remained at Narvik and that shortage of destroyers would ensure that it would stay there for some time, six of those available to the Germans having gone north. The British submarines were therefore re-assigned to new positions.

Both *Tribune* and *Tigris* had given away their positions and would be of little value remaining on their patrol beats for if the last German heavy unit did sail to join the others it would use the same route. The covering line to the north of Norway was only three boats strong and the enemy had heavy units ready to make a sortie, there was no question but to reinforce the covering force as quickly as possible. This intention was conveyed to Admiral Tovey and to the Vice-Chief of Naval Staff, Vice-Admiral Sir Henry Moore, and both approved.

In a final effort at clarification both 'T' boats were asked to report by signal which main unit they had seen and both replied, incorrectly, that it had been the *Tirpitz*. Meanwhile, at 2340, *Unshaken*'s unfortunate signal came in which completely altered the situation and give the impression that the squadron, perhaps upset by the attack of *Tigris*, had taken shelter in Andfiord. *Uredd*'s report, as we have seen was not taken in and therefore *Tigris*, *Unshaken* and *Uredd* were not after all sent north to reinforce the covering force but were concentrated to cover the northern approaches to this, empty, stretch of water.

It was not until the 11th that a report was received from the Spitfires of the Photo Reconnaissance Unit operating from Russia which revealed that *Scheer*, *Hipper* and *Köln* lay at anchor in Altenfiord but that there was no sign of *Tirpitz*. This report was in such stark contrast to the 'T' boats' reports that *Uredd* was asked to confirm her position on the 9th, but she never replied to this signal.

Meanwhile the submarines of the covering force were reinforced on the 12th and 13th and subsequently moved up and down their appointed beats until the 20th with no sight or sign of the German fleet. On the 20th therefore they were recalled to Lerwick.

Meanwhile the *Rubis* had left that harbour early on 12th

September for her patrol position well clear of the Lofoten Islands. On the 16th her orders were modified and she was told to lay mines on a five mile front between three and eight miles of Kjolva Point off the entrance of Malangenfiord, and she did without event on the 19th.

The final movements of the British submarines in this operation, apart from the two of the Convoy Escort Force, were that the *Tigris* and *Tribune* were diverted on the 20th from their homeward passage to Lerwick and sent back to patrol zones K 151 to K 154 once more in the hope that the big German ships would slip back to Narvik now that the operation had concluded. This they did but after a week's fruitless patrolling both were recalled on the 27th and arrived back at Lerwick after spending twenty-eight days at sea.

### III

Yet another factor in the great net of deterrent forces spread around PQ 18 was the contribution of Coastal Command, Royal Air Force, under Air Marshal Sir Philip Joubert. It was thought that the stationing of torpedo-bombers in North Russia would act as a major threat to any sortie by the German battle fleet and, to provide the necessary reconnaissance to enable this striking force to be sent out in time to be effective four PRU Spitfires were also sent out as we have seen. In addition to their patrols additional PRU aircraft were to be operated from bases in the United Kingdom to cover those bases that were out of range of the four Russian based Spitfires. This reconnaissance of course could not extend to full cover, nor was it capable of shadowing the German surface ships once they put to sea; their role was therefore a very limited one.

Enough Catalina flying boats were also despatched to maintain cross-over patrols off the Norwegian fiords so that they could cover the likely courses which the German ships would have to take to locate the convoys. The hope was therefore mainly to ensure that the German fleet did not sail unobserved and secondly to deter it. In the last resort it was hoped that perhaps the Hampdens might score a hit or two on the big ships if they did sail. The flying boats would also of course be able to operate as long-range anti-submarine aircraft to cover the path of the convoys and supplement the efforts of *Avenger*'s valiant Swordfish in this duty.

The total striking force therefore consisted of some thirteen Catalinas of 210 Squadron, thirty-two Hampdens of 144 and 455 (RAAF) Squadrons, the whole force being under the command of Group Captain F. L. Hopps, RAF. The maintenance personnel, and torpedo and photographic equipment for the Hampdens and Spitfires, were sent on ahead by the American cruiser *Tuscaloosa*, and the base was set up at Vaenga on the Kola Inlet. The Catalinas, however, were required to operate from Sullom Voe before flying transit sorties to North Russia, so their maintenance party was flown to Lake Lakhta near Archangel, a Russian Naval Air Service base. However as soon as the Senior RAF Officer arrived there he decided that communications with Lakhta were so bad as to make it necessary to operate the flying-boats instead from Grasnaya, some three miles higher up the Kola Inlet than Vaenga. This new base had the additional advantage of being some four hundred miles nearer the patrol area. Its main disadvantage was that it lay close to the front line and frequent air attacks could be expected; none the less Group Captain Hopps decided that this risk must be accepted.

Hopps himself set up his headquarters at Polyarnoe where the *SBNO* was based together with the most reliable meteorological service in that part of the Soviet Union. The Soviets of course had fighters, long-range reconnaissance, bombers and a small number of torpedo-bombers in the area and they were given details of the British plan of interception each day, and arrangements were made for the Soviet torpedo-bombers to take off at the same time as the Hampdens if a strike became necessary.

In addition to the setting up of this force tentative plans had been made by Bomber Command to assist in some way and an attack on the German battle fleet was considered while these ships were still at Narvik. These vessels were however beyond the range of the aircraft of the period and such an attack would mean that the heavy bombers also would have to land in North Russia, refuel, and then return home after carrying out their attack. Although Admiral Tovey offered to send the necessary ground staff by sea to prepare for such a sortie in the same manner as with the Catalina and Hampden units, the Soviets

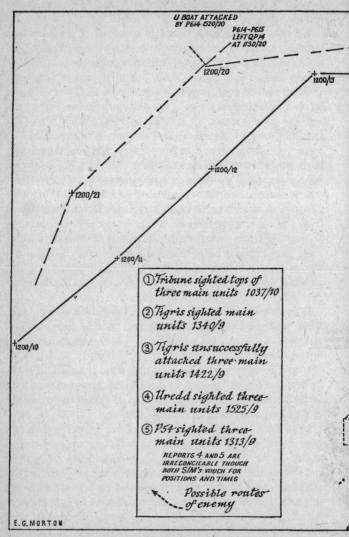

U BOAT ATTACKED
BY P614 1520/20

P614~P615
LEFT QP14
AT 1130/20

1200/20

1200/13

1200/12

1200/21

1200/11

1200/10

① *Tribune sighted tops of three main units 1037/10*

② *Tigris sighted main units 1340/9*

③ *Tigris unsuccessfully attacked three main units 1422/9*

④ *Uredd sighted three main units 1525/9*

⑤ *P54 sighted three main units 1313/9*

REPORTS 4 AND 5 ARE
IRRECONCILABLE THOUGH
BOTH S/M's VOUCH FOR
POSITIONS AND TIMES

- - - → *Possible routes of enemy*

E. G. MORTON

Submarine patrols and the route of German Forces

SPITZBERGEN
1200/19

QP 14    1200/18
          +
1200/14          1200/15
PQ 18

Bear Island

British Submarine
Covering Zones Area

0800/16

URGEON WITH DEFECTS
RETURNS TO LERWICK
1400 6TH.
RUBIS PATROL
POSITION 16·9–19·9
RUBIS MINEFIELD
A.M. 19·9

Alten
Fiord

Tromsö

② ③
④ ⑤

Polyarnoe

Narvik

N O R W A Y

S/M OPERATIONS
Sept., 2nd – Oct., 1st
1942

0        100        200  Miles

refused to allow this and so the contribution of Bomber Command was dropped.

In order that the elderly Hampdens should have sufficient margin of fuel they were routed to Afrikanda airfield to the north-east of Kandalaksha, on the gulf of the same name, in the White Sea. However from their subsequent hair-raising adventures and escapes it would seem that their briefing was not as complete as it might have been.

The Hampden was acting as a stop-gap in the torpedo bomber role and this slim little twin-engined bomber was not really up to such a gruelling role as it found itself in. In truth the RAF was quite unprepared for torpedo-bomber warfare on the outbreak of war and both its active units were equipped at that time with the obsolete Wildebeeste. The change-over from this to the Beaufort had followed but very heavy losses had been taken in the two previous years of operations and most of the torpedo-bomber aces were operational in the Mediterranean theatre. The Hampdens were utilised pending the development fully of the faster Beaufighter as a torpedo dropper. One thing though that the Hampden did have superior to any other British torpedo aircraft and that was range. This was coupled with excellent visibility for the pilot and, although never put to the test, this aircraft might have operated well against poor resistance. Certainly the resourcefulness of the two squadrons was put to the test during the eventful month of September 1942.

Thirty-two Hampdens took off from Sumburgh on the evening of 4th September but only twenty-three reached Afrikanda or any other North Russian airfield. Five of these unfortunate aircraft crashed through lack of fuel or were shot down by German and Finnish fighters in Norway and Sweden, three from 144 Squadron piloted by Pilot Officer E. H. E. Perry, and Sergeants J. C. Bray and L. H. Bertrand, and two from 455 Squadron piloted by Squadron Leader Catanach and Sergeant Smart. About their fate more will be told. Of the other one from 144, piloted by Sergeant E. H. D. Nelson, eventually crash-landed near Afrikanda airfield. Sergeant Nelson described his adventures with his new allies:

At 0232 on 5th September over position Kandalaksha by dead reckoning. Continuous low cloud but a momentary break showed railway, proceding north-east to Barents Sea coast. Flew coast wise through Kildin Isles Channel, heavy flak although wheels down and colour fired. Hit in starboard wing. Fired on by ships in Kola Inlet. Proceded to Ribachi Peninsula, fired on heavily from peninsula and mainland although wheels raised and lowered.[45]

Eventually with his petrol down to twenty minutes, enveloped in ten-tenths cloud and fired on every time he poked his nose out, Nelson decided to force land on a flat soft field near Khibini town. This he did and at 0620 was wheels up in a soft mossy field with no casualties. While they were burning secret papers three children aged between eight and ten came up and the aircrew shouted out *Angliski* and handed out chocolate to the children who promptly demanded cigarettes!

They were subsequently arrested by five workers armed with rifles and searched, the villagers taking a Paybook, *Readers Digest* and a paperback volume entitled *Last Laugh* which, as Nelson recalled, they guarded very carefully. The local commissar arrived but left shortly as no one could make the other understand but friendly relations were finally established after two and a half hours. They were finally taken by truck to Kirossh airfield by some Soviet Ground Staff and next day caught the train to Murmansk. Nelson made a strong point on the arrangements of the flight stating that:

It is considered that had crew been aware of possibility of landing at Vaenga and method of doing so, they could have got down without any trouble. An aircraft which was approx five minutes behind them in vicinity Kildin Island was met and guided in successfully by Russian Hurricanes, although in their case also the pilot had not been given details or briefed on Vaenga as an alternative.[45]

This was a criticism others were to echo. Sergeant Hood, also of 144 had a worse experience. He found himself over hostile Finland at 0250 that same day but later arrived over Murmansk. Light flak was encountered and his Hampden turned north to avoid the worst effects of this. At this moment, when some five miles north of the city two fighters came up on his tail. They were first sighted at 900 yards by Sergeant O'Neil the wireless operator, climbing rapidly. Sergeant Hood fired a recognition cartridge but the two Soviet fighters ignored this, closed and opened fire. Hood threw his aircraft into a steep dive while O'Neil returned fire, but the fighters followed him down to water level, the Hampden touched 350 mph in the dive but it still held together.

Eventually the Hampden was forced to ditch but the air gunner, Sergeant Tabor, had been badly injured by the fighters' fire. He was in the lower rear gun position and the aircraft was sinking rapidly. Sergeant O'Neil tried desperately to get him out as the water rose but he was trapped by his Mae West and his head and shoulders could not be freed. He was believed to be dead and this gallant rescue attempt had to be abandoned as the Hampden sank in about five fathoms of water.

As the British aircrew struggled clear of the sinking aircraft the Russian fighters, which had followed them down, made strafing runs. They survived this hail of fire and swam to the shore which was about forty yards distant. A group of men appeared and fired on them from the shore but desisted when they shouted 'Angliski'. Struggling out of the icy water they were taken to a hut where they were stripped.

Here they found that they were at an inlet called Polyarnoe Zueada to the south-west of Polyarnoe and later an English-speaking Russian Naval Officer arrived and questioned them. When they assured him positively that the flak and the fighters had quite certainly been Russian, he eventually took them with much concern to the SBNO and they spent the night in the sick bay of the Submarine Base. Again this crew stated that they were not briefed on the aerodromes in the northern part of the area, nor had they been told of the Murmansk defences and air corridor.

Another Hampden of this squadron piloted by Pilot Officer D. I. Evans was forced down through engine failure, crashed into a mountain and was burnt out. The navigator, wireless operator and air gunner were killed and only Evans and Corporal B. J. Sowerby survived.

455 Squadron had similar experiences. Pilot Officer Patrick arrived over Afrikanda without incident but could only see the railway and not the aerodrome. By 0545 his petrol was almost exhausted and so he decided to force land. Gliding down he cut his engines at one hundred feet and put his bomber down among

the tree stumps of a thinned out wood with no casualties. They worked out their position as about five miles west of Kandalaksha.

Patrick and Sergeant McIver, the navigator, left the others to guard the aircraft and went to get help. After slogging a mile they saw a Russian soldier and called to him but their reception was far from friendly. Eventually they managed to convince him they were not Germans and after one and half hours a lorry took them to a military camp. Here they found that everyone was very friendly and they were given a meal before being taken to Afrikanda.

Almost every aircraft encountered either flak or fighters on the way in. Pilot Officer Gunton reported that his aircraft was fired on by heavy flak, first by a ship in the Kola Inlet and later by ground fire. He fired his recognition cartridges but without any effect. Flight Lieutenant O'Connor's aircraft was hit in the tail by light accurate flak which did not cease when colours were fired. Heavy flak near Murmansk also continued despite displaying recognition lights and three fighters made a pass at him. O'Connor lowered his wheels and they veered off. Sergeant Gleeson's aircraft crew witnessed the destruction of Sergeant Hood's Hampden as they saw it at a distance of some ten miles being chased and forced down. Sergeant Gleeson 'deemed it prudent to turn away and dive for ground cover!'

On the other hand Sergeant Lord's Hampden had a different encounter with the Soviet fighters. After being fired at over an airfield he proceeded to Kola Inlet where he was sighted by two Airocobras which made feint attacks. He fired his recognition signals and put his wheels down, whereupon the two fighters flew ahead and led him into Murmachi airfield where he landed at 0510.

Eventually the survivors assembled at Vaenga airfield and awaited events. While there they were able to judge their Soviet allies at first hand. Everyone was very courteous and pleasant and the atmosphere was later said to be most cordial with all ranks getting on well with the Russian hosts. The senior ranks were especially co-operative and General Kuznetzov their commander in particular did everything he could to help. In one respect attitudes were noticeable, the junior officers seemed rather frightened to take decisions; however, when a matter was brought before a senior officer things moved very quickly.

The Russian interpreters were very good but communications was in general very poor. This applied to both internal communication and contact with the United Kingdom. The W/T black-out was liable to descend without warning north of sixty degrees north. In these circumstances the RAF unit had to rely on the Russian telephones, which at their best were not good. In one typical incident quoted it took as a rule over an hour to phone to Grasnaya from Polyarnoe via Vaenga, a distance of ten miles and the situation was not helped by the Russian operator's habit of cutting off whenever there was the slightest pause in the conversation.

Again the roads in this region were uniformly bad both round the Kola Inlet and Archangel. The Russians themselves were of course so short of equipment that there was none to spare for the RAF who felt the lack of bowsers and the like acutely. As one officer said, nobody could wait on a bare aerodrome in that climate! Nor was the food any compensation, proving, as expected, extremely monotonous though palatable. Extra rations had been sent out which proved a blessing. The hutments were warm enough but no protection had been provided against the mosquitoes and black fly which swarmed around the area.

With regard to the equipment provided the British seemed to have been no better prepared after three years of war than the Germans had been before Moscow the year before. The kapok-lined 'Tropal' coats were useless in cold weather for the snow froze on them making them so stiff that movement was hampered and the wind blew up beneath them. Leather boots proved equally useless against the cold.

The Catalinas of 210 Squadron meanwhile operated continuous anti-surface ship patrols from the 11th of September onward but this broke down on the night of the 13th/14th September, the most vital period. Many of these aircraft were diverted from their transit patrols to land at Grasnaya but did not receive the message and proceeded as originally instructed to Lake Lakhta. As a result of this only a single operational Catalina was available, A/210 piloted by Flight Lieutenant B. Lewin. She had been long overdue for an inspection and one engine failed to start. It proved impossible to provide a replacement engine from Lake Lakhta because of the usual W/T black-out so the crew worked all night changing the plugs and with the help of the Russians got their aircraft off at dawn. As a result the patrol had to be shifted further out to sea in order to sight any German force that might have left Altenfiord. Unfortunately this patrol was routed so far from the coast that even if the Catalina had sighted the German squadron and reported back the Hampdens would not have got off in time to intercept them.

Up to this date the *Tirpitz* had been quite definitely located and pinpointed at her usual berth at Trondheim and had made no move to join her smaller consorts at Altenfiord. However on this date the Catalina patrol from Britain reported that she was no longer there. A check on Altenfiord revealed that she had not joined the other warships there and as a result there was considerable anxiety at the Admiralty. As a result the panic button was pushed and Group Captain Hopps ordered into the air every serviceable Hampden, twenty-three aircraft in all, to carry out a sweep and reconnaissance in force.

At 0500 on the 14th therefore all hands stood to for the strike at their bleak north Russian base. Their targets were given to them as enemy naval units which were expected to leave Altenfiord. Eleven aircraft of 144 Squadron took off at 0815 in formations of six and five under the leadership of Wing Commander McLaughlin. One of these aircraft, 'T' Tommy, had been loaned by 455 Squadron and they contributed to a total of twelve aircraft to the strike force led by Squadron Leader Holmes.

This force was sent out to the farthest possible position on the probable track of the German force with instructions to return along it until they reached the Catalina patrol area. A few Soviet torpedo bombers were to co-operate in accordance with the arrangement already made but this came to nothing and one Soviet aircraft was lost. The Hampdens were airborne from Vaenga and flew to a point over Kilden Island and then struck north to a point some 120 miles further out from the Kola Inlet. From this point they set course for a position 73° 5′ N, 20° 20′ E. On reaching this point the force then swept to the south down the track to Altenfiord before turning east again assembling over Kilden Island and returning to base. The whole flight was totally without incident; no German ships or submarines were sighted nor were any enemy aircraft met on either the outward or inward search and all aircraft returned to Vaenga at 1500 without loss.

The result of this abortive mission was judged to be a success for the following reasons. It was considered that the convoy had by this date reached a position sufficiently far to the east to make it impossible for the German units to attack without coming into the range of the Squadron's torpedoes. It was believed, though there was no confirmation, that the Squadron had been sighted by an enemy aircraft and, having been reported, may have been a deterrent.

Despite heavy air attacks on their home airfield by German aircraft the Hampdens were hastily refuelled and were all ready for action again the next morning but that afternoon the PRU sortie showed that the German heavy ships still lay serenely at anchor at Altenfiord. *Tirpitz* was however still unlocated and the Hampdens remained ready for action for the next three days.

On the night of the 15th the Squadron's airfield was subjected to continuous air raids. Lack of camouflage nets worried the British commanders as their aircraft were dispersed around the field, but at first the German bombers paid more attention to the half of the base occupied by Soviet aircraft and the PRU Spitfires. The Hampdens at the other end were stationed 150 yards apart and suffered very little, but one of the Spitfires was damaged.

It was a very different story however on the night of the 27th and all through that day. In particular a bombing attack at 1600 was delivered with great skill and during the course of it a Soviet fighter was shot down overhead and crashed into the officers' sleeping quarters causing loss of most of their equipment but no deaths. At 2100 the Junkers returned and this time they hit both the airfield and the Hampden dispersals, severely damaging twelve of the British bombers.

The armoury was set on fire by flying shrapnel and flares, ammunition and equipment destroyed. With half their strength gone in a single attack and the convoy safely through there was no further need for the Hampdens' crews to remain. Their aircraft were handed over to the Russians and a special ceremony was held on 12th October to mark the event, the air and ground crews returning to England aboard the cruiser *Argonaut* later that month.

Meanwhile the Catalinas had provided continuous escort to PQ 18 from the 3rd to 12th September. There was then a gap of three days until Catalinas could be spared from the anti-surface ship searches, and from the 16th to the 19th, when PQ 18 arrived in the White Sea, two Catalinas accompanied the escort. From the 18th onwards these aircraft were switched to help escort the homeward bound QP 14. The only loss these big flying boats suffered was that of Z/330 which was shot down by a U-boat but the crew were picked up by the destroyer *Marne*.

This was the role played by the Royal Air Force in protecting PQ 18.

It is of interest here to see what conclusions were reached by the British about the effectiveness of all their forms of defence in deterring the German surface ships from attacking PQ 18 in conjunction with the submarines and torpedo bombers.

In their final conclusions it can be seen that the combination of all these arms was held to have been responsible. Admiral Tovey made this point quite clearly in his report which was circulated without disagreement after the event. In it he stated that the reason for the failure of the Germans to make any further move after the transfer of the *Scheer*, *Hipper* and *Köln* to Altenfiord could not be definitely established, but was in his opinion due, not to any single factor, but to a combination of :

(a)  The strength of the destroyer covering force.
(b)  The presence, emphasised by the *Tigris*'s attack, of our submarines off the north coast of Norway; and of two submarines with the convoy.
(c)  The presence, known to the enemy, of our torpedo carrying aircraft in North Russia.
(d)  The knowledge that their forces were constantly being reconnoitred by our aircraft.
(e)  The sighting of the battle fleet, north-east of Iceland and steering to the north-eastwards, on 12th September, and doubt as to its subsequent movements.[1]

The RAF of course did not admit to (a), (b) or (e) as having any effect of value so much as their own presence. It was recorded that :

The aircrew were disappointed at not having an opportunity of engaging the enemy but the main purpose of the detachment was achieved, namely the frustration of enemy naval surface units from attacking convoys between Britain and North Russia![56]

Our Soviet ally of course held that the main attack on the convoy was in fact the air raids made *after* the convoy reached the White Sea!

So much for the claims of glory in a surface battle that did not take place. Let us turn to the German records and see what was the real cause of their big ships staying in Altenfiord.

## IV

In fact the decision not to send the German fleet out against PQ 18 had been taken more than a month before when the results of the success against PQ 17 were analysed. It was the false reading of this victory which muzzled the surface fleet later for, as usual with air forces the world over, the Luftwaffe made claims far in excess of their achievements when reporting on PQ 17. The pilots of *Luftflotte V* claimed in all to have despatched one cruiser, one destroyer, two other escort vessels and twenty-two merchant ships. The U-boats made their own claims of sixteen ships totalling 113,963 tons and amended the Luftwaffe total to twenty merchantmen of a total tonnage of 131,000 tons.

Later Colonel-General Stumpff in a letter to Reichsmarschall Goering went further. 'I claim for *Luftflotte V* the sinking of twenty-two merchant vessels together comprising 142,216 tons.' In actual fact PQ 17's losses, ghastly as they were, came out much lower than this for it lost a total of twenty-four ships, of which only eight were sunk by air attack alone, nine U-boats with another seven 'shared' by the combined attacks of both. But, more than the false details, the Germans missed the whole point, which was that it was the fear of the intervention of the German *surface ships* that had caused the convoy to be scattered to its doom. The Luftwaffe thought that its attacks alone had broken the convoy up but this was absolutely wrong. The subsequent German decision was therefore based on this false reading of their greatest victory.

The German Naval Command was no less elated than the

Luftwaffe, and stated that the success was the result of 'exemplary co-operation between aircraft and U-boats.' Because these two arms had achieved as much as any fleet could have hoped to have done, it was decided that this method of attack should be the basis of future operations against the heavily-guarded outward PQ convoys, while the heavy ships should confine their sorties to those mounted against the less well defended homeward QP convoys where their task was felt to be easier. Such operations would be backed up by minelaying operations carried out by the *Ulm* and other vessels, including the *Hipper* and destroyers.

This course of action therefore decided events during the passage of PQ 18 and was not even discussed at the next Naval Conference at the *Wehrwolf* headquarters of the Fuehrer on the Eastern Front held on 26th August. Present at this conference were the C-in-C Navy, Admiral Erich Raeder, Vice-Admiral Krancke, Raeder's permanent representative at the Fuehrer's HQ and Captain Karl-Jesco von Puttkamer, the Fuehrer's naval adjutant.

This conference was held at a time when the Third Reich was the apex of its power. Just the previous day the great summer offensive had reached a spectacular climax as General Kleist's 1st Panzer Army spearheaded Army Group A's magnificent thrust into the Caucasus by taking the town of Mozdok on the river Terek within easy reach of the oil fields at Grozny. Maikop, Nalchik and Novorossisk on the Black Sea coast had already fallen. In the north the Volga had been reached and Astrakhan and Baku on the Caspian seemed certain to fall. The swastika banner was raised high on Mount Erebus. The Navy was also in rare favour after the humiliations heaped on the Allies by the Channel Dash in February, PQ 17 in July and an equally false assumption of victories achieved against the Malta convoys by the Italians. In addition the U-boats were sinking some 700,000 tons of Allied shipping a month in the Atlantic. Little wonder then that Hitler was in a conciliatory mood with his Naval chiefs.

The use of the Navy in the war against Russia naturally came up. In the Arctic Ocean Raeder could report that his searches for the next convoy had drawn a blank. 'Evidently PQ 18 did not sail.' He drew his own conclusions from this which he gave his Fuehrer in concise, and in places, only too accurate form.

We can thus assume that our submarines and aircraft, which totally destroyed convoy PQ 17, have forced the enemy to give up this route temporarily, or even fundamentally to change his whole system of supply lines. Supplies to northern ports of Russia remain decisive for the whole conduct of the war waged by the Anglo-Saxons. They must preserve Russia's strength in order to keep German forces occupied. The enemy will most probably continue to ship supplies to northern Russia, and the Naval Staff must therefore maintain submarines along the same routes.*

The Grand-Admiral continued by detailing the role of the Fleet now based in Norway. The reason for stationing the greater part of the surface navy here, he said, was the twofold one of a constant threat against the Russian convoys and a deterrent against invasion by the Allies, a thought very often in both Hitler's and Churchill's minds at this time. He added that the bonus of this great 'Fleet in being' was that it tied down the British Home Fleet in great strength and this was especially valuable in the light of heavy losses suffered by the Allies in the Mediterranean and the Pacific. With all this Hitler expressed his complete agreement.

Therefore we can see from this that the post-war criticism heaped on Hitler for keeping his fleet in Norway was completely unjustified in that, firstly, he was only accepting proposals put to him by his own Commander-in-Chief and, secondly, by the fact that the success of this strategy on Allied seapower was only too plain to see and has constantly been bemoaned ever since. In this decision the Fuehrer was right.

Thus it was only against QP 14 that the big ships were to be unleashed. What effect did the elaborate British defence measures have on the safety of this homeward convoy, among whose ranks it must be recalled, were the greater part of the survivors, angry and embittered, of PQ 17?

It will be remembered that six of the Coastal Command Hampdens that set out from Sumburgh failed to reach Russia. One of these unfortunates was 'G-George' Squadron Leader Catanach, hit by flak from the German armed trawler *UJ.1105* off the Norwegian coast and crash-landing near Vardo. Only four

* The Fuhrer's Naval Conferences, Brasseys Naval Annual 1948.

of the crew survived and did not have opportunity to destroy the secret documents relating to radio-communications organisation to be used during the passage of the two convoys. The Germans reported that a total of five Hampdens had been shot down, crashing in Lapland and one in northern Sweden. Their crews were said to be a mixture of English, Canadian and Australians and from their documents it was obvious that they were sent to carry out offensive sorties over German controlled seas. Most of these aircraft were hit by flak over Vardo from a group of German escort vessels based there in Varanger Fiord some miles west of Kola Inlet and the Russian naval base of Polyarnoe.

'G-George', hit the side of a hill near the German base and Squadron Leader Catanach, Flying Officer Anderson, Flight Sergeant Cameron and Flight Sergeant Davidson were subsequently made POWs, but Sergeant Hayes was killed in the crash. 'Valuable secret material' was found intact reported the *Skl* to *OKM* next day in a signal timed at 1646. This document was marked 'If forced to land in enemy territory this document must be destroyed', said the German report and among the items decoded were such R/T identifications as the call sign of the Escort of PQ 8, *Eagle*, and the Escort for QP 14 as *Fulmar* with the Senior Officer as *Woodcock*.*

The price the Germans paid for this unique information was one sailor killed by bursting flak aboard the *UJ.1107*. Armed with this information the German and Finnish cryptographical services were soon able to match their findings with their already very comprehensive knowledge of Allied codes and procedures.

Indeed these highly skilled operators had achieved signal success by 1942 and were able to penetrate British cyphers to an alarming degree. The wireless intelligence divisions intercept section, the *B-Dienst*, firstly as 2/*Skl* and later 4/*Skl*, worked hand in hand with the OKM's intelligence division, 3/*Skl*, and the Luftwaffe's own Air Signals section and between them were intercepting and decoding all Admiralty signals so successfully that they had to forward their findings without reference to their sources and methods, lest the British discover to what extent their secrets were being revealed. The head of *B-Dienst*,

* See Appendix Four for a full list of Call Signs contained in this document.

Heinz Bonatz, also operated with the equally efficient Finnish intelligence organisation, whose achievements were later revealed by Jukka L. Makela in his book *Im Rucken des Feindes*. Much of their combined success was also owed to the work of their chief English cryptanalyst, Wilhelm Tranow.

It would appear that PQ 18 probably provided these teams with, if anything, an excess of material to work upon, for Admiral Burnett's report revealed later that the administrative signal traffic of the convoy through the operation was on a very large scale. Signals referring to the oiling programme, the hunting of anti-submarine contacts and investigating of distant U-boat reports together with those in connection with accommodation of survivors, ships requiring medical attention and the like helped contribute to an enormous total of some 1,840 messages.

The fleet band w/t wave was constantly interrupted by German beacon transmissions through the voyage, the call signs CNTH 646, CNTH 495, CNTH 000 and CNTH 750 being used so often that at one period it was considered worthwhile requesting the shift of the fleet wave. Low power w/t, considered safe, was restricted in use for transmissions from both the Home Fleet and the 18th Cruiser Squadron were picked up and Admiral Burnett decided not to risk homing U-boats by this method.

While, conversely, the VHF and H/F transmissions of the Luftwaffe pilots were invaluable to the fleet (this 'headache' transmission being on one occasion the only warning of the approach of attacking aircraft), the Germans had other sources on which to draw. The Soviet torpedo-bomber force belonging to their 95th Naval Air Regiment was, as has been told, to have co-operated with the Hampdens of Coastal Command and so full details of the convoy's movements and the British methods to counter surface attack were made known to them. The Russians had some forty-two short-range, forty-three long-range fighters, nineteen bombers and ten torpedo-bombers on hand for this operation and during the transmission of this information on 7th September to CO of 95th unit from HQ of the various units the signals were picked up and deciphered. This information was quite comprehensive and, added to what the Germans already had, conclusive. It was listed as including the directions, operational plan, code-names and terms to be used.

Thus the Germans knew well in advance the route of the two convoys, the detailed time schedules and the complete composition of the escort forces along their whole journey. The German Group Command North then knew that the best time to sail to strike at the less well escorted QP 14 was on the 13th/14th September, the date it left Russia. By the time their heavy ships reached their intercepting positions on the 14th/15th the convoy would be still far from any assistance that Burnett's force could give them. As we have seen the passage of the *Scheer*, *Hipper* and *Köln* had been the preliminary step in putting into operation this surface sortie and a full and complete mission had been prepared code named Operation 'Double Blow' (*Doppleschlag*). On 7th September at 1006, Group North had signalled their intentions to the Operational Chiefs in Berlin. Briefly they surmised that the running of PQ 18 and QP 14 could not be long delayed and that their intentions were to strike against the QP convoy with the surface strength, holding *Tirpitz*, in reserve and utilising the strengthened air and submarine arms against the PQ convoy as already agreed.

For 'Double Blow' the *Hipper* and *Köln* with available destroyers would sortie out againts QP 14. Operational control of the force was to be in the hands of Admiral Commanding Group North, tactical control with Admiral of Battle Group. Once this force had fallen upon the convoy the *Scheer* would sortie out in support to complete the pincer movement. It was later revealed that *Hipper* and *Köln* with five destroyers, *Richard Beitzen*, Z23, Z27, Z29 and Z30, were ready and waiting to slip their cables and that it only required the issuing of the code word *Meisen-Balz** by Group North to set the operation into motion.

Meanwhile the *Tirpitz* was joined by the destroyers *Erich Steinbrinck* (Z15), *Friedrich Eckoldt* (Z16) and Z28 with torpedo boats T9 and T12 from Narvik.

Despite the reputation for somewhat cringing behaviour in the handling of their warships many members of this Command and the officers of the ships themselves were no cowards and they made strong representations up to the highest level that such a

* *Meisen-Balz* can be translated as 'Stuffed Titmouse', only the word stuffed has no connection with taxidermists but more with the love-life of the little creatures! No doubt this conveyed most admirably just what the Battle Group intended to do to QP 14!

sortie should take place. Rear-Admiral Meisel of the *Hipper* and Captain Ponitz, the destroyer commander, were both known to be in favour of more aggressive use of their ships, as was their immediate superior, Vice-Admiral Kummetz, flying his flag aboard the *Admiral Scheer*, while the nominal leader of the heavy ships as Flag Officer Battleships, Vice-Admiral Ciliax, had won renown as the commander of the Channel dash by *Scharnhorst*, *Gneisenau* and *Prinz Eugen* just seven months earlier, and his successor, Admiral Schniewind was just as eager to give battle.

Therefore their representations were duly passed on by Group Command, North, to Berlin for onward transmission to Hitler. The Fuehrer did not reject the idea out of hand but warned Grand-Admiral Raeder to bear in mind what had been agreed in August, that the defence of Norway was the prime consideration when judging the operational use of the big ships. This was cold-water enough for Raeder who thereupon cancelled the whole operation. Despite the anger of the men on the spot the word from Berlin was as binding on them as had been that of London upon the British seamen of PQ 17. The German Battle Group remained in harbour.

The absence of the *Tirpitz* from Trondheim was later found out to have been due to a mere training exercise in Vestifiord which had been missed by the reconnaissance aircraft. The merchantmen of QP 14 were therefore saved more by the hesitancy of Hitler and the supine attitude of Raeder than any of the British counter-measures.

However there can be little doubt that, had it have come to the test, all would have justified themselves. It is often stated that the 'Fighting Destroyer Escort' was a new facet of defence, but anyone who studied the actions of Admiral Vian's light cruisers and destroyers when faced with Italian battleships and heavy cruisers, while at the same time handicapped by a convoy under heavy air attack to protect, can visualise quite clearly the probable situation that would have arisen had the German Battle Fleet given battle. Whether the result of this similar battle would have been the same will never be known, but the Second Battle of Sirte is an interesting blueprint to base the speculation of 'might-have-beens' upon. And within a few months the Russian convoys were put to just such a test and came through in triumph during the Battle of New Year's Eve.*

We must now turn away from such speculation and return to the actual events taking place around PQ 18 as it battled its way north still shaken by the losses it had taken on the 13th. With one hazard, unknowingly, removed, the convoy and escorts were more than put to it to repulse the massive assaults now mounted by the Germans' other two arms, the bombers and the great concentration of U-boats that were about to make themselves felt.

* In the New Years Eve battle around convoy JW.51B *Lutzow*, with three destroyers, and *Hipper*, with three more, used the same operational plan but were thwarted by the brilliant handling of Sherbrooke's six destroyers.

Chapter Five

# War of Attrition

## I

By the early hours of the morning of the 14th September Lieutenant-Commander Karl Brandenburg had worked his submarine *U-457* into a satisfactory firing position astern of the convoy. At 0328 he pressed the firing button once, twice, three and four times, shooting at targets in the rear of the convoy with deliberately aimed shots from the port quarter. Even as he fired the asdic operators aboard the destroyer *Impulsive* (Lieutenant-Commander E. G. Roper, DSC) were holding a firm echo from *U-457* at a range of under 2,000 yards which was classified as 'positive submarine'. The *Impulsive* had been returning up the port side of the convoy after taking part in an abortive hunt with the *Achates*, leaving that vessel to continue the search, when the echo was first picked up. Having calculated his position in relationship to the screen after careful scrutiny earlier it was mere chance that Brandenburg should now be located by the returning British destroyer.

Lieutenant-Commander Roper immediately carried out attack procedure and a five-charge pattern of depth-charges was set and fired. The charges had staggered settings, those from the two throwers being set at 150 feet, those from the traps at 250, 100 and 250 feet respectively and the echo was held down firmly to within 100 yards of attack position. Despite this only seconds separated *Impulsive*'s firing and *U-457*'s, but the submarine got her salvo off first. As *Impulsive* closed her target the asdic operator picked up clear 'torpedo running' noises as the submarine's missiles sped on their way and, at 0330, seven minutes after *Impulsive* fired, Brandenburg's torpedoes hit home.

Her victim was the freighting tanker *Atheltemplar* which was straggling from her position at the stern of column four. Tankers were particularly vulnerable so it was fortunate that the single

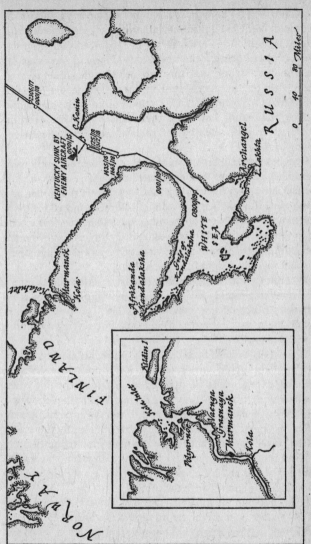

RAF patrol zones and torpedo strikes

torpedo which hit her struck her in her engine room and not in her tanks of highly inflammable cargo. She was actually torpedoed in position 76° 17′ N, 16° 40′ E. The torpedo which struck her had passed *beneath* the rescue ship *Copeland* and astern of the corvette *Bryony* and the two British submarine escorts, hitting her on the port side. Lieutenant-Commander Steward considered the placing of such a valuable ship at the rear of the convoy was wrong but added that *Atheltemplar* had been inclined to straggle, often by the ships ahead of her themselves falling back.

Fires immediately broke out aboard the tanker but these were controlled and there was considered to be a good chance of perhaps saving her by detailing the *Sharpshooter* to tow her into Lowe Sound, Spitzbergen. Admiral Burnett indeed initially ordered this but in view of the numerous submarine contacts he had received, by which it was estimated that at least five more submarines were present in the vicinity, he just could not afford to spare any escort ships from the screen.

Accordingly the minesweeper *Harrier*, also stationed astern of the sinking vessel and the nearest warship to her, was instructed to take off her crew and sink her. This was done and *Atheltemplar* was left astern blazing and in a sinking condition, but still afloat.

Meanwhile Brandenburg had been given no time at all to congratulate himself on his success and it must have been an alarming experience to be attacked so quickly after firing when the nearest destroyers, *Tartar* and *Eskimo*, had been plotted at a safe distance. Both *Impulsive* and *Tartar* now began a new search as contact had been lost in water troubled by the wakes of the whole convoy. Both these destroyers hunted until 0500, without result, before rejoining the screen. Brandenburg was an old hand at this and had shaken off his pursuers well before this without losing contact with the convoy.

It was not until the following morning, however, that he could safely surface and signal to Admiral Kluber in Oslo that he estimated he had sunk a 6,000-ton tanker, hit a 4,000-ton freighter [presumably the *Copeland* whose shallow draught saved her] and had possibly obtained two hits on a 'Javelin' type destroyer [perhaps one of the single funnelled 'Hunt' class boats, *Wilton* and *Wheatland*, had been his target here or he had mistaken the single funnelled *Bryony* for a larger vessel]. This was a reasonable assumption, and he *had* hit the tanker, while the *Copeland* and the *Bryony* had only just been missed. Certainly these were his probable targets and, in the confusion of the counter-attack, explosions must have led him to believe that his whole salvo had struck home. Admiral Commanding Group North was more than satisfied – at last his boats were getting results! He signalled to *U-457* on the afternoon of 14th: 'Bravo! Under water with all the enemies of Brandenburg!' Brandenburg had confirmed his victim's identity already for at dawn he had briefly surfaced alongside the blazing tanker. He was sighted by a patrolling Swordfish at 0615 and forced to dive, but not before he was satisfied that the blazing ship was doomed, though still afloat.

Admiral Burnett's estimate of five U-boats in the vicinity of the convoy was quite reasonable. In addition to *U-457* other submarines reported themselves in contact and several made determined efforts to probe the very strong anti-submarine screen but without success. With eighteen destroyers, six corvettes and minesweepers and four trawlers escorting there were few gaps in the outer screen and the three Swordfish from the *Avenger* were proving themselves invaluable.

*U-405* (Hopmann), with her many aircrew passengers aboard was later to drop out of the hunt and return homeward, but running out against the convoys were *U-251* and *U-601* from Kirkenes and, although these were too far away to be effective, *U-703* commanded by Lieutenant-Commander Heinz Bielfeld also sailed from Narvik at midday.

*U-377* (Koehler), was pressing in towards the convoy during the day as was *U-589* (Horrer). One of these boats paid for their daringness on the 14th. Lieutenant-Commander Horrer had been close to the convoy all night after rescuing four airmen from one of the shot down Heinkel torpedo bombers at 1715 the previous evening in pinpoint 34754. He reported this mercy mission at dusk, then continued to track the convoy. This was the last heard from Horrer at Oslo. Aboard the cramped U-boat that night no doubt spirits were high, especially among the reprieved airmen; alas, their stay of execution was to be a short one.

At 0940 on the morning of the 14th one of the patrolling Swordfish from the *Avenger* sighted *U-589* on the surface some six miles south of the convoy on its starboard bow. The submarine promptly dived but the Swordfish marked the position with a smokefloat and reported her position by W/T and the nearest destroyer, the *Onslow* commanded by 'Beaky' Armstrong, was despatched to carry out a search when *Avenger* notified Admiral Burnett, at 1009.

Meanwhile the Swordfish had been patrolling the area to shadow the submarine until set upon by a Junkers Ju 88 which drove her off with gunfire before *Onslow* could come up. A BV 138 float plane also circled around the Swordfish but did not attack. Every time the German float plane drifted in closer than two miles the 'Stringbag' steered towards the convoy and the flak from the nearest destroyer drove the BV 138 away again; Admiral Burnett described this as a game of 'you can't catch me'.

Having seen the Swordfish driven off, Lieutenant-Commander Horrer duly surfaced once more to continue to replenish his depleted batteries and he was sighted at a range of some 14,000 yards by the *Onslow* as she came storming over the horizon. Her first sighting, at 1019, had been of smoke bearing 215 degrees but shortly afterwards the masthead lookout reported *U-589*'s conning tower and this was also seen a few minutes later from the bridge. The rangefinder had just enough time to lock on to this small target before the lookouts aboard the submarine sighted the bow-wave creaming towards them. A range of 13,700 yards was recorded when, at 1029, the *U-589* dived for the last time in position 75 degrees 40' North, 20 degrees 32' East. With six miles of sea to sweep in any direction the chances of *Onslow*'s asdic operators picking up the scent were estimated at only twenty-four per cent but 'Beaky' Armstrong was an old hand at U-boat hunting and, at 1051, a firm contact was obtained, range 1,900 yards. The unfortunate Horrer had been out-thought by Armstrong and was now to pay the price.

Running straight down the submarine's estimated track for four minutes, with the asdic echo gaining strength, the *Onslow* made her first attack with a six-charge pattern set at the shallow depth of only fifty feet. After the resulting explosions had torn the sea apart in great geysers of dirty grey water and spray the *Onslow*'s asdic operator reported that he had regained contact as firm as ever.

With her victim also stationary the *Onslow* now made further attacks with the utmost precision and skill. After the third, fourth and fifth attacks diesel oil and large bubbles came to the surface indicating that far below her keel the trapped men in the doomed submarine were being crushed to a ghastly death. A sixth and seventh attacks were made with deliberation which resulted in a large underwater explosion three minutes later. Further patches of oil and bubbles came to the surface as well as some wooden gratings and green vegetables.

Still not completely satisfied Armstrong took *Onslow* over the spot once more and a ninth attack was delivered. After this all contact was lost and reluctantly, but with only five depth charges left, the *Onslow* set course to catch up with the convoy again at 1307. En route she passed the wreckage of a still-floating German bomber with its crew of four perched miserably atop of it but no attempt was made to pick them up. They were later perhaps, if they ultimately survived, to feel thankful that they had not been rescued by *U-589* as their compatriots had been the day before.

While *Onslow* had been carrying out her own private war, the German aircraft had been very active around PQ 18 as the next great air attack was prepared and sent out. *Avenger*'s dauntless little Swordfish determinedly kept on with their patrols although German aircraft of all types made their job no sinecure. At 1130 one of them was again attacked by a Ju 88. Despite the German bomber's superior speed and gun power the Swordfish fought back and she made a run for the destroyer screen and claimed to hit the Junkers before flak drove it away. At 1233 groups of German aircraft were seen by this 'Stringbag' to be approaching the convoy from ahead. No radar warning had been given owing to their very low approach but at 1237 *Avenger* went to action stations.

*III/KG 26* was back again but this time Klaus Nocken had twenty fully operational machines with which to attack. However his hands were even more tightly bound than they had been on the 13th for his operational orders were absolutely specific; the carrier was his sole target, with perhaps the anti-aircraft cruiser and other large escorts as last-minute alternatives. They had been informed that the carrier was stationed astern of the convoy and with this in mind the formation thundered at wavecrest level towards the ships which they picked up just after 1230.

In an extended line the Junkers torpedo bombers crossed through the leading ships of the screen as Nocken spotted *Avenger* steaming ahead and *KG 26* slipped into their well-organised routine of deploying aircraft on each wing to synchronise the attack so that no matter which way the carrier turned she would be faced by more than twenty torpedoes.

From the ships it was reported that the main attack, some twelve aircraft, came in from the port side, this was Nocken's group which pressed in further and in fact the ratio was, port to starboard, twelve/eight. At the final moment, when it was realised that the vessel under attack was in fact the carrier, but with fighters aloft, the carefully rehearsed pincher attack was thrown into some confusion as the leading bombers now attempted to re-form in a defensive line once more.

· The *Avenger* had come storming up the convoy and now passed ahead of it, 'peeling off Hurricanes whilst streaking across the front of the convoy from starboard to port inside the screen with her destroyer escorts blazing away with any gun which would bear', as Admiral Burnett later put it.

In addition to the *Wilton* and *Wheatland* the carrier had the added fire support of *Ulster Queen's* formidable battery for Captain Adams thankfully abandoned his enforced defensive position inside the convoy and steamed out to meet the attack also. *Scylla* herself was in a similar role to the previous day and engaged targets at close range. Captain Colvin had decided that absolute freedom of movement was essential to enable his ship to make all available use of speed and manoeuvrability during torpedo bomber attacks and he considered that it was this alone which saved *Avenger* on this day.

At 1240 three sections of Sea Hurricanes had been successfully flown off to engage the oncoming formations but did not have time to get in position as the attack broke over the ship. The bulk of the Junkers 88s of *III/KG 26* now stormed down the convoy's port wing having located the *Avenger*, while the second group passed close down *Scylla's* starboard side and between the convoy's outer starboard columns.

All bedlam now broke out as, her aircraft safely airborne, the *Avenger* scuttled down the port side of the convoy on opposite course seeking sanctuary, with several torpedo bombers in hot pursuit. Again results were confused, the detailed air attack summary reporting that, while *Avenger*'s fighters turned some bombers away and the screen forced others to drop at long range, some eleven aircraft were seen to crash. Many of the torpedoes were seen to somersault in the air after hitting the water.

Commodore Boddam-Whetham once more ordered an alteration in course, to avoid torpedo tracks, of forty-five degrees and this time the merchant ships, not being the direct object of the attack, complied more efficiently. The *Bluebell* had torpedo bombers passing down both sides of her during this attack within three hundred yards, two aircraft passing between her and the next ship of the screen to port, *Intrepid*, and another three between her and the next to starboard, *Faulknor*, and she engaged them first with her 4-inch gun at long range and then, progressively, with every gun available. Many hits were counted by the Oerlikons and Lewis-guns but the majority of the aircraft, intent on their target, brushed aside this barrage and disdainfully carried on past the little corvette. One, however, appeared heavily hit by a great concentration of fire on the port side and was seen emitting great quantities of black smoke.

This attack, reported Lieutenant Waller, broke up soon after penetrating the screen, the aircraft dropping their torpedoes, 'at random', at a range of about 4,000 yards before turning away. The little *Cape Argona* reported, with some indignation, that 'One plane attacked me from astern, dropping two torpedoes at a range of approximately eighty yards.' She claimed this aircraft was definitely damaged by pom-pom and Oerlikon fire as it turned away.

The destroyer *Achates* was in the unenviable position of a man caught with his trousers down for, when the attack developed, she was refuelling alongside the tanker *Black Ranger*. Being only some eight tons short of that required she, not surprisingly, quickly slipped both the short tow and the fuelling hose and hastened back to her position in the screen.

The *Scylla* was under continuous full helm in order to avoid the many torpedoes which crossed her track in her exposed forward position but she was not hit and at least one bomber was seen to crash off her port quarter during this raid.

By 1245 the attack was over and the aircraft had lost two of their number without hitting the *Avenger* or indeed any other ship. Almost immediately after this first torpedo-bomber attack of the day had faded the Junkers Ju 88s of *KG 30* arrived overhead and commenced shallow dive-bombing runs out of the cloud banks, mainly concentrating on the port side of the convoy where their target was once again the *Avenger*.

The Sea Hurricanes that had been flown off, again mostly too late to hinder the torpedo bombers, were now able to harry the dive bombers in and out of the clouds with much more effect, although the number of kills was very low due to the poor penetrating power of their machine-guns. This attack lasted from around 1250 to 1410 and consisted of individual bombing attacks by small groups of Junkers against selected targets. The warships opened fire whenever the bombers appeared briefly below the 6,000-feet cloud base but not much opportunity was afforded to make steady or aimed practice against such tactics. By the same token many of the attacks thus hastily delivered were not accurate either but this was not always the case. The *Scylla* and, especially, the *Avenger*, along with escorts in the vicinity of the carrier like *Wilton* and *Wheatland*, *Eskimo* and *Tartar*, all had very close shaves from time to time and were lucky to escape with more than a severe buffeting.

On occasion also the ships of the convoy, especially in the port hand columns, received near misses from overshoots of salvoes aimed at the escorts. One of the first such misses was close alongside the destroyer *Impulse* at 1259. At 1300 four Sea Hurricanes were flown off *Avenger* to continue the defence above the clouds but thirty-five minutes later a very determined attack was made by a single aircraft diving through broken, thin cloud, cover. This Ju 88 released two heavy bombs which exploded only fifty feet off *Avenger*'s port side and then escaped unscathed. At 1340 another six Sea Hurricanes had been refuelled and re-armed and were sent away in good time to meet an oncoming raid at low level which had been picked up by radar this time. Before this attack had developed the dive-bombing continued, probably in an attempt to once more pre-empt the fighter defences but this time they were not drawn. The *Ulster Queen* had had ample time to circle back to her original position in the second column after her sortie against the first torpedo bomber attack earlier and she opened fire on the Junkers when the opportunity presented itself. She, too, was near missed by two bombs which detonated only thirty yards off her port bow. The minesweeper *Gleaner* had a similar escape, one heavy and one light bomb dropping within fifty yards of her starboard beam.

*Avenger* was now operating on the convoy's starboard quarter, with four Sea Hurricanes aloft, when the next great torpedo bomber attack was detected coming in from right ahead. This was the attack led by Major Klumper with all available aircrews of *I/KG 26*, twenty-two Heinkel 111s took part, six more having aborted the mission due to a variety of technical faults. Co-operating with them were eighteen Junkers Ju 88s, also from Fliegführer Lofoten's command at Bardufoss, *III/KG 30*, led by Major Bloedorn, but again co-operation was not correctly achieved and the torpedo bombers had to face the fighters and flak virtually unsupported.

As they made their approach Klumper was scanning the sea ahead of the convoy to locate the *Avenger*, again the only target to be considered. Reports of the earlier attack had told of how the carrier had steamed out ahead of the convoy and Klumper expected to find her still there, thus, when he sighted *Scylla* out in front on her own behind the main destroyer screen, he naturally assumed *this* ship to be his target. *I/KG 26* therefore deployed in the usual manner in two groups to attack each bow. From the convoy they were seen to split up at a distance of four miles, one group of eleven to port and the other from almost dead ahead.

It was at this point that two things happened which completely ruined *I/KG 26*'s attack plan in a matter of seconds. Firstly the four Sea Hurricanes were sighted closing in on them from astern and apparently undeterred by having to follow the German bombers into the teeth of what was already a vicious barrage. Because of this threat Klumper reversed his order and tried to get the two groups to close up again but in this he was too late. Secondly as they closed their intended target it became obvious that she was *not* the aircraft carrier that they had been told they must concentrate on and, shortly after this realisation, she in fact was spotted to starboard.

Klumper now ordered the attack going in against *Scylla* to be broken off and for as many units as possible to switch target to the carrier. In order to do this the Heinkels now had to cross at close range across the convoy and destroyer screens thus presenting very easy targets to the hundreds of flak guns of the ships. Several of the Heinkels were too far committed to their attacks to comply with this suicidal order, but to their great credit, the majority attempted it and followed Klumper into the barrage towards the carrier and her weaving close escort.

Admiral Burnett duly acknowledged that this attack was fully pressed home but was of the opinion that many of the torpedoes released must have been faulty. The incredible bravery of the German pilots was matched equally by the self-sacrifice of three of the Sea Hurricanes who followed their targets across the convoy and were shot down by the barrage of the fleet.

The destroyer *Faulknor* had been the first ship to open fire on Klumper's squadron as they made their initial deployment, this was at 1410. She was the port-wing ship of the leading screen and, in line with her, the *Malcolm* and the *Achates* were the first escorts over which the torpedo bombers flew, Commander Russell reporting that the bulk of the attackers appeared to fly between his ship and *Achates*, and were heavily engaged. On switching their targets the bombers passed close alongside both sides of *Scylla* giving her close-range weapons ample targets and one Heinkel was claimed shot down at this point crashing amid the convoy columns.

The three gallant Sea Hurricanes were early victims, shells of the barrage aimed at the bombers seeming to explode behind them and in among the pursuing fighters. At 1415 the first Sea Hurricane was seen diving into the sea and the *Faulknor* altered course and picked up her pilot. Within a minute one other fighter came down in a similar manner close to the *Avenger* and was rescued by the *Wheatland*. The third Fleet Air Arm casualty survived until 1425 when he too was badly hit and crashed astern of the convoy, but again the pilot was picked up safely by the *Tartar* off the port flank. Admiral Burrough vividly remembered this episode, as did many others that day.

I shall never forget the reckless gallantry of the Fleet Air Arm pilots in their determination to get in amongst the enemy despite the solid mass of our defensive fire of every type.[2]

The corvette *Bluebell* engaged one Heinkel as it passed down the ship's port side and then switched target as a second passed at zero feet alongside to starboard. Lieutenant Waller recorded how:

> This aircraft was engaged by every close range weapon on the ship except the port bridge oerlikon which could not bear, and every gun appeared to be hitting; the aircraft was being torn to ribbons by the concentrated fire as it passed overhead and pieces of debris were seen flying off from the vicinity of its two torpedoes. As it passed overhead it attempted to drop one torpedo but only the nose was released, the tail of the torpedo remaining fast to the aircraft. This aircraft crashed into the sea about half a mile from the port quarter of the ship; it did not catch fire when it crashed although internal fires had been observed as it passed overhead.[20]

As the Heinkel flew past its gunners returned the fire with their machine-guns and an explosive bullet struck the brass wind chute of the foreside of the starboard armoured position on the *Bluebell*'s bridge. Nobody on the bridge noticed it, not even the starboard look-out inside, who must have had his face within 18-inches of the explosion!

Captain Adams found that *Ulster Queen*'s fire was again being masked by the port wing column of the convoy and so took his ship out on the flank to meet the bombers. Those engaged were still flying low but he thought they had unloaded their torpedoes for none were sighted. In fact the majority of the Heinkels had retained them for use against *Avenger* but many were unable to find suitable release positions and so did not drop. Only Klumper himself and one wingman managed to get a suitable position to release against *Avenger* but in both instances the angle of launch was too acute and the carrier was able to turn in towards them just in time to avoid all tracks.

Not surprisingly then some of the torpedoes dropped ran into the convoy itself even though this was not the target. No turn was ordered by the convoy commodore on this occasion for just this reason and many torpedo tracks passed harmlessly down the convoy lanes. One ship, however, did cross the track of a torpedo running in from the starboard side; this was the *Mary Luckenbach* the only survivor of the ill-fated starboard columns from the previous day's attack.

She was an ammunition ship and the result of this one torpedo hit on her thin sides was awe-inspiring.

> She completely detonated. A huge column of black and grey
> smoke went up to the cloud base and there mushroomed out.[3]

Thus wrote Commodore Boddam-Whetham and it made a deep
impression on him. It was thought that the aircraft which caused
this devastating hit was engulfed itself in the resulting explosion;
Captain Adams for example wrote:

> . . . the *Mary Luckenbach* blew up with the most tremendous
> explosion sending a vast column of fire and smoke many thou-
> sands of feet high, which carried one enemy aircraft away with
> it.[25]

On the other hand from the bridge of the *Harrier* this Heinkel
was seen to pass through the convoy and crash into the sea
about half a mile on the starboard beam. Motor Minesweeper
212 stated quite definitely that this was the aircraft which torpedoed the *Mary Luckenbach*.

Ensign Daniel Rooker of the *Campfire* gave another version:

> Three enemy planes broke through the barrage and came
> directly down column six. Our forward machine gunners suc-
> ceeded in driving them off our bow with effective firing. Two
> of these planes swerved over to column seven dropping their
> load on the *Mary Luckenbach*, which ship immediately ex-
> ploded, only one survivor being picked up. The three planes
> went no further into the convoy. One was blown up with the
> *Luckenbach* and the other two were shot down, all ships in the
> area contributing with their fire.[34]

Lieutenant John Landers, USNR, aboard the *Virginia Dare*
reported this tragedy thus:

> The planes attacking the port side were turned by the heavy fire
> of the escort and six came madly down the columns between
> ships towards our end of the convoy, flying only about twenty
> to thirty feet above the water and hopping in a peculiar fashion.
> As the first came down between our column and the one to port
> our gunners set the port engine afire and the AA ship astern to
> port [*Alynbank*] finished him off.
>   The second plane attempted to pass between this ship and the
> ship ahead [*Luckenbach*] but our gunners set him afire. This
> plane turned toward the ship ahead, turned again and headed

for our bow in a crash dive. The 3 inch guns crew followed him in and fired when the plane was at the point blank range of sixty yards. The plane blew up.

Three more aircraft passed across our bow ridiculously close. Hits were scored on all three and two were brought down. The planes crashed a little abaft our starboard beam about half a mile out.

The sixth plane crossed in front of the ship ahead in the next column to port [*Nathaniel Green*] then headed straight for this ship. We hit with our 20-mm and the plane burst into flames crashing into the *Mary Luckenbach* which was 400 yards from us. The *Mary Luckenbach* immediately blew up, a terrible sight. Meanwhile the attack on our starboard beam had materialised. These were low flying aircraft. These planes passed astern of us. They were fired upon but no positive result could be observed. One plane came in a little abaft the starboard beam. The plane turned slightly and headed for the *Mary Luckenbach*; released its torpedoes tried to gain elevation and then crashed. The *Luckenbach* blew up.[36]

Thus from five accounts of this one episode, picked at random, we had five quite different stories, perhaps with John Landers' as the most comprehensive one. On one thing there was no doubt however, the loss of the *Lukenbach* was a mind-stunning tragedy. For the ships in the immediate vicinity the effect was quite catastrophic. Again John Landers:

The ship was severely shaken, the bow was thrown violently up and we were pelted with debris and large shells.[36]

Lieutenant Billings of the *Nathaniel Green* recalled how:

All the cargo boxes on deck were smashed by the concussion. About ten doors and some bulkheads were blown down and smashed. The insides of many rooms (mine included) were a shambles. The cast iron ventilators buckled. Shrapnel and scraps were covering the deck. A piece of angle-iron penetrated my starboard four-inch ready-box and went through a shell, missing the primer by less than an eighth of an inch. Glass ports were smashed. The hospital aft was practically demolished. The compasses were all out of adjustment. The pointer's platform on the 4-inch gun had completely disappeared and the pointer's sight was nearly ruined. A side plate about two feet square was found on deck. Bullets were picked up all over the deck (both tank ammunition from the *Luckenbach* and bullets fired at us by the planes). How everyone topside was not killed or injured seriously I don't know. It is impossible to put into words the force of the explosion or the amount of debris to hit the ship.[39]

In fact it was thought aboard *Nathaniel Green* initially that they had been torpedoed as well. Boat stations were sounded off by the Master and wounded and injured men brought to the boats. The engines were stopped and a life raft dropped over the side. On learning that the engines were sound and that no major leaks had started in the hull, Captain Vickers rejoined his position in the convoy. His handling of the attack brought warm praise for he had avoided four torpedoes and resumed his position despite the great shock his crew had experienced. Two of the armed guard party were badly injured and these were later taken off by the destroyer *Onslaught* who came alongside when *Nathaniel Green* temporarily dropped back to check her damage.

From the body of one of the broken Heinkels, as it lay sluggishly on the surface between the leading convoy lanes, the surviving members of a very brave crew scrambled out on to the wing and raised their hands. The response from the ships towering above them was instant as Robert Hughes was to recall:

> From the bow Oerlikons of the leading merchant ships long arcs of tracer jumped towards the men on the wing. Far from below us a Bren gun chattered momentarily, and an angry voice screamed, 'Cut it out, for Christ's sake! Give them a chance!'
> But the tracers from the merchantmen were still firing, and one by one the black figures topped off the wing into the icy sea, and the plane floated on down the convoy lane.*

Altogether I/KG 26 was listed as having five Heinkels destroyed in this attack and a further nine of the *Lion* Geschwader were damaged so severely that although they limped home they were written off. On the evening of the second day's battle this crack unit was reduced to a total of eight operational aircraft, although others were to be made ready within a short time for the surviving aircrew.

The target of their wrath, the little stubby *Avenger* had emerged from this attack unscathed, both her own gunners and those of the two 'Hunts' having contributed to her defence in no

* *Through the Waters*, William Kimber, 1956.

small measure. Her signal lamp began to wink at *Scylla* and she told Admiral Burnett that she considered she could claim the 'honour of being the sole object of the attack'. She estimated that seventeen torpedoes had been aimed at her during this action. Her Hurricanes later claimed five certain kills, three probables and fourteen damaged while her gunners claimed shares in another four. The score began to clock up; even the little Motor Minesweeper 212 reported she shot down one He 111 at 1440.

Meanwhile, at 1432 the eighteen Junkers Ju 88s of *III/KG 30* had arrived overhead and continued the attack for a further hour. This attack followed the earlier pattern with the Junkers Ju 88s bombing through the clouds and with the odd one or two more determined than the others who ventured lower to make shallow dive-bombing attacks. Again *Avenger*, *Scylla* and the escorts were the main targets and one aircraft was seen to crash. Although many bombs were dropped no damage was in fact done. The *Avenger* had a fire break out in the catapult room caused by an electrical switch defect but this was soon under control.

Between 1240 and 1520 the Sea Hurricanes carried out sixteen sorties and Captain Colthurst was especially impressed by the speed with which the shot down pilots had been rescued by the destroyers, 'All pilots in *Avenger* now realise that they have nothing to fear if they are forced to abandon their aircraft,' he wrote.

The Type 79.M. radar with which the carrier was equipped was working perfectly and with this the fighter direction had improved beyond all expectations by the 14th.

The *Bluebell* was subjected at this time to one of the few serious attacks, and Lieutenant Waller recorded:

One dive-bombing attack was apparently commenced on the ship and seemed fairly determined, but when the aircraft was engaged by the close range weapons it turned away and dropped its bombs fairly near HMS *Faulknor*, three-quarters of a mile away on our starboard bow.[20]

Lieutenant-Commander A. H. Jones of the *Achates* wrote of how an attack was made on his ship at 1451, the bombs dropping about one cable away and although the aircraft was engaged by short range weapons no hits were observed.

From the merchant ships Ensign Rooker paid a welcome tribute to the largely unseen work of the Sea Hurricanes.

I have not given much verbal credit throughout my report to the planes from the aircraft carrier. This is not because I didn't think that they contributed much, but mainly due to the fact that of necessity they operated above the clouds and outside the range of our barrage. Therefore it was difficult to see what their action was. It is common knowledge to those of us in the convoy that their contribution to our defence was the major factor in our success.[34]

By 1520 the screen was finally clear and the air attacks died away, although, as always, the shadowing aircraft were always on the horizon. The Luftwaffe estimate of the damage inflicted by all their aircraft this day was wildly inaccurate. No less than six merchant ships and one tanker were claimed to have been sunk, totalling some 49,000 BRT, and a destroyer was also claimed destroyed. In addition to this damage was reported to have been inflicted on a further three freighters, totalling some 29,000 BRT, and another destroyer was reported hit and damaged. In fact the *Mary Luckenbach* was their only victim.

With the lull in aerial activity stretching on into the evening Admiral Burnett took the opportunity to transfer the majority of the merchant navy survivors from the smaller escorts and rescue ships to the *Scylla* or the Home Fleet destroyers. This was a warm humanitarian gesture made with the knowledge of the appalling conditions that awaited these men if they had to endure several months of waiting at Archangel in the very primitive conditions the Soviets were using at this time. It was a gesture that was fully appreciated by those who knew about this. Captain Maund was to recall:

The lot of survivors landed here is, despite the efforts of the Soviet Authorities, not a happy one. Lack of food, clothing and sanitary arrangements all contribute to deterioration of their morale, and it was indeed a pleasant surprise to receive only those from the *Kentucky* torpedoed off Kanin Nos after R.A. (D) and his destroyers had parted company with the convoy.

In addition to the *Copeland*, the official rescue ship, the three little motor minesweepers were reported to be invaluable and it was in fact suggested that at least one similar craft should be attached to each future convoy to act as a ferry between the ships torpedoed and the rescue ship. However the passage of PQ 18 was blest with fine weather and it was doubtful whether in winter conditions the motor minesweepers would have been so happy in Arctic waters.

The *Harrier* transferred survivors to the Scylla and in the sea then running, and at only eight knots, damage was caused as they grated together, although this was not serious. Again Robert Hughes remembered the scene:

> 'Over you go!' came the sharp command from the minesweeper and the first wave jumped for our guard rails. We reached out and grabbed them, pulling them over willy-nilly to clear the rails for the next wave. The next batch scrambled over, followed by another, then stopped as the ships parted for a moment. Slowly they came together again and the transfer continued. I grabbed a seaman who was holding on to the guard rail with one hand, the other hand held protectively over his coat.
>
> 'All right, chum, go easy,' he complained good-naturedly.
>
> 'Wounded?' I enquired.
>
> 'Nah! Look!' He opened his jacket and pointed. 'Brought me li'l pup!'
>
> There snuggled against his rough jersey was a little puppy, innocent, unknowing, but not forgotten and dearly loved.*

The trawler *St Kenan* transferred thirty-nine survivors from the *Macbeth* to the destroyer *Offa* and the remainder to the *Onslow*. The *Sharpshooter* followed *Harrier* alongside *Scylla* and transferred ninety-five survivors and in all the cruiser embarked some 209 men and the destroyers another 234. The 124 Russian survivors of course, plus the eleven British or American cot cases, were left in the rescue ships. A total of 578 survivors were saved from the twelve ships sunk up to that time.

As dusk grew deeper PQ 18's remaining ships congratulated themselves on surviving one more day of constant attack despite all that the Germans could throw at them. There were still another five days to go however.

Hope Island was sighted at 1800 and the *Malcolm* reported numerous H/F and M/F D/F bearings which suggested that the U-boat pack would attack again during the short period of darkness.

* *Through the Waters*, William Kimber, 1956.

151

In fact only three U-boats were still in contact with PQ 18 at this time. All were following in close contact with the eight-knot assembly of ships but with a healthy respect for the size of the escort and their efficiency. The three boats that were still trailing the convoy were the *U-457* (Brandenburg), *U-255* (Reche) and *U-405* (Hopmann) but the latter was about to return to his base to replenish. However at least seven other submarines were on their way to the operational area or had only lost contact for a while, including *U-403* (Claussen), *U-703* (Bielefeld), *U-606* (von Esch), *U-212* (Vogler) and *U-436* (Terchert).

Despite this concentration, and some determined attempts to penetrate the screen, their best efforts failed. Next morning the Swordfish were early astir and, sure enough, the inevitable sight of a surfaced submarine was reported by one of them at 0453, some fifteen miles off the convoy's port bow. Unfortunately the take-off wind speed was only fifteen knots and to get off the deck at all the Swordfish had to forgo her depth-charges so she could only report her sighting and take no action. She returned to *Avenger* an hour later reporting fog banks ahead. A second Swordfish airborne later sighted no submarines and was attacked by a Junkers Ju 88 but managed to evade her attacker by hiding among the clouds. The first shadower was picked up on the radar screens at 0800 and from then on there were always two hovering around out of range. The cloudbase was at 3,000 feet with a few clear patches. The morning passed uneventfully until, at 1225, the expected air attack was reported on the screens. A large group of bombers was detected in good time and the *Avenger* opened what was to be a busy day for her by flying off ten Sea Hurricanes. The *Avenger* and other ships had a great deal of success this day in monitoring the Luftwaffe's communications and homing signals on 5610 kc/s and adjacent frequencies.

The frequent chat between the various aircraft proved a valuable aid in anticipating their next moves. Admiral Burnett later recalled how, from these intercepted reports, the German pilots were not at all happy, being harassed by the fighters above the clouds and being forced to bomb either blind or through cloud which made spotting targets and bomb-aiming difficult in the extreme. Some surprise was expressed by one formation leader who reported later in the day, with a hint of exasperation: 'I have just been counting. There are still thirty-four ships – big ones too!'

This indicated just how far the Luftwaffe had been over-estimating their success rate during the previous two days. Further transmissions revealed that the *Gruppe* was circling and waiting overhead for the convoy to come out clear of the clouds. An estimated forty-five aircraft took part in this attack arriving in small groups and many bombs were dropped over the ships, mostly from above the clouds. As usual a few, more bold than the others, made shallow dive-bombing runs through the odd clear patches in the overcast sky, but as these potential danger spots were few and far between and could therefore be watched closely by the lookouts aboard the ships, these aircraft were usually met by a hot, if inaccurate barrage, directly they poked their noses out. As a result the bomb aiming was of a poor quality even though some very large bombs were dropped. In all the attack lasted over a period of three hours.

At one point an emergency turn was being considered to keep the convoy under cloud but before this was put into effect the R/T transmissions from the circling bombers indicated that their limit of endurance had been reached and that they were forced to return to base. When this happened there was a general jettisoning of bomb loads which resulted in both some incredibly distant bomb splashes far from any ships or else a completely unexpected and unavoidable near miss.

Between the first sighting by *Harrier* at 1255 and 1640 the Fleet Air Arm fighters flew twenty-one sorties but despite this, and the large numbers of Junkers Ju 88s overhead, just about every serviceable aircraft that *KG* 30's three Gruppen could muster, very few interceptions were in fact made. This was not due to any lack of enthusiasm by the young Sea Hurricane pilots but to a combination of several factors. The German bombers were more interested in evading the fighters and looking for openings in the cloud than in offering aerial combat. The German bombers were as fast, and more heavily armoured and armed than the Fleet Air Arm fighters, and when the Sea Hurricanes did manage to close the Junkers, they merely took refuge in the very thick cloud. Even when cornered the useless machine-guns again had great difficulty in penetrating the bombers' thick hides.

None the less the effect of the fighters was to complicate the German bombers' already unsatisfactory mission. Further groups of aircraft approached the convoy steadily within twenty miles range, after which they commenced circling at this distance. Very few dived below the 500 feet thick cloud cover to face the guns of the escort. Another theory was that by thus circling it was hoped that the Sea Hurricanes would run out of fuel and be forced to land, thus leading the bombers to the carrier. In fact the new method adopted by the *Avenger* on the 14th frustrated this, for the continuing cycle of take-offs and landings at twenty-five minute intervals ensured that there were always at least four Sea Hurricanes available with adequate fuel and ammunition.

During their brief combats on this day the fighters claimed to have damaged three aircraft, but from the convoy at least three were seen to crash, perhaps hit by lucky flak bursts. During all the time the BV 138s kept the ships in sight and relayed any alterations up to the bombers.

At least one of the German casualties was caused by skilful gunnery by the *Ulster Queen*. Her after control utilised the Type 285 radar on an unseen target and was fortunate in obtaining a most useful correction as the aircraft passed a small gap in the cloud exactly where the guns were tracking as instructed. The barrage followed on and caught up with this aircraft, who must have felt completely safe, scoring a hit. The aircraft was seen rapidly losing height and at least one parachute was seen to open. The *Ulster Queen* claimed this kill in absolute confidence for not only were no other ships firing at this time but no Sea Hurricanes were in the vicinity either.

The *Achates* was one of the few escorts this day who had the opportunity of engaging aircraft targets with her close-range arament but no results were recorded. By 1530 this attack had died away save for the shadowers and the radar screens went black at 1646 as the weather started to worsen. In fact this attack was the last mounted by the Luftwaffe for several days, since because of this change in weather conditions they were grounded. In the attacks to date they had sunk eight ships, but this was far from the overwhelming blow that they had expected to deliver and, to their intense disappointment, and to the lasting chagrin of Reichsmarschall Goering, the carrier had come through unharmed. *Avenger's* only casualty, a very minor one, was caused by the pom-pom fire from an escorting ship. Nor had the massed torpedo bomber attacks broken the convoy up into scattered fragments as it had been thought was the case with PQ 17. Baffled for the moment, the Luftwaffe withdrew from the fray and turned the attack over to the Arctic weather and the U-boats again.

Although they had not been over active during the preceding night the German submarines now made more serious efforts to close with the convoy and this resulted in a day full of alarms and counter-attacks. Not all the sightings of periscopes in the convoy, torpedo tracks and the like, were considered genuine but nevertheless the escort had a very full and busy day.

A submarine was reported astern of the *Hollywood* at 0700. It was seen by lookouts aboard the *Exford* and the Armed Guard manned the 4-inch gun but were unable to open fire due to other ships masking their fire. They called to a destroyer which dropped depth charges over the spot. The *Campfire* transferred a badly wounded crewman to a destroyer during the day for urgent attention but reported nothing else untoward. The *Virginia Dare*, however, reported that a torpedo passed directly under her counter and she opened fire with her 20-mm Oerlikons in a vain attempt to explode it. Again a destroyer closed and dropped two depth charges, without result.

The threat of surface attack was still very much a possibility as far as the convoy and escort was concerned so it was with something of alarm that smoke was sighted on the horizon at 1341. Immediately the destroyer *Opportune* was detached to investigate along her reported bearing of 120 degrees. Within five minutes she was able to confirm that the smoke was not the lethal indications of German heavy units but in fact a pair of U-boats on the surface in visual communication with each other.

The nearest U-boat immediately dived at a distance of some 8,000 yards but *Opportune* was able to open fire with her 'A' and 'B' mountings on the second at 1305, getting in four salvoes before this boat also went under in a crash-dive, the range being down to 10,000 yards. The *Opportune* carried out a series of runs through the broad general area where the two submarines had gone under using a broad zigzag under continuous helm varying speeds between fifteen and eighteen knots.

This caution was justified for one of the German submarines, *U-457*, immediately worked herself into an attacking position and as the *Opportune* went past, intent on her other prey, fired two torpedoes at her, both of which were misses and not reported by the destroyer. She kept up the hunt and, on being approached by one of the BV 138s which were acting as homing aircraft and guardian angels to the U-boats, she also vented her wrath into the sky as well as below the waves, loosening off a fierce barrage which quickly drove the aircraft away. At 1545 the *Opportune* called off her hunt and rejoined the convoy.

As night drew on once more these submarines grew even more bold and more determined in their probings. There were still five U-boats in close contact with PQ 18 as dusk deepened, including the *U-403* (Claussen) and *U-408* (von Hymen). At 2050 Captain Allan Scott-Moncrieff reported that his superior detection devices, HF/DF and MF/DF, had indicated that five U-boats were making attack reports and we now know that this was exactly correct.

At 2220 the destroyer *Meteor* (Lieutenant-Commander D. J. B. Jewitt) had just finished fuelling and was crossing across the head of the convoy to regain her screening position ahead in the centre to the starboard of *Malcolm*, the guide of the fleet, when she sighted a suspicious object bearing Red 70 degrees. An immediate counter-attack was made and a line of three depth-charges was laid by eye with settings of fifty feet. Lieutenant-Commander Jewitt's one concern was to put this possible submarine off its aim for it was situated in an ideal situation for a spread across the leading ships of the convoy. After the charges had detonated a more precise hunt was made with the asdic which resulted in a contact but this was later confirmed as a 'non-sub'. *Meteor* therefore re-joined the screen. It was not clear from German reports whether this was in fact a submarine but if it was then *Meteor* was quite justified in claiming that she had prevented a torpedo attack on the convoy.

The submarines, however, continued to press in for a kill. Following up his earlier success and in keeping with his aggressive conduct so far Lieutenant-Commander Brandenburg refused to be deterred and by 0255 on the 16th had worked *U-457* up ahead of the port side of the convoy in readiness for another attempt to spend his remaining torpedoes in a final blow before retiring. He had penetrated through the outer screen with his usual skill and care but at 0255 the *U-457* was picked out as a firm echo on the asdic set of the destroyer *Impulsive* (Lieutenant-Commander E. G. Roper) which was occupying a bow wing position inside the main screen. When first detected Brandenburg was some eight hundred yards off the *Impulsive*'s port bow.

Lieutenant-Commander Roper at once initiated a counter attack in the recognised procedure to keep the submarine off target, the asdic operator holding his contact firmly down to within fifty yards of depth-charge release. A standard pattern was fired with fifty foot settings and, as these charges exploded in her wake, *Impulsive* was rapidly closing the line of merchant vessels in column one on the convoy's port quarter and contact was lost amidst the noise of their combined washes and propeller noise.

Passing between two ships of this outer column, the *Impulsive* wheeled under helm and picked up speed as Lieutenant-Commander Roper brought her around to carry out a detailed hunt astern of the convoy but no further contact was picked up, despite an intensive search lasting over an hour. Eventually however, in position 73° 05′ N, 43° 15′ E, the destroyer came upon the scene of her first and only attack. Here the surface of the sea was befouled by evil smelling diesel oil and air bubbles were observed rising to the surface from a stationary source.

Roper edged his ship in over this grim marker and they fished out several pieces of freshly shattered wooden wreckage as well as a black leather glove and pieces of paper. An all-round sweep in this position revealed no further evidence. After five minutes Roper fired a single depth charge set to explode at 500 feet right over the spot where the oil still seeped up to the surface, after ascertaining that the depth of water below *Impulsive*'s keel at this position was some 120 fathoms. There was no further reaction to this charge and Roper steered his ship to re-join the convoy. At the time there seemed little doubt that he had detected a U-boat trying to penetrate the screen and that his accurate counter attack not only prevented *U-457* from making her last attack but sank her. Roper in his report was more modest stating only that:

. . . the U-boat was either destroyed or else damaged and bottomed as oil and air were rising in the position of the attack 45-minutes later and no echo was obtained.[10]

There was no doubt however and post-war it was confirmed that Lieutenant-Commander Brandenburg, his command and crew met their fate here. Group North was in fact bemoaning their loss within twenty-four hours. Brandenburg was a brave and skilful commander but the escort screen was just too large. His fate did not deter his comrades from their further efforts however. Numerous anti-submarine contacts were obtained and Rear-Admiral Burnett had constantly to order 'Grab', but he was later of the opinion that no submarines actually penetrated the screen but merely fired, 'browning shots', from outside, at long range, a view which the Director of Anti-Submarine Warfare later failed to agree with, and indeed this now seems rather optimistic. We can certainly agree with the Rear-Admiral, however, that a large proportion of these alarms and excursions were false and in one instance 'Grab' was put into effect after the sighting of a broom handle dropped by one of the leading merchantmen!

During the forenoon these alarms continued but some at least were genuine. At 1034 the destroyer *Offa* (Lieutenant-Commander R. A. Ewing) reported sighting a U-boat on the surface some five miles away. The *Opportune* (Commander M. L. Power, DSO) was detached to join her sister in the hunt and both at once altered to the bearing of the sighting to make their attack.

At 7,000 yards range the U-boat crash-dived at 1045 in the approximate position 75° 30′ N, 45° 25′ E, and, at 1113 after a diligent search, the *Opportune* obtained a contact with wake echoes ahead and then obtained a firm contact dead ahead which was classified as 'Submarine', range 400 yards and closing. The asdic operator held his contact cleanly down to within the last hundred yards of the attack before Commander Power fired a six-charge pattern with staggered depth settings from 100 to 250 feet. There was visible result to be seen after the depth charges had exploded.

This boat was probably the *U-408* which reported herself in contact with PQ 18 earlier, in pinpoint 6337. Lieutenant-Commander von Hymen now began a battle to save his boat as the two destroyers sniffed purposefully about overhead. As *Opportune* ran out from the position of the first attack the U-boat's echo, moving swiftly, was obtained but quickly lost again after 'double' echoes at 600 yards and it was never re-obtained.

Both destroyers, however, continued to hunt methodically for fresh clues as the convoy plodded on towards the far horizon. Two further attacks were made without result and at 1300 the two ships reluctantly gave up the hunt and steered to overtake the convoy. In his report Burnett credits the escape of this submarine by clever use of the *Pillenwerfer* device. Lieutenant-Commander von Hymen and his submariners called this useful piece of apparatus *Bolde*, after the mediaeval magician who had a magic cloak which made him invisible. Briefly it ejected simulated bubbles into the sea in a sort of chemical 'Eno's' to throw the hunters off the scent.

Although the shadowing aircraft was heard early in the day sending out homing signals no air attacks developed. The convoy had altered course southward for the final leg at 0900 this day thus, inevitably closing the gap between them and Banak airfield but as if to compensate for this the weather closed in to one mile visibility, shielding the convoy in its own version of Bolde's cloak and the shadowing ceased. A solitary Catalina which was sighted early in the morning was most likely *VA728* of 210 Squadron, piloted by Flight Lieutenant G. G. Potier, which had been airborne from Grasnaya since 1803 on the 15th on anti-shipping patrol. She had sighted an unidentified submarine at 0600 that morning on an easterly course at five knots and at the same time an enemy aircraft was also seen at 6,000 feet. Potier took his great flying boat in a swoop towards the submarine but, while still some four miles from this target, the U-boat dived.

Within half an hour a submarine was picked up on the surface at a range indicated as fifteen miles. The Catalina was homed in on the contact and, at 0644 in position 71° 55′ N, 35° 00′ E, they were rewarded again with the sighting of a U-boat running on the top of the water directly below them at twelve knots. Again, before an attack could be made, the U-boat submerged. Potier continued his frustrating patrol and at 0716 only one thousand yards ahead of his lumbering aircraft, yet a third submarine surfaced and then immediately submerged. It was the last straw and by 1230 a very infuriated Catalina turned its almost empty wings towards base. The weather ensured that this was the last operational flying conducted by 210 during the 16th.

The time was now rapidly approaching when the 'Fighting Destroyer Escort' was due to part company with the convoy and transfer their protection to the homeward bound QP 14, and with the weather turning in their favour by protecting them from the Luftwaffe there must have been many who felt that their troubles were almost over.

### III

Although not concerned with our story in great detail, the passage of QP 14 must merit some brief attention. Comprising a total of fifteen merchant ships led by Commodore Dowding, a large proportion of them being the survivors from the PQ 17 debacle of July, this convoy had as its close escort two anti-aircraft ships, two Hunt class destroyers, *Blankney* and *Middleton*, four corvettes, three minesweepers and four trawlers. In command of the close escort for this force was Captain Crombie in one of the minesweepers, the *Bramble*. Also included were two rescue ships.

For most of these vessels the perils and fears of July had been followed by two gloomy and depressing months isolated at Archangel, where the general mood especially among the Americans, gradually festered into sullen insolence. Although there were many who did not understand the course of action followed by their escorts but none the less tried to understand that what was done was done on higher authority, there were many who were already very reluctant voyagers into these distant waters and among these discontent was widespread.

Not surprisingly then there was some difficulty in getting the wholehearted co-operation of all these crews in organising themselves for the equally perilous voyage home again. As we have seen their fears were not altogether unfounded for only last minute alterations to the Germans' plans prevented their heavy ships from descending on these already exhausted merchantmen. None the less the voyage had to be made and it was arranged that the convoy should assemble off the Dvina Bar and sail at 0915 on 13th September.

A combination of strong winds and reluctant travellers made

this deadline completely unobtainable, while other mishaps beset these jinxed vessels. Due to the wind for example part of the convoy to be sailed to the assembly point from the jetties at Molotevsk were unable to be warped away from their berths. One of the merchant ships, the *Ironclad*, had trouble with her steering gear and eventually dropped anchor smack in the centre of the channel effectively blocking the exit for all the other merchantmen. Another vessel, the *Ocean Voice*, went hard ashore off Modyugski Island.

However eventually the wind moderated and, with the aid of Russian tugs, the convoy was finally assembled at the rendezvous and sailed at 1600, some seven hours behind schedule. It was fortunate that their passage through the White Sea during the 14th was completely uneventful as it enabled the ships to settle down a little before the going got rough. However at 0730 on the 15th their worst fears were realised, for a Junkers Ju 88 started to shadow them and from then on they were under constant watch.

Although still well within easy range of Soviet air cover the convoy was ill protected against this permanent bird of ill-omen whose immunity began to play on the already taut nerves of the merchant navy crews. Two Soviet fighters were orbiting the convoy but, despite crossing and re-crossing the flight path of the German bomber, they made not the slightest attempt to attack him. The British escorts frantically tried every way they knew how to attract the attention of these two fighters by visual signals but to no effect whatsoever; the fighters ignored the ships equally and as completely as they did the Junkers. Captain Crombie was becoming understandably cross with such stupidity and a message from the British Liaison Officer in one of the Soviet destroyers, the *Uritzki*, which stated that the Russians had just confessed that they were unable to communicate with their own fighters in any way, did nothing to lessen that feeling.

Finally the destroyer *Middleton* tried the last possible method of waking the fighter pilots out of their trance as they spiralled around and around in their futile circles. One round of 4-inch HA was loosened off in their direction to attract their attention. The response was immediate. The two fighters put their noses down and streaked at full speed for the shore, vanishing in a matter of minutes and were never seen near the convoy again!

The Junkers continued his shadowing no doubt puzzled by the example of Allied co-operation he had just witnessed!

Captain Crombie could do little but crack on at full speed and make up the leeway in order to get under the cover of *Avenger*'s Sea Hurricanes as quickly as possible. In this QP 14 needed little bidding, and, by early afternoon, they were well ahead of their estimated position as signalled by the Senior British Naval Officer, North Russia, although still of course behind their original schedule. The weather deteriorated somewhat during the afternoon and Captain Crombie decided that he would be revealing no secrets to the enemy by revealing his true position to Rear-Admiral Burnett and thus facilitating the junction of the convoy and the 'Fighting Destroyer Escort' due for the next day, the 17th. This was accordingly done.

The weather, as we have seen, got steadily worse during the night and the already not too brilliant formation of QP 14 suffered severely as a result. Even before this the *Troubadour* had been a straggler and had fallen away from the convoy to pursue her own solitary course. Commodore Dowding knew enough not to bother waiting for her but during the night of the 16th/17th the *Winston Salem* and *Silver Sword*, yet again American vessels, went adrift also and the minesweeper *Seagull* (Lieutenant C. H. Pollock) was sent back along the convoy's track to try and locate them.

Meanwhile back with PQ 18 during the early afternoon of this same day Rear-Admiral Burnett had been making his plans for leaving one convoy and joining the other. He had obviously to do this in the most discreet way possible so as not to make it too easy for the shadowing submarines to gauge what was afoot. He therefore decided to take leave of the convoy by stages, at intervals, in three distinct groups.

At 1515 the *Scylla* with one flotilla was to leave PQ 18, followed a little later by two more flotillas with the *Alynbank*, the two submarines and the two fleet oilers. Finally the *Avenger*, her two Hunt class destroyers and the last flotilla, the 6th, would depart. Patchy snow squalls were by this time making visibility poor and, as we have seen, the Catalina flying boats from Russia were unable to assist in this vital cross-over period as arranged, although, in the event, it did not matter. Rear-Admiral Burnett had meanwhile received Captain Crombie's signal announcing that QP 14 was now ahead of the re-estimated time by some five hours and in view of the bad visibility Burnett decided not to meet QP 14 until first light on the 17th.

Before the 'Fighting Destroyer Escort' left PQ 18 there was an evocative exchange of signals between the Rear-Admiral and the convoy commodore. As recorded earlier he had already sent a letter to Burnett in which he expressed his hopes and fears:

> You will agree, I think that it is on the cards that I won't get home, so am writing this to suggest a few things which you may be willing to bring to My Lords' notice.[3]

This he did but he also included the message that:

> I'll be sending a signal to you before we part company and though you'll laugh and accuse me of hot air, I really mean it all. What we would have done without you and your chaps I don't know. They must be dead to the world now and have still got to fight their way back.[2]

This signal was in fact sent at 0700 on the 16th and concluded with a quotation from the Bible, Proverbs, Chapter Six, Verse Ten, which Commodore Boddam-Whetham hoped, would shortly come true for everyone.

> Yet a little sleep, a little slumber, a little folding of the hands to sleep.

Rear-Admiral Burnett replied at 0825 expressing his admiration for the convoy as a whole. He thought that the Home Fleet Destroyers felt that 'the likes of you' taught 'the likes of us', for Boddam-Whetham was an old destroyer man, and that they were proud of his approbation. He likewise concluded with a Bible quotation, Isaiah, Chapter 43, verse 2.

> When thou passest through the waters, I will be with thee; and through the rivers, they shall not overflow thee; when thou walkest through the fire, though shalt not be burned; neither shall the flame kindle upon thee.

## IV

The 'Fighting Destroyer Escort' and accompanying vessels left PQ 18 with a very attenuated defence. One anti-aircraft ship, the *Ulster Queen*, two destroyers, *Malcolm* and *Achates* and an assortment of minesweepers and trawlers. This now comprised the total escort force until or unless Russian reinforcements arrived, but past experience had shown that this was not likely to be enormous, not even for the last few miles in sight of land.

Commander A. B. Russell now resumed overall command of the Through Escort, although junior in rank to Captain Adams of the *Ulster Queen*. Routine duties now occupied them, punctuated with the usual submarine alarms. The *Achates* closed the *Ocean Faith* and *Dan-y-Bryn* and embarked two slightly wounded men, *Gleaner* reported two instances of firm radar contacts in poor visibility which were probably U-boats shadowing on the surface but brief hunts proved fruitless.

The merchant ships were still somewhat jittery despite the lack of hard action. John Currant of the *Exford* recalled:

At 0200 No. 42 [*Patrick Henry*] reports mines floating thru convoy. We soon found out they were right, five of them were reported to the bridge by our lookouts. One air raid warning today but nothing came in sight. We had lots of cross fire from other ships, as soon as anything is sighted in the water and resembles a periscope it is showered with lead and steel. Plenty of seals found that out. Our starboard life boats have been damaged by the cross fire. No. 1 boat had a dozen or more holes in it and No. 3 has three or four. This was done by a 20-mm burst under No. 1 boat.[30]

As Captain Adams later reported, some of the merchantmen were horribly dangerous with their uncontrolled fire. The wind had shifted to the south-east and was blowing with increased ferocity bringing with it fog and rain as the afternoon wore on into the short night.

Chapter Six

# The Final Effort

## I

On Thursday 17th the weather continued poor with low visibility shielding the convoy from all but a few persistent shadowers and preventing the Luftwaffe from intruding. Apart from the customary Junkers Ju 88 which arrived at 0915, the day passed without any sign of the Germans. More welcome was the arrival at 1030 of the two Soviet destroyers *Gremyaschi* and *Sokrushitelni* under the command of Flotilla Commander Kolchin. This was the first actual sign of Russian assistance to aid this convoy although in fact Soviet submarines had been operational, three off Persanger, four off Nordkyn and six more in Veranger Fiord. Because of their superior A/A armaments these two new arrivals were stationed one on either beam some five cables off to act as A/A ships.

A further sign of assistance arrived that afternoon in the ungainly shape of Catalina 'G-George' at 1530, piloted by Flying Officer N. W. Wright. She had been airborne from Lake Lakhta. After an exchange of visual signals she settled down to carry out an anti-submarine patrol. At 1637 she sighted a German shadower, which she took to be a Heinkel He 111 off her port beam and when this aircraft turned towards her to attack she sought the protection of cloud cover. She resumed her patrolling later but the weather closed in so much that she eventually lost contact and returned to base. 'F-Freddie' had meanwhile never gained contact and 'K-King', piloted by Flying Officer G. L. Maxton, had similar problems. However no U-boats put in an appearance this day, although the *Exford* was logging the fact that floating mines and submarines were in the area and that depth charges were being dropped all around and through the convoy.

The Armed Guard commander reported that his crew were

getting a much needed rest sleeping by their guns. Daniel Rooker of the *Campfire* wrote tersely, 'All quiet, no enemy action', and the same tone of relief could be detected in Blake Hughes' comments, 'Sky two-thirds filled with squally grey clouds. During the morning two Russian destroyers joined us.'

Both these large destroyers were welcome additions to the escort for as related their main and secondary armaments consisted of four 5-inch guns which could elevate to 45-degrees and two 3-inch A/A guns. Apart from the *Ulster Queen* no British ship could match this for firepower. However if the Americans thought that they were now out of the wood disillusionment awaited them on 18th September.

However in one respect the worst *was* over for PQ 18 for on this day Group North threw in the towel and conceded defeat for their U-boats. Only one boat still reported herself in touch with the convoy as the weather worsened; this was Koehler in *U-377* and he had claimed, without any justification, a hit on an *Afridi*-type destroyer. Operation *Ice Palace* was not the success expected and gloomily Group North took stock. They had lost outright, with few survivors, three submarines, *U-88* (Bohmann), *U-457* (Brandenburg) and *U-589* (Horrer). In addition *U-403* (Clausen) had been badly damaged. They had little to compensate for this on the balance sheet they drew up this day. Four merchant vessels, with a combined total tonnage of 24,000 tons, were claimed as sunk, with another hit and damaged. They also claimed, as certain, one torpedo hit on an *Afridi*-type destroyer (presumably a *Tribal* of which four accompanied PQ 18) and two hits on a *Javelin*-class destroyer (none were present but the ships of the *M* and *O* classes had similar hull lines), with possible hits on two small escorts, corvettes or minesweepers. The hard facts were that only three merchant vessels were sunk and *no* naval craft. In an exchange rate of one submarine for one merchant vessel the Germans were obviously taking unacceptable returns.

The British, for their part, had estimated that up to thirty U-boats had carried out attacks against PQ 18 when in fact only twelve had actually done so. The submarine arm was now switched against QP 14, and already hopes of easy pickings there were bolstering their morale. Timm in *U-251* reported, at 1350, sighting the *Avenger* with three destroyers in pinpoint 4468 so it was obvious she was reinforcing the escort. But in a similar manner the U-boats were concentrated in a new pack, with fresh boats out from Norway, and fresh crews. Against the homeward convoy the U-boats were to regain afresh their old confidence. But against PQ 18 it was once more to be the turn of the Luftwaffe to try and snatch a last-minute victory against the odds.

The withdrawal of the German submarines coincided with the mounting, at last, of the Russian effort to help the convoy through the last short stage. The Soviet Admiral later recorded how :

> Enemy U-boats are stalking the convoy. [*Apparent surprise at this*]. Although they have been found today in different areas, they are still concentrated mainly off Novaya Zemlya. To seek them out I have ordered Simonov to steam there with a detachment of his ships, *Kuibyshev*, *Uritsky* and *Karl Liebknecht*, and join the convoy tomorrow. Besides this, patrol ships and trawlers from the White Sea flotilla have been sent to the region. Catalina aircraft have also been sent.*

Indeed Catalina aircraft were on patrol but they were from 210 Squadron. First into the air was *N* piloted by Sergeant J. Fish. They left Lake Lakhta at 0820 and sighted the convoy at 1110 at twenty miles range. They were therefore too late to take part in the first of the day's air attacks, perhaps fortunately for them.

In fact only two more of the Soviet destroyers joined the convoy, this was at 0415, and these were stationed ahead and astern of the convoy by Commander Russell. At 0600 the convoy sighted Cape Kanin and at the same time the first German shadower appeared in the murky, but clearing, sky. Some two-and-a-quarter hours later M/F D/F homing signals were picked up, which *Ulster Queen* interpreted as firm warning of an impending air attack, but this first assault did not in fact break over the convoy until 1025.

An earlier alert had taken place when the Commodore hoisted the 'Enemy warship' pendant but after this scare nothing happened. But the lifting weather had made the *Fliegerführer Nordost*, Colonel Alexander Holle at Kirkenes, determined to make one last effort with what few serviceable aircraft remained at Banak. The first of these units was *III/KG 30*, led by Captain

* With the Red Fleet, Putnam & Co., 1965.

Hajo Herrmann, transferred from Bardufoss to Banak, Herrmann had already established a record for outstanding leadership and was later in the war to become a top ace night-fighting pilot in defence of his homeland against area bombing raids. His Junkers Ju 88s were to co-operate in the usual manner by making low-level bombing runs through the low cloud base to divert the attention of the gunners. Round the clock sorties were to be made to coincide with two blows to be delivered by the torpedo bombers.

The first of these latter attacks was delivered by twelve Heinkel He 111s of I/KG 26, all that could be scraped together at this stage, once again led with grim determination by Werner Klumper. It was the attacks delivered this day by the somewhat threadbare remnant of Stumff's élite force, a mere fraction of the numbers thrown in with such confidence four days earlier, that the Russians later persuaded themselves was the Germans' 'main blow'. They described it as a planned blow conceived by the German command in the form of a simultaneous attack by U-boats and aircraft.

> However the aircraft were late arriving. Our ships drove off the enemy U-boats with depth-charges and forced them to fall behind. A second Nazi reconnaissance plane appeared over the convoy at 1000. Half an hour afterwards the lookouts on *Gremyaschi*, Listenev and Luzhkov, noticed simultaneously the first echelon of enemy machines – four-engined torpedo-planes coming in at sea-level to attack the convoy in the rear.

Thus did good, comradely eyes spot the four-engined He 111s (sic), well ahead of *Ulster Queen*'s Type 279 radar apparently, which, we are informed by her report, plotted a large group of aircraft coming in from the westward at 1000. Anyway at 1020 He 111s flying low were sighted by the ships visually on the starboard quarter. The captain of the *Gremyaschi* immediately despatched a message to Fleet headquarters and opened fire with all guns, which, it was said, surprised the English particularly, as they had never seen main-calibre guns used against low-flying aircraft! (sic).

Herrmann's Ju 88s were overhead bombing through the clouds but this did not deter most of the rear escorts from engaging the torpedo bombers. Captain Adams had earlier stationed *Ulster*

*Queen* astern of the convoy and so, when this torpedo bomber threat developed, turned her to bring his entire main armament to bear and commenced firing at 10,000 yards. The Soviet ships opened fire with broadsides at four miles.

Klumper's twelve Heinkels deployed in line abreast across the rear of the convoy and were met by the combined fire of *Ulster Queen*, *Gremyaschi* and *Sharpshooter* as well as the rear merchant ships in each column. Most of the Heinkels launched at between 3 and 4,000 yards range before veering off unharmed. Many of the torpedoes seemed to break the surface after dropping and finish their runs among the rear ships of the convoy without damage but one found its mark on the number two ship up in the port wing column. This was the American vessel *Kentucky*.

She was a 5,466-ton cargo vessel owned by the States Steamship Company. She was steering at the convoy speed of nine knots, not zig-zagging but the captain had just ordered an alteration in course when the torpedo was sighted, about 100 yards away, approaching at about fifteen degrees to the ship's course from the starboard side. Some of the Heinkels, which flew down between the convoy lanes, were clearly visible and, being painted dark green, stood out easily, but the gunners held their fire for fear of hitting other ships in the convoy. The captain just had time to order everyone to take cover before the torpedo struck home just before the bridge on the starboard side. Luckily no one was in the open for the resulting explosion blew the cover of number two hatch up into the ship's rigging as if it were made of paper and the port side of the bridge was carried away by the blast.

All communication lines were broken and fire immediately broke out in the officers' quarters, nevertheless the ship's engines were immediately stopped and the crew ordered up on deck by the captain. Two minutes after the detonation the captain ordered 'Abandon Ship'.

In all some fifty-five men of the crew and the armed guard party of fourteen got away in the lifeboats and the rafts. The *Kentucky*, however, remained afloat. This fact caused much adverse comment from the Americans' two allies; the Russian Admiral stated, quite reasonably, that: 'Although she was still capable of making way and remained on an even keel, the vessel nevertheless left her station in the column.' Of course this account then has to go further and distort the true events out of all recognition. 'No sooner had the turn been completed than the *Kentucky*'s crew abandoned ship and a British patrol ship and a Nazi bomber rushed at it together. In the course of ten minutes the British ship bombarded the vessel with its guns, after which the Nazi finished it off with bombs. A singular unanimity of action!'*

A ghastly and twisted way in which to describe what was in fact a very determined effort by the minesweeper *Sharpshooter* to rescue and bring in the *Kentucky*. The cargo vessel in fact remained afloat for some three quarters of an hour after the crew left her. The minesweeper *Harrier* had proceeded to the van of the convoy earlier and had ordered Lieutenant-Commander O'Hara of the *Sharpshooter* to organise any rescue work with the trawlers and the three little motor minesweepers, and, in fact, *Kentucky*'s crew were picked up by these latter vessels. Meanwhile *Ulster Queen* had radioed to Archangel for two rescue tugs and *Sharpshooter* was ordered to stand by the *Kentucky* until they arrived with the trawler *Cape Mariato* as an additional escort.

While turning to proceed alongside the *Kentucky* and put a salvage party aboard both *Sharpshooter* and *Kentucky* were bombed by one of the *III/KG 30*'s Junkers Ju 88s in what Captain Adams described as 'a well-executed dive'. Two bombs struck the disabled *Kentucky* aft and fierce fires broke out. *Sharpshooter* herself suffered from the blasts of near misses and it proved impossible to proceed alongside the blazing American vessel as more bombers appeared overhead and commenced their attacks. Consequently *Sharpshooter* and *Cape Mariato* rejoined the main convoy, the little trawler surviving three set attacks as they did so. The rescue tugs from Iokanka were later cancelled at 1130 when the *Kentucky* was seen to blow up.

*Ulster Queen* had meanwhile broadcast a 'Help' signal for fighter cover, but the Soviet fighters did not arrive overhead until 1230, by which time the attacks were well over. High-level bombing continued until 1210 but, as Lieutenant John Laird aboard the *Virginia Dare* recalled, 'they hit nothing and nor did we.' As did several others, Ensign Daniel Rooker aboard the *Campfire*

* *With the Red Fleet*, Putnam & Co., 1965.

considered that the convoy was extremely lucky to come through the torpedo bomber attack with the loss of only one ship for the attacks by *I/KG 26* were pressed well home.

Many of the torpedoes must have been duds. Three torpedoes were dropped at point-blank range near a Liberty Ship in column seven and none of them exploded.[34]

The attack he is referring to here was against the *Virginia Dare*, let John Landers tell the story :

This ship was astern and to the right of the convoy. Hence we were without the covering fire of other ships. Three of the attacking planes wheeled to starboard, then turned and came at us on our starboard quarter, flying about thirty feet above the water. Our 3-inch would not bear, so we fired four shrapnel shells that the British gave us in the 4-inch. This turned the leading aircraft, and he turned, coming on a parallel course, pulling ahead, and coming in on the starboard bow. The two remaining planes came on in, releasing their torpedoes at about 1000 yards. We gave the ship hard right rudder and the two torpedoes passed close astern. The two planes then banked to starboard, strafing as they did so – the shots were wild – and flew out on the starboard beam. As we turned, the plane that was coming in on the bow released its torpedo and flew off to starboard. We were unable to bring any of these planes down as they would not come within our range.[36]

The *Patrick Henry* also had a narrow escape in this attack, and not only from the German aircraft.

One Heinkel flew up our column on a level with our flying bridge at a distance of about 150 yards when abeam. As he approached our ship our 4-inch shrapnel tore his tail plane. Shortly thereafter he dropped two torpedoes just astern of us both of which missed, and as he came abreast of us two or three of our 20-mm guns scored hits. Shortly afterwards he crashed in flames about 1,000 yards ahead of us. One sailor was severely injured by gunfire and several planes on our deck [Deck cargo for Russia] were riddled by 20-mm fire from other ships.[35]

Several of the escorts managed to get in good shots as these aircraft left the convoy lines at deck-level. The *Achates* in particular was well placed to engage several Heinkels at ranges of around

1,000 yards. The trawler *Cape Argonia* was straffed in return by the Heinkels at very close range and one of the 4-inch guns crew was hit by a bullet.

Some postwar accounts give the impression that these attacks were half-hearted affairs but the descriptions we have given from eye-witnesses would seem to refute these statements as being entirely incorrect.

At 1130 another wave of Heinkels appeared and delivered a second attack. By this time air cover, of a kind, had arrived, in the lumbering shape of Catalina *N* which arrived over the convoy at 1110. Sergeant Fish circled the ships, which were flying their balloon barrage with little effect, at 800 feet and watched the *Kentucky* sink but, beyond noting a possible Junkers Ju 87 dive-bomber passing over the convoy, he made no reference to this second attack although the sky around him must have been thick with German bombers.

This second wave also consisted of twelve Heinkels and these divided into two sections to attack the port and starboard wings of the convoy respectively. Those attacking from the port were seen to drop their torpedoes from at least 4,000 yards out and at heights which varied between fifty and 150 feet. It was noticeable that the torpedoes released from such a height tended to shoot into the air after impact which probably contributed to their inaccuracy. In their later comments the Russians considered that the low-level approach favoured by the Germans was a mistake. They considered that the convoy's losses would have been considerably larger if the high-level approach, as used by their own torpedo aircraft, had been favoured. However there was no conspicuous record of success achieved by the Soviet high-level tactics, although the Japanese had certainly utilised this method quite effectively when sinking the *Prince of Wales* and *Repulse* ten months earlier.

The starboard group of aircraft pressed their attack home with a greater determination, closing to within 1,000 yards before release. Despite this most of the torpedoes seemed to finish their runs amongst the rear ships and eight were noted to have broken the surface in the vicinity of the *Ulster Queen* who turned stern-on to avoid the worst effects.

Again casualties among the aircraft were claimed as high. The *Ulster Queen* was at one stage of this attack laying down an effective splash barrage with 'Y' mounting astern and one He III was seen to capsize and crash after bumping one of these, while another was seen banking steeply in the barrage. Captain Adams reported that only nine of the twelve appeared emerging from the convoy. One Heinkel penetrated at low level right into the convoy and this aircraft was fired on by all and sundry as it flew up between columns three and four, 'fired on by all ships irrespective of good neigbourliness', was how Captain Adams described it later, and this aircraft crashed among the forward screen after a round from 'B' mounting was seen to hit her. Such a spectacular attack was of course noted by most of the ships and clearly all appeared to claim this victim as their own.

The Soviet destroyers claimed five aircraft destroyed, two by *Gremyaschi*, two by *Sokrushitelny* and one by *Kuibyshev*, but Captain Adams put the score at two destroyed, one probable and two possible, with the total for all the convoy as four certains. Lieutenant-Commander A. H. Jones of the *Achates* logged one Heinkel which was heavily engaged by all his guns to starboard from a range of 500 yards. This aircraft turned towards *Achates* and crashed in flames about ninety yards away. This would appear to be confirmed by the report of Lieutenant Walker of the corvette *Bluebell* who logged:

A Heinkel III which emerged from the convoy was seen to be engaged by HMS *Achates*, the next ship on the screen to starboard, and was shot down, bursting into flames as it struck the water.[20]

*Harrier* was of the opinion that, although her Oerlikons were seen to be hitting, the aircraft had already passed through a hail of fire from the convoy and other escorts, so considered that these victories should be shared by a large number of ships.

Aboard the *Exford* Coxswain John H. Currant, USNR noted:

Most of them came in to the port wing of the convoy. One bomber made for the *Hollywood* which was right astern of this ship. It let two torpedoes go at the *Hollywood* and missed. Then he tried to get us and our gunners on the stern and filled him full of 20mms. He was soon abeam of the bridge and we fired five .303 calibre machine guns at him. When he was a little beyond our bow he made a wingover and crashed into the sea. For some reason he didn't let any torpedoes go at us. We think he con-

contracted lead poison before he had a chance to.[30] [The Heinkel He 111s of course only carried two torpedoes.]

On the *Patrick Henry* Blake Hughes thought several German aircraft were destroyed, but was not specific, but in his opinion a determined attack by a large number of torpedo planes could have wiped out the rest of the convoy at this stage, because of the much depleted escort and with the fire of the ships becoming noticeably ragged because of the long period of action.

Lieutenant Stansel E. De Foe of the *Esek Hopkins*'s Armed Guard claimed one Heinkel destroyed by his guns crews, again he described the fate of the same outstandingly brave crew mentioned earlier.

The second group of about five planes then began a beam attack on the last two ships in the eighth column. These planes and those from the starboard side re-formed. This group of four planes then flew as if to attack from astern on columns three and four. All but one of these were diverted by the Hurricane from the CAM ship. The remaining Heinkel flew between columns three and four as if to attack ship 44 [*Hollywood*], then banking away from that ship as if to attack this ship. The attacker apparently having been diverted by the fire of the two ships (44 and 43) then began to fall off to port with all torpedoes still not launched. The plane was met with a devastating crossfire from all the ships in columns three and four and crashed into the sea ahead of the convoy.[31]

Many of the Americans and Russians reported the Heinkels as four-engined aircraft, or 'Kuriers' but the reason for this is not known except perhaps because of extremely poor aircraft recognition. If the reader feels that it is unlikely for such a mistake to be made by AA gunners then the fate of the CAM Hurricane is perhaps the obvious answer. This aircraft had been sitting on its catapult aboard the *Empire Moon* for the whole voyage, awaiting its opportunity to engage the enemy. With the *Avenger* gone and still no sign of any Russian fighter cover arriving, it was decided to unleash her. Flying Officer A. H. Burr was already seated strapped-in and ready to go.

In fact he had been so since 1015 that morning but the SO had not thought the time was ready for the Hurricane to show her paces. At 1100 the second high altitude attack developed and his

Fighter Direction Officer, Lieutenant Carrique, gave Burr's Captain aboard the *Empire Morn* instructions to fire off the Hurricane to make an interception, but as the ship was not clear ahead this could not be done and a red flag was given the firing officer, Pilot Officer Davies.

In this delay Burr was perhaps fortunate for, while still sitting impatiently in his cockpit, he ran another instrument check and found that his electrical installation had broken down entirely. The RTO and the other members of his crew very calmly proceeded to check the fuses and then they changed the battery while bombs from the Junkers Ju 88s continued to fall close to the ship.

At 1150 the second torpedo-bomber attack came in from the post quarter and Burr was launched off immediately and cleanly. Once airborne he was deluged with a hail of shells from trigger-happy gunners on ships all around him. Captain Adams later wrote that:

> It was a disgrace to see two of the convoy open up close range weapons on the Hurricane from the moment it was launched until it was out of range, happily intact; and there was no way to stop the imbeciles.[25]

The Commodore was more specific claiming that it was American ships which opened fire on the Hurricane as soon as she was airborne. Fortunately Burr got clear and he was soon in action. The FDO directed him up to 700 feet and then out to the port quarter of the convoy. At once Burr counted an estimated fifteen He 111s coming in line abreast about three miles astern of the convoy at a height of fifty feet.

> I dived on them and carried out a head-on and port beam attack on a He 111 opening fire at 300 yards and closing to 150 yards. I noticed my shots striking the engine and nose of the Heinkel and as I turned above and behind to the left I noticed white smoke coming from his starboard engine. I closed again to 250 yards and gave him the rest of my ammunition in a beam attack carried out from his starboard side. I then noticed that white smoke was coming from both his engines, but as I was interfering with the flak from the ships I broke to the right and went round the stern to the starboard side of the convoy.[11]

After this the FDO sent him to patrol the starboard side of the convoy. Although Burr had no ammunition left he intended to make mock attacks on the next formation and break it up, but no further attack took place other than the Ju 88s bombing through the clouds. Burr checked his petrol and found he had seventy gallons left so asked Lieutenant Carrique for the distance and vector of the nearest airfield in order to save the aircraft instead of the usual method of ditching alongside an escort. On learning that the nearest base was some 240 miles Burr set off, but it wasn't that easy.

> I ran into a fog bank about forty miles wide after fifteen minutes flying but managed to make a landfall and pinpoint my position. I flew at heights between 200 and 2,000 feet and arriving over Archangel fired the recognition signal and found Keg Ostrov aerodrome where I landed at 1415 hours with five gallons in my reserve tank left.[11]

It was a gallant sortie.

This ended the torpedo bombing effort, although the Junkers Ju 88s continued to drone in and out of the cloud banks until after midday and some ships were lucky to escape with no more than a severe shaking. The master of the Russian freighter *Tbilisi* for example was wounded and the ship was subsequently handled very efficiently by the mate. The *Empire Tristram* was severely shaken by two near miss bombs and it was thought aboard her that they had been torpedoed. Captain W. H. Miller, her Master, ordered his crew to stand by the boats but this order was misinterpreted. The ship's confidential books were thrown overboard and a boat was lowered; she subsequently re-joined however. The master of the *William Moultrie*, Captain Hocken, demanded that his ship be placed in a safer position in the convoy so Commodore Boddam-Whetham instructed the British *Goolistan* to change places with her.

> I informed Master of *William Moultrie*, however, that the only difference I could see between 4,000 tons of TNT and 2,000 tons was a fractional part of a second should she be hit.[3]

It was certainly evident that the appalling examples of the annihilation of the *Empire Stevenson* and *Mary Luckenbach* had affected the nerves of other officers and men in the vicinity of ammunition ships but *William Moultrie* was the only ship to change position. Others, however, were none too keen, and understandably so, to maintain close formation as required. Certainly Captain Russell was to report that the station-keeping left much to be desired. He subsequently discussed this question with some of the Merchant Navy officers and came to the conclusion that more trouble should be taken at the pre-sailing Convoy Conferences to explain the value of close station-keeping.

The attacks gradually died out after midday although the *Ulster Queen* was reporting various distant groups of aircraft and M/F D/F homing signals were being monitored continuously. This tailing off of effort was thought to be due to deteriorating visibility and later in the afternoon two Russian PE 3 fighters arrived overhead.

This final effort by the torpedo bombers had failed and never again were they to influence the passage of Russian Convoys. Their action against PQ 18 was their last major mission in Arctic waters, for towards the end of October the whole of *KG 26* started to transfer to the Mediterranean where better results were expected from them. In fact their arrival there coincided with the Allied invasion of Vichy-French North Africa and they were able to contribute to its defence. Luftflotte 5 claimed that the torpedo bombers had sunk two freighters and damaged a third this day, while *KG 30* had thought they had destroyed three merchant ships and an escort (presumably *Sharpshooter*), and damaged another two freighters.

Thus ended the fighting of the 18th September which the Russians elevated into a major conflict and victory. As the 'Fight off Kanin Nos' it thus passed into history as proof of the White Sea's Fleet defeat of the major attack on a Russian Convoy. Admiral Arseni Golovko's book has been cited before but one last extract must be included to show to what lengths this minor action has been distorted and dished up as a major Soviet victory.

The battle for the September Allied convoy constitutes the most conclusive answer to all objections to the despatch of cargoes to Soviet northern ports. The tragic affair of the July convoy (PQ 17) occurred, as we know, through the fault of the allies who abandoned the ships to their fate without forewarning us. This time, when we were able to take timely steps to secure the safety of the convoy in our operational zone, everything went differently. The enemy received the proper rebuff, and the convoy's losses (one transport out of twenty-nine which reached our zone) must be regarded as minimal, bearing in mind the very substantial blow delivered by the enemy. The battle at Kanin Nos will long be remembered by us, the allies and the Nazis.*

This, it must be borne in mind, describes the contribution by four destroyers in beating off three air attacks in sight of their own coasts and the subsequent arrival, when the battle was over, of two fighter aircraft as escorts!

## II

Even now the weary ships' crews were not granted a respite for with the departure of the last German bomber the weather took up the fight in the vicious and evil way that only the Arctic storms could. Men who had been at action stations for a week in the face of the heaviest air attacks mounted on this convoy route now found their numb minds having to cope with heavy seas and icy winds which battered them and their ships into the last stages of complete exhaustion. Little wonder then that the strain began to tell, not least on the man with the greatest responsibility on his shoulders, the convoy commodore.

The signs of the impending storm had begun while the last attacks were still taking place and were instrumental in preventing further assaults. In the air conditions became quickly impossible as the escorting Catalinas from 210 Squadron were to find out. Sergeant Fish in N had logged sighting two Russian MB seaplanes at 1318 which passed overhead of convoy and disappeared in a north-westerly direction and two minutes later she sighted 'S' piloted by Flight Lieutenant Healey and the two exchanged signals. Sergeant Fish was told that S's intentions were to stay with the convoy until first light and he flashed back, 'Leaving for base'.

Flight Lieutenant Healey continued his lonely patrol until 1603 by which time the weather was deteriorating rapidly and he was forced to leave the convoy and head for Cape Kanin and safety. As the convoy approached the Dvina Bar preparations were made to form the convoy into two columns and the minesweepers began to organise themselves to sweep a clear path along the Russians' front door to allow the convoy to enter Arch-

* *With the Red Fleet*, Putnam & Co., 1965.

angel safely. The *Harrier*, Commander A. D. H. Jay, DSO, was therefore stationed ahead of the convoy because of Commander Jay's knowledge of local conditions hereabouts, so that she could lead in when the local minesweeping flotilla joined.

These four ships, *Britomart*, *Halcyon*, *Hazard* and *Salamander*, were duly sighted at 1620 and Jay signalled to Lieutenant-Commander C. H. Corbett-Singleton in *Halcyon*:

'Do you consider it necessary for convoy to be swept through channel?'

To which the reply was received that it was not considered necessary for the local flotilla had been sweeping that area for the past seven days. Lieutenant-Commander Corbett-Singleton suggested, however, that the flotilla be detached to go ahead to sweep the Dvina approaches for ground mines as German air minelaying had been reported active recently. This suggestion was passed on to Commander Russell who, in view of the weather conditions, approved it. Accordingly the four boats were detached at 1740 for this purpose.

Off Cape Gorodetski two columns were therefore formed but considerable navigational problems now beset the elongated convoy during the night due to the combination of an exceptionally strong tide which was setting against the convoy and the fact that the Group 1A shore lights marking the channel were not shown as requested. Instead, following Russian objections, the lights at Cape Orlovterski and Three Island were out. Their penetration of this tricky channel then was very much a heart-in-mouth affair.

Commander Jay thought that it was almost impossible to keep such a large group of ships within the searched channel without shore lights under the conditions of the 18/19th; a dark night, low visibility and strong tides. Radio beacons alone were not sufficient for accurate navigation. He meanwhile had signalled ahead to Senior British Naval Officer at Archangel, Captain Maund, his arrangements to ensure safe passage of the convoy through the Dvina approach channel. One minesweeper was to be stationed at the entrance to mark its position and due to the weather it was anticipated that the convoy would need to anchor near the Fairway Buoy. He planned to use the game little MMSs to help the five pilot boats distribute the pilots to the merchant ships and *Achates* was detached to organise a head-count in

179

readiness for this. The four big minesweepers were to anchor at three-mile intervals to mark the swept channel and act as visual signal links. Alas for his good intentions and plans, by the afternoon of the 19th conditions were becoming impossible at sea.

By the time the convoy reached the North Dvina approaches and tried to anchor a full gale was blowing from the north-west. The Russian pilot boats wisely ran for shelter. There was nothing for it but to mark time and try to ride the gale out and for thirty-six hours the long straggling lines of the merchant ships and their little escorts rolled and plunged in heavy seas. Many were soon in trouble.

The minesweeper *Harrier* was forced to weigh anchor by 1650 and steam to seaward. At 0203 on the 20th the steering engine failed and the little vessel hove-to in hand steering in ghastly conditions. The after ballast tank of 32 tons was already full to reduce racing but now the forepeak and double bottom compartments were also flooded to give an extra twenty-two tons ballast which made steering easier until emergency repairs were completed at 1250 that afternoon which enabled her to re-join the convoy.

The little trawler *Cape Argonia* was in a worse state for by the time the convoy hove-to she had already started to use her permanent coal ballast of thirty tons and Lieutenant Pate could do nothing more but stem the sea and conserve as much coal as possible. Happily she survived berthing, at No. 19 Sawmill Berth at 1700 on the 21st with just five tons of coal left, this despite the fact that she had embarked 210 tons when she left Iceland against the 170 tons she was limited to.

*St Kenan* was in a similar way with only sixty tons of coal remaining on the 19th which made the ship dangerously unstable. On the 20th she was caught in the trough of the sea and went over in an exceptionally heavy roll. The lifeboat had earlier been swung out in case she broached to and this was carried away and the davits bent badly.

The *Exford* lost both her anchors and her No. 3 lifeboat and davits and had to call for a pilot. He very bravely got aboard, the pilot boat bending *Exford*'s starboard life-raft frame in doing so. Once they had him embarked they set off down the swept channel in the still raging seas and after an hour came upon three American freighters hard and fast ashore. The wind had taken control and the *Exford* veered across the channel towards this group until it seemed certain that she would collide with them. She managed to avoid this but in doing so also went ashore. Strenuous efforts got her afloat again and she continued down the channel but at 2200 she again went ashore where she remained all night.

The *Campfire* lost one anchor just after midnight and had to haul in the other and keep underway until 1730 when she took on a pilot. *Campfire* then proceeded up channel behind the pilot boat. At 1900 the *Sahale* signalled that she was aground and shortly after this *Campfire* followed her ashore. At 2030 she floated off once more and was back in the swept channel when another ship thrust through and, in avoiding her, *Campfire* went aground again and her engines were rendered useless by clogged condensers.

The trawler *Daneman*, the little rescue ship that had performed so valiantly and so well, was another storm victim. On the night of the 19/20th she reported that she had exhausted all her fuel and that her anchor was dragging. Commander Russell sent the corvettes to try and help her. The *Bergamot* (Lieutenant R. T. Horan), established visual contact at 0025 when the *Daneman* reported that she was still coping with the situation, but an hour later her anchors continued to drag and it seemed possible that she would collide with one of the merchantmen. The freighter was told to up anchor and move, which she did in a commendably short time, and *Bergamot* got ready to take *Daneman* in tow despite the appalling weather conditions.

Between 0104 and 0654 repeated attempts were made to pass lines into the trawler, both by costa gun line and by anchoring ahead and down lines on buoys, but none of these were successful. The corvette *Bluebell* then arrived to assist and anchored ahead of the trawler and at 1655 succeeded in passing a tow line into her. *Bergamot* did not get clear again until 1952 with the loss of her anti-submarine asdic dome.

A third escort then arrived, the minesweeper *Gleaner* (Lieutenant-Commander Hewitt, DSC), and found *Daneman* hard and fast. In the conditions prevailing in the darkness, with two ships already damaged, he considered that nothing further could be done that night. Commander Russell therefore ordered all attempts at towing to be postponed until daybreak.

By dawn of the 21st *Daneman* was still ashore near the Modyugski Light and *Campfire*, *Sahale* and *Lafayette* were hard aground on the Dvina Bar, mainly as a result of two of them not having embarked a pilot. In the words of Captain Maund (who was SBNO, at Archangel):* 'Some difficulty was experienced with regard to their crews.' Ensign Daniel Rooker of the Armed Guard party told what exactly this meant.

> Shortly afterwards the general alarm sounded. I asked the Captain what it meant. He replied that inasmuch as the ship was defenceless against high altitude bombers that for the safety of the crew he was going to abandon the ship. I replied that I didn't think the armed guard should leave the ship. I asked if this were an order. He said it was and to get my crew to the boats.[34]

Both *Campfire*'s boats got away safely and landed the entire crew on Mudyugski Island, her Captain remaining despite the danger, until the last possible moment. Rooker meanwhile proceeded to the lighthouse and contacted the US Naval Attaché at Archangel, Commander Frenkel, on the phone and informed him that he felt it was wrong for his party to be ashore. The Naval Attaché agreed and promised to send a boat to take them back to defend the ship. A high-level bomber dropped a single bomb close to the *Campfire* at this time and it was this that persuaded the captain to join the others ashore which he did. The American crew joined up with the crew of the *Daneman* and all spent the night in the lighthouse, although Rooker and *Campfire*'s skipper spent the night aboard the trawler. On the morning of the 22nd Rooker informed the captain he was going back to the ship and the captain agreed to return with them. The Naval Attaché arrived and Rooker, the captain, the armed guard and seven of the merchant crew reboarded their vessel. However the bulk of the crew refused point-blank to go until the explosive cargo had been unloaded, and this attitude they kept to. Captain Maund wryly reported that, in an effort to get them back aboard, he told them that if they stayed ashore they would probably all be devoured by wolves, but even this had no effect!

These three ships were still aground on the 25th and were

* The Senior British Officer.

discharging into lighters. The Derrick Ships *Empire Bard* and *Empire Elgar* were despatched to the bar with heavy equipment together with the Soviet salvage vessel *Schval*. These salvage operations were carried out by a very able team of experts led by Colonel Petrov who was attached to the staff at Admiral Golovko's White Sea Force. Captain Maund paid strong tributes to his efficiency and indeed by the 27th all three ships had been refloated. The *Daneman* proved a more difficult problem for she was still fast aground on this date but Captain Maund expressed the opinion that Colonel Petrov would succeed in refloating her eventually, and he did. A letter of appreciation was later forwarded by Their Lordships to Admiral Khalamov at the Soviet Embassy in London for Petrov's work.

As if the gale were not enough to contend with at 1540 on the 20th came warnings of German air activity once more and Junkers Ju 88s commenced a prolonged bombing attack on the storm tossed ships, but fortunately the aircraft must have been equally troubled by the conditions, and the attacks were not very effective. These aircraft, twelve strong, approached at 2,000 feet through 8/10ths cloud. The convoy was very split up but *Ulster Queen* closed the largest section of about ten merchant ships and put up a controlled long range barrage. The attacks continued for half an hour. The *Exford* was near missed by two heavy bombs which fell about 100 yards astern. The ship shook like a leaf from stem to stern and the crew went below to look for leaks in the holds but found none.

Again the twin-engined Ju 88s are often described by the Americans as Focke-Wulf 'Kuriers' (sic) as in the account of the action by Lieutenant De Foe of the *Esek Hopkins*:

> The planes flew above the clouds and came below the banks at times to sight and drop bombs. For the first time in any of the attacks the 'Kuriers' were observed to have released their bombs both from a level flight and also from a shallow dive. The last bomb was dropped at 1620. No hits were observed on the ships of the convoy or escort. One of the shells we fired was seen to have a direct hit on one of the Focke-Wulfs. The shell was reported to have burst in the area between the nose of the ship and the starboard engines. The plane then began to lose altitude and smoke from the leading edge of the starboard wing.[37]

The *Nathaniel Green* observed at least three planes, one of which crashed. The Russians reported that a total of twenty-four bombers were involved in this attack and, on being met by Soviet fighters, 'dropped their bombs in disorder in the water'. The Russians claimed the destruction of two of the Junkers bombers. There is some direct evidence that Russian fighter cover was indeed effective this day, several of the American ships comment on it while Captain Adams of the *Ulster Queen* thought that many of likely attacks plotted never materialised due to the interception by the PE 3s.

Captain Maund commented that no better target could have presented itself but that the attacks were ineffective. The German pilots claimed to have sunk two merchantmen and damaged another in this attack but no ship was in fact hit. This marked the final effort by the Luftwaffe and it is appropriate here to summarise the total credit and loss account as compiled during the passage of PQ 18, on both sides, it will be seen gross miscalculations of results achieved abounded.

Luftwaffe estimates and final claims were for twenty-three merchant ships sunk, nineteen of these by torpedo, with a total estimated tonnage of 162,000 BRT. In addition one destroyer and two smaller escorts had been sunk. Furthermore another ten freighters were claimed as damaged, six of these by torpedoes, adding another 77,000 BRT to the total. In fact they had sunk ten merchant ships only, totalling 54,669 tons, and *no* warship had been even slightly damaged.

On the other hand the British, American and Russian estimates of aircraft destroyed were equally unrealistic. The British estimates were the most modest and carefully detailed and they claimed a total of forty-two German aircraft confirmed destroyed. The figures were broken down in this manner:

By ships' gunfire: 36. By Fleet Air Arm: 5.
By CAM Hurricane: 1. Total confirmed: 42.

German records however, which were always carefully documented, give the total losses for the whole operation against PQ 18 as 44 aircraft, including thirty-eight torpedo bombers.

It is interesting to see how quickly and how often figures are distorted. Perhaps the most simple example of this is the attack made by the CAM Ship Hurricane IA flown by Flying Officer A. H. Burr, RAF. We quoted from his own report in his own words and he reported hitting a single Heinkel 111 but does not claim it destroyed for certain because he had to break off the attack. And yet, in the official estimate made a fortnight later, this *possible* damage has already become 'One certain Heinkel'.

Unfortunately the story does not stop there but grows with the telling over the years. In the Commodore's report it becomes 'one enemy *at least*', which implies even if it does not claim outright that perhaps more than one was brought down. By 1956 Burr's *intention* to make dummy attacks when he was out of ammunition had become an established fact in the Official History, *The War At Sea*, Volume II, when it is stated that, 'the fighter pilot then drove off other enemies by making dummy attacks'. But in fact Flying Officer Burr stated at the time, 'no other aircraft appeared.' By 1973 his score had quite positively doubled although his victims had changed, for in *Carrier Operations of World War II, Volume I* it is stated that : 'the Sea Hurricane IA from the *Empire Morn* destroyed two Heinkel torpedo bombers and saved the convoy from further damage.'

Therefore it is easy to see from just this one simple example that even when the basic facts are well documented and available gross distortion can take place unless checked at source and verified. Both books quoted, it should be added, were written by individuals or teams with the fullest access to all available material. No book will ever be free of such errors but at least the impression can be corrected that if it is 'official' then it is automatically and without question correct.

The Kriegsmarine was doubtful, even at the time, whether the figures claimed by Stumff were correct. They examined these figures and came up with the conclusion that if the Luftwaffe were correct then the convoy must have contained at least forty-five ships and not the thirty-eight that had been constantly reported all through. They did some juggling with what they knew and came up with the more realistic, but still highly inaccurate figures, of twenty-three ships sunk out of thirty-eight.

Finally, as we leave for the moment the surviving ships of PQ 18 picking their way into the White Sea, some consideration must be given to the strain that the survivors had undergone during nineteen days of continuous action. It must be born in mind that for almost all the American crews this was the very first action they had seen even though their country had been in the war for ten months. Fresh gun-crews and inexperienced crews, no wonder Commodore Boddam-Whetham was to write in one account:

These Americans must be persuaded to:
(a) obey orders
(b) look out for signals
(c) learn the Morse Code
(d) know what distance a cable is!
(e) realise that the Commodore's orders are given to get the Convoy home safely and not for amusement or to show his authority.
(f) Read and learn the elementary paragraphs in Mersigs on the various methods of turning etc.
(g) Understand that they are at war and that the motto 'It can't happen here' does not apply to convoy work.[3]

This was not an isolated opinion by any means. Captain Adams of the *Ulster Queen* was to write:

The wild firing of some of the merchant ships was at times highly dangerous, being particularly noticeable amongst the Americans – indeed *Ulster Queen* had one man at Y gun very slightly wounded, and sustained her only damage in this manner.
Finally it should go on record that in the first few and last few miles of the passage, two decided and almost successful but quite unnecessary attempts were made to ram *Ulster Queen* also, alas, by our allies.[25]

The majority should not be marred by the actions of the few and considering that this was their first action and that the *Luftwaffe* made their greatest effort against them the Americans came through the test well. Lieutenant Wesley N. Miller, USNR armed guard commander about the *St Olaf* gave this impression of the operation as seen by his men, on 15th September mid-way through the battle:

I have not slept longer than two hours at night for the past three nights. My food is brought to the bridge. I do not leave even to visit the head. And so it went with the majority of the ships crew, including the merchant crew. It was 21 hours duty out of every 24, if one wanted to live. There is nineteen hours continuous daylight. The rubber suits are torturing our weary bodies, but they must be endured as the water is cold and ships must be abandoned too quickly to take time to put them on later . . .

Blake Hughes of the *Patrick Henry* also summarised the feeling of many of his countrymen which was in strict contrast to some of the opinions being expressed elsewhere.

Upon arriving in Archangel I heard one seaman exclaim, 'If I ever hear anyone knock the limey navy I'll knock his block off!' (A sentiment shared by all the men on my ship.) The bang-up, courageous job done by our British escort has instilled in our men who participated in this convoy a deep respect for the British navy. As a result of a common experience relations between American and British seamen and officers were the most cordial I have ever seen.[35]

And he added a tip on how to bolster morale which he had learned.

After a gruelling engagement with enemy planes British destroyers on several occasions steamed up and down our columns, and our men and theirs shouted words of encouragement to one another, waving, wisecracking, making the 'V' and 'thumbs up' signs. There was something in that business that bolstered morale all around.[35]

Among survivors morale was high also. Robert Hughes described an incident aboard the *Scylla* where a survivors' show was being organised to raise spirits.

The forrard messdecks seemed to bulge with men haunched in little groups, talking, playing cards, sleeping or eating. There were seamen of many nations – British, Americans, Norwegian – with quite a sprinkling of American negroes. Three of them sat quietly humming some song in their velvet voices, and on being approached they agreed to sing in Shirkers Gaytime.

'If you're looking for talent, sir,' drawled one, 'there's a coloured boy just right here who sure can sing. Yes sir!' He pointed to a short fat man at the end of the table, who smiled broadly.

'He says he comes from the *Mary Luckenbach*,' added my informant.

In amazement I approached him. Surely nobody could have survived that tremendous explosion, but here it seemed was one who had been spared.

'You come from the *Mary Luckenbach*?' I enquired.

'Yes, suh,' nodded the little man, smiling shyly.

'But surely,' I asked, 'no one could have survived her?'

'Sure I did,' asserted the little man. 'I was walking along the deck with a cup of cawfee for the Old Man, when "Whoom" I find myself half a mile down the convoy!'*

### III

Meanwhile QP 14 was having a mixed reception on their homeward journey, the Luftwaffe did not bother to participate in attacks on this convoy but the U-boats were out for revenge.

It will be recalled that the 'Fighting Destroyer Escort' together with the *Avenger*, her two destroyers and the AA ship *Alynbank*, in addition to the two escorting submarines, had all parted company from PQ 18 during the afternoon of the 16th in three groups. The first of these, the *Scylla* and two destroyer flotillas joined up with QP 14 at 0300 on the 17th and Rear-Admiral Burnett took over the command of the escort from the commanding officer of the close escort in the minesweeper *Bramble*. As each group arrived they took up the planned screening diagram (No. 30) altering it only to compensate for the fact that QP 14 had only six columns. At this time only sixteen merchant vessels remained with the convoy for as we have seen *Ironclad* remained at Archangel, the *Troubadour* had dropped out at dusk on the 15th September† and *Winston Salem* had been left behind when she straggled during the night.

Despite the fact that *Avenger* flew off Swordfish to search for the two missing vessels no trace was found. Meanwhile the little carrier had, by a magnificent feat of improvisation, and with very hard work and dedication by her hangar crews, managed to rectify the many minor defects in her surviving aircraft and reported this day that she had thirteen Sea Hurricanes and three Swordfish now ready for operations. This was a splendid achievement when it is recalled that she started Operation 'EV' with only twelve Sea Hurricanes assembled and had lost four in action. Rear-Admiral Burnett signalled to Commander Colthurst:

'You are a good father to your children.'

* *Through the Waters*, William Kimber, 1956.

† She was later wrongly reported as having been damaged by bombing on her return to Soviet waters 'she was eventually broken up there'!

To which he received the reply:

'The nursery door is now finally closed.'

Also on the 17th her Swordfish located *Intrepid* and an oiler and the *Alynbank* group and homed them to the convoy. Their pilots subsequently reported severe icing conditions from sea-level upwards in a slight mist. It was indeed very cold throughout this day and the visibility was variable with snow storms and clear intervals; however no shadowing aircraft were observed either visually or on the radar screens.

This pattern of weather remained the same during the 18th but QP 14 was sighted early on and two shadowing aircraft remained fixed astern from 1005 onward despite the fact that a few rounds were fired at them when they ventured in too close during snow storms. Visibility however closed down later in the afternoon and they later lost touch. This was the day of the last great air attack on PQ 18 and no forces were detached to strike at the homeward convoy. The U-boat pack was now however closing in, fresh boats and fresh crews.

Icebergs were reported on several occasions and the convoy was forced to make emergency turns to avoid them. At 1630 that afternoon Hope Island was in sight and thirty minutes later one of the Catalinas homed on the convoy bringing with her the unpalatable news that she had sighted two U-boats at very long range to the north-west. The destroyer *Onslow* was despatched post-haste to investigate this but found no trace. A curious case of friction arose between the Rear-Admiral and this unfortunate aircraft; Burnett later reported that:

This aircraft gave the wrong identification, failed to tell me the name of my flagship and requested the number, formation, course and speed of the convoy though Hope Island was in sight close to starboard and the convoy clearly visible; altogether a most suspicious character.[2]

This 'suspicious character' was in fact Flight-Lieutenant G. G. Potier flying Catalina 'H' (VA728) from Grasnaya. He later reported that he twice requested composition and speed of the convoy from the Senior Naval Officer and received no reply. After reporting his two submarine sightings and seeing the destroyer despatched he was asked for his identity letter and replied 'H'. Burnett then signalled him:

You used wrong identification signal on approaching convoy, what is name of this cruiser?

Potier replied by visual signal:

We used signal laid down for use with warships east of 15 degrees.[2]

He later commented that this procedure was checked when he returned to base and was found correct. An interesting sidelight on the still far from happy inter-relationship of the RN/RAF liaison even at this stage of the war. Fortunately for the British the German formations got on even worse!

Rear-Admiral Burnett seemed inclined to believe that the convoy had at this stage, Potier's reports notwithstanding, shaken off any possible U-boat packs or else thought that they had been ordered to proceed ahead and await the arrival of the convoy off South Cape. Burnett had noted previously that after passing South Cape he would accordingly edge his ships to the north in the hope of keeping at the extreme range of the torpedo bombers and thus avoiding another tragic day like that of the 13th. He therefore decided to round South Cape as close as possible and the most northerly course steered. He commented:

If the alteration of course to the northward could be carried out without observation there seemed every chance of our eluding the enemy, at least in time to get clear.[2]

He was soon to learn otherwise.

It had also been the original intention to send all the destroyers into Bell Sound to refuel, but as this would have seriously depleted the escort at the most critical period, and as so far all the destroyers had managed to keep topped up, Rear-Admiral Burnett decided that one of the two oilers stationed there should be winkled out and brought into the convoy to help oil the destroyers at sea.

Accordingly the destroyers *Fury* and *Impulsive* were detached at dusk to proceed ahead and duly collect the *Oligarch* and rendezvous in 77° N, 11° E. The usual anti-submarine patrols were maintained by the Swordfish during the 18th and initially their only sighting was of a large iceberg. However at **1715 one of them scuppered Burnett's theory of elusiveness** when she sighted a U-boat on the surface, conning tower awash, patiently pacing the convoy twenty miles astern. The submarine dived on sighting but the Swordfish pressed on to drop two depth charges in the diving swirl one and a half minutes later; one charge however failed to detonate. No attack resulted from below the surface that night however, but the sands were running out.

Dawn on the 19th brought a grim reminder that the German battle-fleet was still a menace to be considered by the homeward-bound convoy. At 0430 the *Onslow* reported two masts over the horizon to the north-east. The *Offa* was sent off to investigate this and tense minutes ticked away as the British destroyers awaited the sighting of the fighting tops of the Altenfiord squadron to lift up over the horizon. It was a relief when it was revealed by Lieutenant-Commander Ewing that the culprit was the *Winston Salem*, the straying lamb returning to the fold. Her commanding officer reported that she had 'gone north and followed the ice edge'.

All hopes of turning north undetected and throwing the Germans off the scent were finally scotched at 0550 when the first aerial shadower appeared. She was joined later by a second and all subsequent alterations in course were dutifully reported and marked down precisely on the great charts on the tables and walls in Oslo.

Meanwhile the afternoon brought shrill word of the second wandering American for at 1300 a distress message was picked up from the *Troubadour*. She reported herself under heavy attack by submarine some seventy miles south-east of the convoy. The *Onslaught* was therefore despatched at high speed to her aid and Commander Selby was instructed to escort her into Bell Sound and, after refuelling, for him to add his destroyer to Force 'P' bound for Scapa Flow.

*Onslaught* dashed off on her rescue mission and when some thirty miles clear of the convoy Commander Selby broadcast to the *Troubadour* that he was on his way. 'Thanks a million' was his reply. The *Avenger* flew off one of her Swordfish to patrol over the ship until *Onslaught* arrived. She escorted her for an hour until Commander Selby arrived on the scene but there was absolutely no sign of the U-boat. At dusk the *Oligarch* joined the convoy with *Fury*, *Impulsive* and the destroyer *Worcester* from

Bell Sound, the latter taking *Onslaught*'s place on the screen. Numerous anti-submarine contacts were obtained, and hunted, during the night which it was clear were from a strong force of U-boats and all further need for W/T silence was abandoned.

At 0530 the U-boats struck.

The minesweeper *Leda* (Commander A. H. Wynne-Edwards) was stationed astern of the convoy, always an unenviable position because any submarine frustrated from approaching from ahead would tend to fire consolation shots astern. Such was the case with *U-435* (Lieutenant-Commander Strelow) and his salvo struck the little minesweeper with two torpedoes. Despite the devastation of this attack the sturdy little ship took an hour and a half to sink. Rescue ships and escorts were soon on the scene and Commander Wynne-Edwards, eighty-six officers and men and two merchant navy officers were subsequently rescued, although six sailors died of their wounds and exposure later. The bulk of these survivors were transferred to the official rescue ships *Rathlin* and *Zamelek*, while a few more remained aboard the *Seagull*.

By mid-morning it was plain that at least five U-boats were stalking QP 14 with others joining and, because the two British submarines, *P.614* and *P.615* were due to shortly depart anyway, Burnett decided to give them an opportunity to try their skill against their underwater opponents before they left. The destroyer *Opportune* therefore escorted the two boats to twenty miles astern of the convoy and turned their young skippers loose to do their worse.

At 1350 the two British submarines opened up some five miles apart and dived into the area through which the five following German submarines must pass. Unfortunately visibility was continually hampered by snow storms. None the less at 1509 Lieutenant D. J. Beckley of *P.614* heard the distinctive sound of a diesel engine on a bearing of Green 150. Eight minutes later their unsuspecting prey was sighted in a clear patch in the snow storm at a range of about one thousand yards. This was the *U-408* (Lieutenant-Commander von Hymen) and he was blissfully unaware of his terribly exposed position.

Lieutenant Beckley immediately turned *P.614* to attack and at 1520 he fired four torpedoes. Twelve long seconds passed and then an explosion was heard, followed fourteen seconds later by a second and, five seconds after that, a third. A look through the murk revealed the stern of a completely surprised U-boat disappearing in a large patch of foam at a range of between 500 and 600 yards. Von Hymen probably never had such a nasty shock in his life, but fate spared him and his crew the split-second annihilation that was almost his certain end. It was evident that the first explosion heard by Beckley was the premature ignition from one of the CCR pistols used which set off the warheads.

Two of the torpedoes were thought to have exploded right under *U-408* but Beckley quite correctly did not surface to hunt for wreckage or survivors of his attack as there were still four more U-boats in the vicinity and he would probably have shared his apparent victim's fate. Nor did Lieutenant Newstead of *P.615* sight anything. In fact von Hymen had sighted the oncoming torpedo tracks and had crash-dived *U-408* to safety, but it was a remarkable example of early work in the field of using submarine to hunt submarine. During World War I a special class of submarines had been built for just this purpose, the 'R' class, but they arrived too late to give results. Later in the second war several successful attacks of this kind took place and of course postwar one of the main objectives of British nuclear submarines has been this role. The two British submarines had no further adventures and both eventually arrived back safely at Lerwick on the 24th and 25th September.

Meanwhile attacks from the surface and the air had also been made in attempts to beat off this determined concentration. At 1120 one of the Swordfish sighted another U-boat on the surface some fifteen miles to the east. This submarine did not dive and the Swordfish was able to make an attack with two 40-lb general-purpose bombs which forced it to go under. A promising attack with three depth-charges was made against the submerged target.

The position was reported by W/T to the convoy. Meanwhile the destroyer *Ashanti* sighted another U-boat at the range of eight miles and proceeded to hunt her. Two destroyers had been sent out to aid the Swordfish but while they were still approaching the scene of her attack she sighted yet a third and re-directed the destroyers to it before returning to *Avenger* to re-arm. This hunt was unsuccessful. The *Ashanti* meanwhile had sighted a periscope at a range of one mile and Commander Onslow proceeded to carry out five attacks which at first produced air bubbles and a streak of oil. A heavy explosion was felt a few seconds after the last of these attacks and the contact was subsequently lost. Although there was no visual evidence of a success it was hoped that this signified the destruction of this German submarine but in fact this was not subsequently confirmed.

All this vigorous counter-attack activity failed to deter the wolf pack however and at 1725 the *Silver Sword* in the rear of the centre column was hit by two torpedoes from one of them which had penetrated the screen. At once the nearest escorts closed her but she was doomed. Badly hit, her survivors were taken off and her blazing hulk was finally sunk by the destroyer *Worcester* (Lieutenant-Commander W. A. Juniper, DSO) at 1830.

With the U-boat attacks gradually building up and with no indication of a repetition of the heavy air attacks suffered by PQ 18 Rear-Admiral Burnett made yet another hard decision. Commander Colthurst had already indicated that his three Swordfish crews were reaching the limits of their endurance. They had been in constant action taking their frail little 'Stringbags' into the Arctic skies from the tiny deck of the *Avenger* and had been instrumental in locating and keeping down many submarines, but now their effectiveness was lessening as the strain began to tell. The mere fact that they had to fly such obsolete old aircraft as these antiquated biplanes speaks volumes for their achievements. The Swordfish was a much-loved aircraft that performed wonders in the hands of the young Fleet Air Arm crews from Taranto onward, but it was far from being a modern weapon of war, and, even more than the obsolete Sea Hurricanes, showed just how far the Fleet Air Arm had fallen behind its foreign equivalents during the 1930s.

In fact Commander Colthurst was quite adamant that, in his opinion, the operation of Swordfish on anti-submarine patrols from escort carriers was completely inadequate. The *Avenger* only had a 440-foot flight deck and a maximum speed of only sixteen knots. To get the Swordfish airborne with a full load of depth-charges or torpedoes was extremely difficult, and this during an operation when the weather was kind. Despite these handicaps the Swordfish sighted U-boats sixteen times and of these twelve were on the surface and three had conning towers awash. The clumsy methods of visually signalling such sightings meant that often the Swordfish were unable to communicate with the ships of the screen and had to return to *Avenger* to report, thus losing contact. These were all teething troubles that had to be ironed out before the operations of escort carriers as part of a viable striking force against wolf packs could become efficient.

Both *Scylla* and *Avenger* were therefore now little more than valuable targets for the German submariners and able to contribute little or nothing to the defence of the merchantmen. Rear-Admiral Burnett decided to send them home before the pack, growing ever more bolder, sank both. They were to be sent to the sanctuary of Seidesfiord initially. Accordingly therefore at 1830, the destroyer leader *Milne* (Captain I. M. R. Campbell, Captain (D3)), came alongside the *Scylla* to enable Rear-Admiral Burnett to transfer his flag to her. Robert Hughes described the scene:

> Slowly the Fleet destroyer *Milne* edged her way into *Scylla*'s port side, her wickedly-raked bows rising and falling in the swell, and her bow wave mingling with our wash to form a disturbed lane of prickly little waves. Both crews lined the decks, muffled in a variety of garments, and looking much as Willem Barents' men must have looked three and a half centuries before, when then, as now, cold and survival dictated the apparel, and fashion mattered little.
>
> Down on our deck the crane was poised over a steel chair from the crew's recreation space, fittted with slings, and hooked to the crane. The Admiral moved smiling to the chair, seated himself, adjusted the ropes to his satisfaction, passed some jocular remarks, and turned his hands in a winding motion. The torpedo man moved the lever, and the chair and Admiral Burnett rose from the deck and slowly slung across to the waiting destroyer. As the crane began to train left, the Boatswain's mates on *Scylla*'s deck raised their calls and piped the Admiral over the side. Sideways the crane moved until it plumbed the destroyer's deck, and then slowly and carefully it lowered the Admiral until, touching the deck, it was unhooked and the boatswain's pipes of the destroyers piped him aboard.*

Shortly after this the *Scylla* and *Avenger* parted company from QP 14, and, with the escorting destroyers *Fury*, *Wheatland* and *Wilton*, proceeded independently.

* *Through the Waters*, William Kimber, 1956.

However the departure of *Avenger*'s faithful Swordfish was not compensated for in any way by the arrival of Coastal Command aircraft and the waiting U-boats soon took advantage of this new situation and the sudden freedom of movement granted them. First to feel their wrath was another of the faithful escorts, the 'Tribal' class destroyer *Somali* (Lieutenant-Commander C. Maud, DSC). She was stationed on the port beam of the convoy and at 1900 a torpedo from *U-408* hit her in her port side in the engine room. Her number three boiler room, the engine room and the gearing room were all immediately flooded and the destroyer immediately took on a heavy list to starboard. The *Opportune* and *Lord Middleton* closed her and began to take off survivors while the *Eskimo* and *Intrepid* made a fruitless hunt for her assailant.

These vessels continued to stand by her while Richard Onslow of the *Ashanti* attempted to tow his sister ship to safety. This tow lasted for 420 anxious miles and took four nights and three days under very difficult conditions. It was a wartime epic in itself and finally a gale arose which cheated Onslow of his victory for the poor damaged *Somali* broke in half and foundered.*

With the departure of yet another large group of destroyers to protect these vessels the once formidable screen of QP 14 was rapidly melting away but despite this, for a time, the German submarines failed to inflict any further casualties although their constant presence was always menacing. By 2030 wireless transmissions were being picked up around the convoy from at least three U-boats.

On the morning of the 21st September, at 0600, the convoy changed course to 199 degrees but the two shadowing Blohm and Voss seaplanes remained glued to their tracks. Hopes of the RAF providing an alternate anti-submarine escort were raised by the arrival of a Catalina an hour later but this protection was short lived indeed.

The destroyer *Milne* had meanwhile carried out a sweep to north-east in an attempt to locate the *Somali* and see how the tow had progressed during the night, but she failed to locate her at all. When she gave her actual position it was some forty miles to the north-east and Rear-Admiral Burnett decided to re-join the

---

* Sir Richard Onslow was to write the full story of this epic voyage which is included n my anthology *Destroyer Action* (Kimber, 1974).

convoy's escort without further delay. At 0850, on her return, she sighted a U-boat on the surface which she immediately steered towards, the submarine going under at four miles range and being unlocated on the asdic sweep.

Meanwhile, at 1040 Catalina 'Z-Zebra' of 330 Squadron had been sniffing around the convoy's fringes and was rewarded with the sighting of a surfaced submarine which she duly attacked. However the *U-378* (Lieutenant-Commander Zetsche) manned her anti-aircraft guns and handled these with very good effect and hit 'Z-Zebra' in the petrol tank. Despite this the Catalina managed to release four depth charges in the vicinity of the submarine forcing her to dive before the seaplane made a forced landing. The destroyer *Marne* (Lieutenant-Commander H. N. A. Richardson) immediately closed her and rescued her crew. Once more QP 14 was without air protection.

At 1430 the minesweeper *Bramble* and the destroyer *Worcester* obtained firm asdic contacts and delivered a promising attack. Underwater explosions were heard before the second attack and a large air bubble observed, but the submarine in fact escaped.

By 0530 the convoy had reached position 'Q' and Admiral Burnett parted company and left in the *Milne* to proceed to Seidisfiord, handing over command of the convoy to the senior officer of the much reduced screen, Captain A. K. Scott-Moncrieff, aboard the *Faulknor*. Within a short time the screen was penetrated by the submarine pack and the 22nd September was marked by this brilliant attack by *U-435* (Lieutenant-Commander Strelow).

He made his attack at 0625 and the starboard wing ship of the convoy, the *Bellingham*, was hit, followed immediately afterwards by the torpedoing of the *Ocean Voice*, the Convoy Commodore's ship (Commander Dowding), and the valuable fleet oiler *Grey Ranger*. Long considered one of the most vulnerable vessels and her fate, along with that of the *Atheltemplar*, again emphasised how exposed tankers were in convoys such as this. The minesweeper *Seagull* rescued Commander Dowding and had instructions to convey him to any ship of the convoy he wished but Commander Dowding decided to remain aboard *Seagull*. Responsibility for the convoy therefore devolved upon the Vice-Commodore, Captain Walker of the *Ocean Freedom*.

Captain Scott-Moncrieff now made arrangements to tighten up his small screen to prevent a repetition of this episode. The *Bramble* and *Seagull* were placed on each quarter of the convoy, with the corvettes *La Malouine* and *Dianella* two miles on either bow. The trawlers were allocated as close anti-submarine vessels on the beams of the rear-wing ships and astern, while the corvettes *Lotus* and *Poppy* were placed on either bow. Captain Scott-Moncrieff placed his *Faulknor* ahead of the convoy as close ahead cover while his remaining destroyers he spread across the face of the convoy as advance screen two miles out.

For night screening he arranged it that depth charges would be dropped continuously each mile. The *Worcester* was to patrol across the convoy's stern at sixteen knots and the *Impulsive* and *Middleton* had random roving positions using radar to sweep on either flank. This new tactic appeared to be successful and by the morning of the 23rd the rescue ships *Rathlin* and *Zamelek* were detached to Seidesfiord for provisions. Yet a further three destroyers went with them as escorts, *Onslow*, *Offa* and *Worcester*. On the 23rd the Catalinas of 210 Squadron were able to show their worth and hit back in some measure against these successes by the U-boat pack. Catalina 'U-Uncle' piloted by Flight-Sergeant J. W. Semmens had been airborne from Sullom Voe just before midnight on the 22nd. At 0553 she had located QP 14 and began patrolling back along its track. A U-boat was sighted on the surface in the classical trailing position astern awaiting nightfall for its attack. When first seen the submarine was only ¾-mile away and the surprise was mutual. This was the *U-253* and she was making a speed of six knots, course 160 degrees when attacked.

There was no escape for Semmens made his attack instantly and at a height of only fifty feet six 250-lb Torpex depth-charges were released which straddled *U-253* which had crash dived and had already submerged when they exploded all around her. The stricken submarine was forced back to the surface in a great upheaval of water and spray and then disappeared for an instant. Out of control the *U-253* re-emerged again on her side, rolled over and her bows dipped and her stern rose. At an almost vertical angle she took her final plunge to the bed of the Arctic Ocean. There were no survivors.

However the skeleton escort was saved from further attacks

by the weather which now broke in a NNE gale. At 1718 Langanes Point, Iceland, was sighted.

The *Marne* was also detached to land her survivors from the Catalina aircraft at Seidisfiord, for the nine airmen were based at Akureyri, and she re-joined later. The convoy was formed into four columns at dawn and by now regular shore-based air cover was overhead. During the storm the *Winston Salem* again acted up, and, she being hove-to, was left behind. The *Martin* was later sent back to look after her. It was now blowing a full gale from the north. This died away during the 25th but a heavy swell was still running which made navigation by the big merchant ships in ballast difficult. On this day the *Offa*, *Onslow*, *Worcester* and the two rescue ships re-joined the convoy.

On the 26th September the *Bramble* and *Seagull* were sent into Scapa and later the *Blankney* and *Middleton* took *Oligarch* and *Black Ranger* in there also. Finally the remaining Home Fleet destroyers parted company handing over the convoy to the close escort under *La Malouine* and proceeded to Scapa Flow. The final chapter of QP 14's long ordeal had been reached.

Far, far astern, in the empty waters off the North Cape, the heavy cruiser *Admiral Hipper* and the destroyers *Richard Beitzen*, Z.29, Z.30 and Z.23 were carrying out Operation *Zarin*. This watered-down, final version of the great attack consisted of the laying of a minefield by these vessels along the known convoy route to Archangel, while, on the completion of this by the 8th Flotilla, the *Hipper* laid an additional field north-west of Nowaya Zemlya. A classic case of closing the stable door well after the horse had bolted.

Chapter Seven

# Home is the Sailor

I

Despite their safe arrival at Archangel the troubles and difficulties of the surviving merchant vesels of PQ 18 were not over, far from it. Nor were they yet to be free of air attacks.

The arrangements for handling the unloading and turn round of all such Russian convoys was in the hands of the Soviet authorities with small parties of the Royal Navy at various ports to act in a liaison capacity. Although these convoys to north Russia have been identified as the 'the Murmansk convoys' or 'the Kola run' in some books in fact the port of destination most utilised by these convoys was that known collectively as Archangel.

The three British Naval Parties in north Russia at this time, all subordinate to Admiral Miles in Moscow, were dispersed about these main complexes. The senior party was under Rear-Admiral Douglas B. Fisher and was based at Polyarnoye (formerly Alexandrovsk) the main HQ of the Soviet White Sea Fleet. This naval base was some ten miles from the sea on the western bank of the Kola Inlet and sheltered by a small island. On the western head of the inlet was the large island of Kildin often used as a reference marker for aircraft strikes, like that mounted by the Hampdens for example. Below Polyarnoe were a string of small islets and, where the river bends to the west, on the eastern bank, was Vaenga with, just below it, Grasnaya.

The river turns a dog-leg again and on the east bank again below this point was Murmansk harbour which was almost entirely a commercial port. It was the only north Russian port that never froze over because it received the tail-end of the Gulf Stream, which did not reach as far east as Archangel. Even further down the river, at its confluence with a small tributary, again on the eastern bank, lay Kola itself after which the Inlet was named. In 1942 this town had lost most of its former importance and was little used. The SBNO at Murmansk was Commander Dickson, who had with him a small party only.

The entrance to the White Sea is marked by the Cape Kanin peninsular on a long promontory to the east of the entrance. The White Sea opened up to the eastward into the Gulf of Kandalaksha and at the head of this inlet was the town of the same name and, just north of that, was the Afrikanda air base. Archangel itself, with Ekonomia, Bakharitsa and Solombola, was the largest port, a complex built along the northern coast of the Northern Dvina, but it suffered the disadvantage during the winter months of freezing over. Beyond the head of the estuary lay Lake Lakhta.

At Archangel in the summer of 1942 was the junior British naval party under Captain Maund, RN. Whenever Archangel was not frozen up the Russian convoys were routed there for it was the port furthest away from the nearest German airfield, at Loustari, very close to Petsamo. Sometimes large convoys were divided between Archangel and the Kola Inlet. In July 1942, very heavy air attacks on Murmansk had reduced the town to a heap of rubble and so there was never any question of PQ 18 being routed to the Kola Inlet at all.

A member of the Polyarnoe party recalls however that:

I could never understand why the Germans concentrated on bombing the town and docks of Murmansk – I once spent a night there and very unpleasant it was – instead of mining the harbour.[52]

Certainly on reflection this would have been a simple and very effective way of reducing this port to impotence, which the widespread destruction of wooden houses and wharves never did. However, as we have seen, it was on Captain Maund's party that the main burden of the reception of the large number of heavily-laden merchant ships rested.

As already noted, the majority of the convoy got underway on the final lap of their outward journey during the afternoon of the 21st September. The *Malcolm*, *Achates* and some other escorts were piloted up to find berths at the Vorosenski Quay: Commander Russell wryly noted at the time how:

The Commanding Officer of the *Bryony* whom I passed coming up channel, appeared to have had his sense of propriety considerably upset by having a female Pilot on board.[25]

The minesweeper *Harrier* was piloted up harbour by the master of the *Stalingrad*, one of the many Russian survivors she had on board, and, arriving at the Krasny Quay, disembarked them safely at 0845. The *Ulster Queen* however decided to remain to the seaward of three stranded merchant vessels on the bar to give them a measure of anti-aircraft protection, for as they lay there they were sitting ducks. In this duty, throughout the 21st, she was joined by a Soviet destroyer and the *Britomart*. It was as well she did so, for at 1545 two Junkers Ju 88s made a surprise attack from the landward side. One of them dropped a stick of bombs right in among the stranded vessels while the second made a dive on the *Ulster Queen*, despite the fierce barrage put up. This latter attack missed by some forty yards off the port quarter and no damage was done and fortunately the merchant vessels were undamaged also, as were the bombers.

It was decided by the *Ulster Queen*'s captain that his crew needed some rest from their continuous action and accordingly he weighed and proceeded up harbour towards Archangel, anchoring eight miles further in at dusk. However his weary crew would probably have got more rest had they stayed out to sea.

The Germans mounted a heavy air attack on Archangel that night, and, as Captain Maund was later to point out, no better targets could have been asked for than the line of eleven ships alongside the Bakharitsa Quay, itself piled high with explosives. The other half of the convoy's merchant vessels berthed at Ekonomia and were equally as vulnerable.

The heavy raid on the night of 21st/22nd extended right the way down river as far as Mogjugski Island but was not very successful from the German point of view. It is thought that some minelaying was attempted, Captain Adams reporting how a heavy detonation was seen on the mudflats about a mile across the river, while at midnight a heavy object fell close to the *Ulster Queen*'s starboard bow. He assessed this as either an unexploded bomb or a mine.

For some of the merchantmen this heavy raid was just about the last straw for many had felt themselves secure once they had tied up at the quays. It was not generally realised just how close the front line fighting was to Archangel and how easy a flight it was for the German and Finnish air forces. They were once more disillusioned.

John Currant aboard the *Exford* told later how:

We did not open fire from the ships. The Russians are filling the sky with shrapnel. We were told not to open fire unless attacked. Many incendiary bombs and flares were dropped.[30]

Blake Hughes was even more specific.

Night bombers came with high explosive and incendiary loads on several occasions after the convoy reached Archangel. On these raids they levelled six to eight city blocks, but to everyone's surprise, although the docks laden with newly transported war material were brightly illuminated by parachute flares more than once, *no attempt was made to bomb ships or docks*.[35]

Hughes added that he had no obvious explanation to account for this but the best conjecture he had heard was to the effect that the bombers might have been Finnish, and the Finns may have preferred to bomb Russians rather than Americans. Whatever the real reason the Luftwaffe missed their last opportunity to inflict lasting damage on the PQ 18 and thus justify their long standing claims of supremacy over the sea.

In view of the dangers and hazards to which forty valuable cargo vessels had been exposed along with their crews and the equal amount of effort put in by the fifty warships involved in this operation it might appear strange to a layman to wonder why, after all this time (the Russia convoys had been running for over a year and the Soviets were avidly demanding more and more supplies), the valuable cargoes worth many hundreds of thousands of pounds were unloaded from the freighters after passing all dangers and left stacked on the dockside within fifty miles of Axis airfields. We can be sure that many of the Allied seamen bitterly asked the same question at the time. The Soviet Admiral, so vehement in his accusations of the Allies eagerly scuppering their ships without a fight, fails to mention this aspect at all of course but Captain Maund offers his explanation.

The discharge of vessels was slow in the early stages and considerable congestion and confusion prevailed at Bakharitsa and Ekonomia. After more wagons had arrived and tanks and aeroplanes had been got away, discharge proceeded more smoothly.[6]

Indeed after the ambulances and other medical supplies had had their loving captions of 'A gift to the Soviet people from the citizens of Coventry' and other such indications of origin carefully and immediately painted out as they were unloaded, they were rushed away by rail to the seething cauldron of Stalingrad, on the far distant Volga, where the fate of the Soviet Union was being decided in that bitter and bloody battle. The attentions of the Luftwaffe, ineffective as they were, seemed to have been the spur to hurry this process up for later it was a very different story as again Captain Maund's report indicates.

The Russians were, quite rightly, anxious to remove all explosives from the quays and in their efforts to do so, a considerable amount of ammunition consigned to me for distribution to HM Ships and Merchant Ships was whisked away. I have located the greater part, some of which had been removed by rail to Vologda.[6]

Despite sour postwar propaganda at the time the ordinary Russian citizen seemed to appreciate the help that was being brought to him at great danger by the much maligned 'capitalist lackeys' from across the sea. Blake Hughes once more:

Of course there is a language barrier, and a standard of living barrier but my men and myself found the Russians very friendly and desirous of making our stay with them a pleasant one. The facilities of the International Club in Archangel and the Navy Club in Salombala were available to all. There were dances, comforts, movies – and, if you dared – Russian lessons! I visited the Navy Club on several occasions and someone always made the effort to see that I was having an enjoyable time.[35]

This report has been quoted to show the other side of the coin; nor was this the only one of its kind on file.

Commodore Boddam-Whetham paid tribute to the work of the Soviet skippers in this convoy, a marked contrast to his pungent opinions on some of the American masters. The Master of the *Tbilisi* for example had been wounded but his ship was subsequently very ably handled by the Mate. He also commented on the endurance of some of the British skippers some of who were old hands on this run.

This is Captain Lamont's third Arctic Convoy [he wrote of the skipper of the *Temple Arch*] and he and his Chief Engineer – Currey – have already been awarded the OBE. Captain Lamont's calm on the bridge, his assistance to me in looking out for approaching aircraft and his control of his ship's gunfire deserve the highest commendation and I submit his name for further award.[3]

Certainly ashore in Archangel during September and October 1942 there was no lack of co-operation and the feeling of the fact that they were allies in a common war. This feeling reached its highest pitch when things looked bleak on the Eastern front and the friendliness decreased in proportion to subsequent Soviet successes and ambitions. In October 1942, however, even the highest officials of the party radiated warmth and friendship.

On 22nd October there was a meeting of American, British and Soviet seamen at the City Theatre in Archangel, the purpose of which was, the Mayor of Archangel emphasised at the time, 'the closer acquaintance of the men of the allied powers.' The main speech was made by M. Papani, a famous Arctic explorer and Hero of the Soviet Union. He spoke highly of the courage of the men who fought the convoy through and expressed Russia's deep appreciation for the equipment delivered, the first of which, he stated, had already arrived at the front and been used against Germany. He stressed the fact that Russia required even more and ever increasing quantities of such supplies and equipment. Portraits of Roosevelt, Churchill and Stalin were on display along with the flags of all three nations and at the end of the speech all three national anthems were played. It was quite an event.

Meanwhile discharging had continued and Captain Maund was able to report that it was completed by 20th October, just under a month after their arrival!

In general the Allied view of the Russians seen at close range was similar to that arrived at by one of the RAF officers serving with the striking force. He later wrote that the Russian powers of improvisation, coupled with their capacity for hard work, seemed to be the main factors in their efficiency. Once the word 'go' was given the Russian went on working until the job was done. His final comment today has a prophetic ring to it.

> If they were a little slow in starting at times, they soon made up
> for that by their staying power.

While all the celebrations were in progress, both at Archangel
and at home, the one final casualty of Operation 'EV' went
almost unnoticed and unremembered by the many men whose
welfare and safe arrival had been largely brought about by his
untiring efforts. Commodore Boddam-Whetham had borne the
strain of the largest Russia convoy then mounted upon his own
shoulders. With scant co-operation from a few of the brand-new
captains, who had never sailed in such a convoy before and
thought they knew all the answers, he had carefully and
patiently nursed his forty charges through their initial period of
learning and, with infinite patience, had knitted them in an ever
more confident team. The measure of his success lay in the fact
that the convoy reformed after the traumatic experience of the
great torpedo-bomber attack and kept going, not one ship had
turned back.

All this he had achieved, and each loss of a ship or a life he had
felt very deeply inside, as his letter to Burnett made clear. He put
everything into the safe arrival of his charges, and, for a man of
his years, this enormous strain eventually proved just too much.

Captain Maund reported how some belated realisation had
manifested itself to the seamen of PQ 18, as to how much they
owed him.

> At a banquet held by the Mayor of this City in honour of Officers
> of HM Ships and Merchant Ships of PQ 18, the spontaneous and
> whole-hearted reception accorded to Rear Admiral Boddam-
> Whetham proved more than any written words the appreciation
> of his splendid achievement under such arduous conditions.[6]

Unfortunately this proved the last occasion for the great
strain, not surprisingly, later made itself obvious and, in a report
from Norway House, Archangel, signed by Surgeon Lieutenant-
Commander W. M. Hamilton, RN, and Captains C. J. Roberts and
H. Goodwin of the RAMC, Rear-Admiral Boddam-Whetham was
recorded as being temporarily unfit to carry out his duties.
Morphia and bromide did something to relieve the strain but
these doctors stated that a relapse could occur and Captain

Maund was forced to signal the Admiralty to that effect and ask that a Vice-Commodore be sent to help him during the return journey.

Rear-Admiral Boddam-Whetham was justly awarded the CBE for his part in fighting through PQ 18, part of the citation reading that he displayed bravery and resolution as commodore of a north Russian convoy. During an interview in Moscow on his way home he is said to have remarked, 'The Germans claimed we cannot use the northern route, but the answer simply is – we do.' Indeed we did but only because of men like Boddam-Whetham. After the North Africa landings Rear-Admiral Boddam-Whetham died at Gibraltar in March 1943, still on active service.

In recounting great events and actions it is as well to remember such unsung individuals on who so much depended and whose maximum effort was taken completely for granted.

## II

There was some considerable relief in British circles that the losses in this operation were not on the same ghastly scale as those suffered by the preceding convoy to Russia. In fact the break-down of the cold, hard figures makes interesting reading, although, like all such statistics, they could be and were used to depict whichever facet was most liable to make good copy for the home press.

PQ 17 contained thirty-four ships of which twenty-three were lost. PQ 18 contained forty ships from which only thirteen were lost. These bald facts alone need no embroidery. Unfortunately Dr Goebbels in Germany and the Ministry of Information, a misnomer if ever there was one, in Britain immediately got to work and, as usual, the facts became blurred at the time, and an immense amount of postwar publication has muddled rather than cleared the scene as we have seen from earlier examples.

Fortunately the servicemen of both combatants at the time were more honest and revealing and from their reports and opinions we can evaluate the operation more readily than from such sources.

Commodore Boddam-Whetham, as we have already noted, thought that the convoy was lucky to have got away with the casualties it did considering the scale of air and submarine attacks made, but, as has also been observed, the scale of submarine attacks had been greatly overestimated, thirty boats against an actual twelve.

Rear-Admiral Robert Burnett was equally as frank in his summing-up of the operation.

> I do not know how far this operation may be considered to have been a success or failure, but I am convinced that had any of six circumstances been otherwise it must have proved a tragic failure.

He listed these six circumstances as follows:

1. *Weather*. Had this have been bad, instead of calm all the way from Jan Mayen island outwards and during the return, then the constant oiling could not have taken place in the smooth manner in which it did. The supporting destroyer force would then have had to have been withdrawn.

2. *Oilers*. Had either, or more especially, both, the vital oilers been hit, especially during the first days heavy attacks, then the covering force would have had to withdraw, which might have necessitated the turning back of the convoy. The result of such an action, hard on the heels of PQ 17, are not difficult to imagine, especially the effect on the Soviet Union, then at the nadir of its fortunes.

3. Had there been the least delay on the part of the escorts in reaching Bell Sound, or had their oiling have been disrupted by enemy action in any way, the *Scylla* and five of the destroyers (including the four with the most effective anti-aircraft capacity), would have been missing from the screen during the first heavy torpedo-bomber attack. Merchant ship casualties can hardly have failed therefore to have been much more severe than they were.

4. Had the Luftwaffe followed up this torpedo bomber attack on the same scale as the first then not only would casualties have grown unbearable but the anti-aircraft ammunition in the escorts would most likely have been exhausted before the convoy reached safety.

5. The most obvious point of all was that had the Germans synchronised the torpedo bomber, dive-bomber, submarine

and surface ships attacks losses would have been very heavy indeed.

6. The final point again concerned the oilers for had they have been among the casualties, even later on, in the operation when PQ 18 had reached Russia, the resultant effect on the screen of QP 14 during the heavy and sustained U-boat attacks would have been significant.[2]

All these points were given detailed examination, first by Admiral Tovey and then by the specialists at the Admiralty. Admiral Tovey's conclusions agreed with Rear-Admiral Burnett's except on a few of these points and his comments are of interest.

With regard to 1 and 2, the sinking of one of the convoy oilers or the weather being too bad for oiling, would not, in his opinion, have necessarily have entailed to turning back of the convoy, provided fuelling facilities still remained available at Spitzbergen. As he pointed out it was specifically to guard against this possibility that the Spitzbergen force had been included and yet another spare oiler held ready at Iceland. What would have been more likely he felt in this circumstance would have been the cancellation of the sailing of QP 14, while the Fighting Destroyer Escort returned home on its own.

Although he had not the returns of ammunition expenditure to hand he felt that enough remained to fight off several more attacks. It is felt that Admiral Tovey missed the point here for Rear-Admiral Burnett was especially thinking of the result on ammunition stocks of more attacks like the first rather than additional small attacks. Surely in this instance he was right, in that the ammunition just would not have lasted long in the destroyers.

Tovey also added that it was by no means certain that the Germans knew of the use of Lowe Sound as a fuelling anchorage, and here, once more, there can be little doubt that he was being optimistic.

For Rear-Admiral Burnett the safe arrival of two-thirds of PQ 18 was a triumph despite his cautious assessment. In December 1942, he was made CB for 'his daring skill and resolution in taking a convoy to north Russia in the face of sustained and relentless attacks by enemy aircraft and submarines'. That month, in command of the cruiser escort for yet another Russian convoy, he took his two ships to drive off the *Lutzow* and *Hipper* in the New Year's Eve battle but perhaps his most famous action of the Russia convoy trilogy was his handling of the 10th Cruiser Squadron at the sinking of the *Scharnhorst* in 1943.

He was then a Vice-Admiral and has been awarded the Order of Souverov by the Russians in gratitude. He later went on to become C-in-C South Atlantic between 1944 and 1946 and C-in-C Plymouth, before retiring in 1950 as Admiral. After some years as Chairman of the White Fish Authority Admiral Burnett was to die in London in July 1959, aged seventy-one.

The Director of Anti-Submarine Warfare commented on 28th November, that the best protection for convoys was undoubtedly a combination of air and surface escorts. The Director of the Gunnery Division commented on the ineffectiveness of the bombing attacks and on the fact that the majority of losses to air attack happened while the guns crews were still inexperienced at the beginning of the fighting. The improved figures for the tonnage lost/aircraft destroyed on this convoy he put down to better gunnery equipment with which the Fleet, as distinct from the Western Approaches, destroyers were fitted and the improved Control methods. He also drew attention to the fact that one third of British fighter strength was shot down by our own barrage, but in fairness it was the bravery of the Fleet Air pilots which accounted for this rather than lack of control by the escorts. With the merchantmen it was of course another thing altogether.

The Director of the Trade Division thought that the 'formidable nature' of the close range armament of merchant vessels was a major factor in the shooting down of more aircraft, a conjecture with which few of the escorts who witnessed their wild firing would agree. With regard to the latter the DTD merely commented that action was proceeding.

What this action was, was revealed in a series of notes passed between DTD and the US Navy in London later, when convoy PQ 18 was already a dusty file overtaken and eclipsed by such matters as the Allied landings in North Africa, El Alamein and Guadalcanal.

A letter dated 2nd February, 1943, from John D. Higham of the Military Branch, Admiralty, enclosed Commodore Boddam-

Whetham's report and his acid comments on the standard of the American vessels, and was sent to Commander R. H Errington, for the attention of the Flag Officer Liaison with the Commander United States Naval Forces in Europe, Admiral Blake.

In spite of the elapse of some five months since the operation, the letter, in the true spirit of Whitehall, commented that the Naval Staff, 'are eager that it should be passed to the Americans, so that, if possible, some action may be taken to improve the situation described.'

Higham added that although the report was getting, 'pretty white in the beard now', there was still, 'plenty of scope for improvement in the station keeping of American Merchant Ships'. No comment was made of the standard of fire discipline.

The American attitude was predictable enough. Commander Errington replied, on 6th February, that Admiral Blake was, 'Glad it has come to his notice!' He felt however that Commodore Boddam-Whetham's comments were too vague. General accusations, he felt, were of no value, one needed the facts and names of defaulters. He commented that there were twenty-two American ships in the convoy and that the faults must have been committed by specific ships. 'There may have been some ships that behaved well and they would resent any general charge.'

He also commented pithily that it was a pity that Commodore Boddam-Whetham had not been instructed to come and see Admiral Blake (and Admiral Kirk, USN), when he was in London.

Nor was the Commodore's adoption of a special 'Emergency Turn Procedure' any better received by the Western Approaches command. The Commander-in-Chief, represented by A. S. Russell, noting in a letter dated 9th February, 1943, that this procedure was not considered necessary or desirable in Western Approaches conditions.

For it to be successful the convoy must be very well drilled and exercised. It is interesting to note that on this particular occasion it was not a success at the first attempt.[9]

These points apart some positive, although slow, progress resulted from the lessons absorbed by PQ 18 and were applied to the Royal Navy in later months. The Director of the Naval Air Division noted how:

For months past efforts have been directed to obtaining Hurricane II.C (20-mm cannon) aircraft with which to equip Auxiliary cruisers. [He, one assumes, meant to say Auxiliary carriers, later known under the more apt title Escort Carriers.] It is hoped that these aircraft will be available to protect the future PQ convoys, if not, Martlets (0.5-inch guns) must be used in lieu.[8]

The Director of Gunnery and Anti-Aircraft Warfare noted how an estimated 220 aircraft torpedoes had produced only hits on nine merchant ships, eight of which were hit the first attack. Also that 100 aircraft made bombing attacks and failed to score a single hit. Although these figures are questionable today the fact remained that with this convoy and *Pedestal* it was becoming apparent that the supply of 20-mm Oerlikon guns was giving ships a good degree of close-range protection and the future supplying of these vessels with 40-mm Bofors would be an even greater step forward. Unfortunately another two years were to pass before these desirable goals were largely achieved.

On the anti-submarine front the Director of Anti-Submarine Warfare thought that the amount of flying achieved by the *Avenger's* three Swordfish was a good omen for the future once escort carriers became available in large enough numbers to accompany each major convoy.

The dependence of the destroyers on oilers was given some comment, which is not strange, and the DA/SW considered that this was the chief factor in restricting the searching teams of destroyers from pressing home their hunts, but, as noted before, the ships were given precise instructions to limit this activity.

But from these operations sprang one of the most important facets of anti-submarine warfare, the carrier/destroyer hunting group which a year later were operating in the Atlantic battlefield, going from convoy to convoy to bolster the escort, and which scored the great triumph of the Royal Navy over the U-boats by this method. PQ 18 can be seen as a trial run for this type of operation. It had of course been tried at the beginning of the war with the fleet carriers, resulting in the loss of *Courageous*, but the escort carriers were to be both more expendable and more numerous.

DACD noted in his report dated 8th December, 1942, that more long-range aircraft should be available to Coastal Command by the spring of 1943. Certainly the U-boat would have been beaten earlier, British losses made less and the war shortened if the 1,000-bomber raids directed against civilian targets throughout Greater Germany in 1942 to 1944 had been concentrated instead on submarine building slips, fuel supplies and sea patrols, but Coastal Command itself cannot be held at fault for the false direction of available resources and the old Catalinas had certainly proved their worth.

On one point all those who were involved with PQ 18 were as adamant at the end of the operation as they had been at the beginning, and this was that the convoy was too big, the number of ships to be handled was far too large.

Admiral Tovey again made this point in his accompanying notes on the Commodore's Report, which were dated 11th November, 1942:

> There is no doubt that a convoy of forty ships is too large to handle during air attacks; this has been frequently pointed out.[1]

The Admiral could have added, though of course he did not, that it had just as equally often been ignored. Captain Maund said much the same thing.

> The number of ships (40) was too large especially, as mentioned above, a large proportion of these ships were American and unaccustomed to convoy work and were bad station keepers.[2]

And Commodore Boddham-Whetham.

> I expressed to the Admiralty before sailing the opinion that the convoy was too large. Ten columns of four ships, including as they did 22 USA ships and 6 Russians are most difficult to handle in attack.[3]

The very experienced voice of Commander A. B. Russell in charge of the Close Escort.

> I feel most strongly that the number of ships in the convoy was too great. Had all the ships of the convoy been British, and accustomed to convoy work, a convoy of this size might have been accepted. But when the convoy consists of American, Panamanian, Russian and British ships the station-keeping and communication problems become acute.[27]

At last, at long, long last, this fact appears to have finally got through to the impatient and intolerant Premier, although the American President continued with his heady plans regardless for a while longer and the Soviets never tried to understand. The lesson learnt, according to Admiral Golovko, was that the fighting off of the single air attack by the convoy, on 18th September, would,

> . . . confirm once more that given resolute action by covering forces and adequate preliminary combat measures, the enemy's surface ships can be neutralized, while the attacks of U-boats and aircraft can be repulsed – and with heavy loss to the enemy – by a correctly organized order of battle. By deploying forces in good time along the convoy's route at places where the enemy is mounting his attacks, and by changing the course of the convoy at the right moment, it is possible to reduce its losses to a minimum, even in conditions which are most unfavourable to the side under attack.
>
> It will be interesting to hear what the opponents of allied convoys to Soviet northern ports will say to all this.*

Interesting indeed. Again it must be pointed out that all the dispenser of this meaningless jargon had contributed was four destroyers, to the 'correct order of battle', and this when the fighting, save for one air raid, was already over.

Roosevelt commented in typical fashion that he regarded the maintenance of the PQ convoys as an operation of equal magnitude with 'Torch' [the North African landings], although he was ready to skip one, or perhaps two, for the sake of 'Torch'.

The Prime Minister had finally had to face the fact that some things were just *not* possible. The launching of an invasion of Vichy North Africa coupled with providing an escort for the planned PQ 19 was one time when he had to see this as so. The Royal Navy was at full stretch. He cabled Roosevelt accordingly. On the 27th he had his reply, the President conceding the argument, although somewhat uneasy at Stalin's wrath.

> While I think that is a tough blow for the Russians, I nevertheless think that the purposes for which the escorts are to be used both as to time and place make the decision inevitable. PQ 19 however would not have sailed under any circumstances for another ten days, and I feel very strongly that time arrives and we know with finality that the convoy will not go.[61]

* *With the Red Fleet*, Putnam & Co., 1965.

Churchill was made of sterner stuff however and wished to tell their Dictator partner as soon as possible. Again Roosevelt preferred to await events; on 2nd October he wrote:

So far as PQ 19 is concerned, I feel most strongly that we should not tell Stalin that the convoy will not sail.[62]

Anxious to sustain the Soviet leader, no matter what, the President wished to sail the convoy anyway, despite 'Torch', in . . . 'successive groups comprising the fastest ships . . .'

But Churchill had now decided that, after all, his Naval Advisers were right and the sooner Stalin was told the better. He let the Soviet leader know as gently as he could on 9th October to which Stalin replied, 'I received your message of October 9th. Thank you.' As Churchill was to later comment on this reply, 'It was neither informative nor helpful.'

The Germans also drew lessons from PQ 18, somewhat different lessons however to those that were subsequently accredited to them. For example in the *War at Sea* Captain Roskill wrote that:

Before the next pair of convoys sailed, events in Africa had forced him to send south his entire heavy bomber and torpedo striking force of Ju.88s and He.111s. Thus did a strategic success obtained thousands of miles away, when the Allied soldiers landed in North Africa, have favourable repercussions inside the Arctic Circle.*

There are indications however that this interpretation might not be quite accurate, for the North African landings did not take place until dawn on 7th December. However the torpedo bomber units of the Luftwaffe in Norway started to move south to the Mediterranean as early as the 2nd November, the order being given on that date, and the transfer taking five days. As the landings came as a great surprise to the Axis it is not thought that the official British version can therefore be correct, for it would have required a week's advance knowledge of the operation. The German version, which, in this instance and for that reason, rings more true, is that the failure of the torpedo-bomber force to repeat the outstanding success of PQ 17 against PQ 18 resulted in the re-think of policy and it was decided that these

* Vol. II, H.M.S.O.

*Gruppen* would have greater scope in attacking shipping in the Mediterranean than in operating on the convoy route to Russia. There can be little doubt that an attack would be pushed home with greater tenacity in the knowledge that a warm ocean awaited any aircrew forced to ditch rather than an icy grave. One *Staffel* is reported to have completed its transfer from Bardufoss to Grosseto, on the west coast of Italy, in forty-eight hours. The units based at Banak, further north, moved even further south, being initially based on Comiso and Catania airfields in Sicily.

Meanwhile the staff of Naval Group North were determined to sortie out against the next PQ convoy with *Hipper* and *Köln* and did in fact do so (with *Hipper* and *Lutzow*). Again therefore the incredible lack of co-ordination resulted in failure.

Only against PQ 17 had all three arms, Luftwaffe, U-boats and surface fleet, operationed in anything like harmony and the result had been a massacre. Far from drawing the correct conclusion, that they had a winning team on their hands, the German forces in Norway vacillated. Against PQ 18 they used aircraft as the main force, against QP 14 the submarines had the premier role and against JW 51 B the surface ships attacked. As a result each single facet of their effort was rendered ineffective by acting alone and each could be countered successfully in turn by the still limited escorts available to the Royal Navy. The destruction of every Russian convoy was in their power briefly during the brief months of the autumn of 1942, but, by failing to unite against PQ 18, the Germans threw away for ever their greatest opportunity to split asunder the strange alliance ranged against them. Three years later the results of that hesitancy came home to roost with a vengeance of terrible magnitude.

On this result, and all that it implied, the defence of convoy PQ 18 must be acclaimed as a victory for sea-power as significant as any in Britain's long history of maritime supremacy.

# Appendices

# Composition of Convoy PQ 18

| | | | | |
|---|---|---|---|---|
| 11 | *Empire Baffin* | British | 6,800 | |
| 12 | *Kentucky* | American | 5,446 | Sunk |
| 13 | *Charles R. McCormick* | American | 6,027 | |
| 14 | *Andre Marti* | Soviet | 2,352 | |
| 21 | *Komiles* | Soviet | 3,962 | |
| 22 | *Petrovsky* | Soviet | 3,771 | |
| 23 | *White Clover* | Panamanian | 5,497 | |
| 31 | *Empire Snow* | British | 6,327 | |
| 32 | *St Olaf* | American | 7,191 | |
| 33 | *Exford* | American | 4,969 | |
| 34 | *Hollywood* | American | 5,498 | |
| 41 | *Empire Beaumont* | British | 7,044 | Sunk |
| 42 | *Patrick Henry* | American | 7,190 | |
| 43 | *Esek Hopkins* | American | 7,191 | |
| 44 | *Meanticut* | American | 6,061 | |
| 45 | *Atheltemplar* | British | 8,992 | Sunk |
| 51 | *Empire Tristram* | British | 7,167 | |
| 52 | *Sahale* | American | 5,028 | |
| 53 | *Empire Morn* | British | 7,092 | |
| 61 | *Temple Arch* | British | 5,138 | |
| 62 | *Lafayette* | American | 5,887 | |
| 63 | *Campfire* | American | 5,671 | |
| 64 | *Schoharie* | American | 4,971 | |
| 71 | *Ocean Faith* | British | 7,173 | |
| 72 | *Nathaniel Green* | American | 7,176 | |
| 73 | *John Penn* | American | 7,177 | Sunk |
| 74 | *Goolistan* | British | 5,851 | |
| 75 | *Tbitisi* | Soviet | 7,169 | |
| 81 | *Dan-y-Bryn* | British | 5,117 | |
| 82 | *Virginia Dare* | American | 7,177 | |

| 83 | William Moultrie | American | 7,177 | |
| 91 | Empire Stevenson | British | 6,209 | Sunk |
| 92 | Wacosta | American | 5,432 | Sunk |
| 93 | Mary Luckenbach | American | 5,049 | Sunk |
| 94 | Afrikander | Panamanian | 5,441 | Sunk |
| 101 | Oregonian | American | 4,862 | Sunk |
| 102 | Macbeth | Panamanian | 4,885 | Sunk |
| 103 | Stalingrad | Soviet | 3,569 | Sunk |
| 104 | Sukhona | Soviet | 3,124 | Sunk |
| 105 | Oliver Ellsworth | American | 7,191 | Sunk |

# Composition of the Naval Escort Forces for PQ 18

1: *Initial Close Escort for Loch Ewe portion of convoy to rendezvous with Through Escort*

Destroyers:

| L.36 | Eskdale | Lieutenant M. J. W. Pausey |
| I.60 | Campbell | Commander E. C. Coates, DSO, DSC |
| L.70 | Farndale | Commander D. P. Trentham |
| I.70 | Mackay | Lieutenant J. B. Marjoribanks |
| I.01 | Montrose | Commander W. J. Phipps |
| H.23 | Echo | Lieutenant-Commander N. Layton |
| I.41 | Walpole | Lieutenant A. S. Pomeroy, DSC |

Trawlers:

| FY.202 | Arab | Lieutenant F. M. Procter, RNVR |
| FY.220 | Duncton | Lieutenant J. P. Kilbee, RNR |
| FY.102 | Hugh Walpole | Lieutenant J. Mackenzie, RNR |
| FY.235 | King Sol | Lieutenant P. A. Read |
| FY.242 | Paynter | Lieutenant R. H. Nositter, DSC, RANVR |

2: *Through Escort*

Destroyers:

| I.19 | Malcolm | Commander A. B. Russell |
| I.39 | Amazon | Lieutenant-Commander Lord Teynham |
| H.12 | Achates | Lieutenant-Commander A. H. T. Johns |

Anti-Aircraft Ships:

| F.118 | Ulster Queen | Captain C. K. Adams |
| F.84 | Alynbank | Captain H. F. Nash |

Corvettes:

| K.192 | Bryony | Lieutenant-Commander J. P. Stewart, DSC, RNR |
| K.80 | Bluebell | Lieutenant G. H. Walker, RNVR |
| K.189 | Bergamot | Lieutenant R. T. Horan, RNR |
| K.31 | Camellia | Lieutenant R. F. J. Maberley, RNVR |

Minesweepers:

| N.71 | *Harrier* | Commander A. D. H. Jay, DSO |
| N.83 | *Gleaner* | Lieutenant-Commander F. J. G. Hewitt, DSC |
| N.68 | *Sharpshooter* | Lieutenant-Commander W. L. O'Mara |

Submarines:

| P.614 | | Lieutenant D. J. Beckley |
| P.615 | | Lieutenant P. E. Newstead |

Trawlers:

| FY.190 | *Cape Argona* | Lieutenant E. R. Pate, RNR |
| FY.264 | *St Kenan* | Lieutenant R. R. Simpson, RNR |
| FY.123 | *Daneman* | Lieutenant T. D. Henderson, RNVR |
| FY.172 | *Cape Mariato* | Lieutenant H. T. S. Clouston, RNVR |

Motor Minesweepers:

| MMS.90 | | Lieutenant J. Dinwoodie, RNR |
| MMS.203 | | Lieutenant J. H. Petherbridge, DSC, RNR |
| MMS.212 | | Lieutenant W. J. Walker, RNR |

Fleet Oilers:

| | *Black Ranger* | Master L. J. Mack |
| | *Grey Ranger* | Master H. D. Gausden |

3 : *Carrier Force*
Escort Carrier:

| D.14 | *Avenger* | Commander A. P. Colthurst |

Destroyers:

| L.22 | *Wheatland* | Lieutenant-Commander R. de L. Brooke |
| L.128 | *Wilton* | Lieutenant A. P. Northey, DSC |

4 : *Fighting Destroyer Escort*
Anti-Aircraft Cruiser:

| C.98 | *Scylla* | Flag of Rear-Admiral R. L. Burnett |
| | | Captain I. A. P. Macintyre, CBE |

Destroyers:

| G.14 | *Milne* | Captain I. M. R. Campbell |
| H.62 | *Faulknor* | Captain A. K. Scott Moncrieff |
| G.11 | *Onslow* | Captain H. T. Armstrong, DSC |

| G.33 | *Somali* | Lieutenant-Commander C. C. Maud, DSC |
|------|----------|--------------------------------------|
| G.04 | *Onslaught* | Commander W. H. Selby |
| G.51 | *Ashanti* | Commander R. G. Onslow, DSO |
| G.80 | *Opportune* | Commander M. L. Power, DSO |
| G.43 | *Tarta* | Commander St J. R. J. Tyrwhitt, DSC |
| G.44 | *Martin* | Commander C. R. P. Thomson, DSO |
| I.10 | *Intrepid* | Commander C. A. De W. Kitcat |
| G.75 | *Eskimo* | Commander E. G. Le Geyt |
| G.35 | *Marne* | Lieutenant-Commander H. N. A. Richardson, DSC |
| H.76 | *Fury* | Lieutenant-Commander C. H. Campbell, DSC |
| G.73 | *Meteor* | Lieutenant-Commander D. J. B. Jewitt |
| G.29 | *Offa* | Lieutenant-Commander R. A. Ewing |
| I.11 | *Impulsive* | Lieutenant-Commander E. G. Roper, DSC |

## 5 : Spitzbergen Fuelling Force

Fleet Oilers :

| | *Oligarch* | Master A. V. Barton |
|---|-----------|---------------------|
| | *Blue Ranger* | Master H. F. Colbourne |

Destroyers :

| L.98 | *Oakley* | Lieutenant-Commander R. C. V. Thomson |
|------|----------|----------------------------------------|
| L.52 | *Cowdray* | Lieutenant-Commander C. W. North |
| I.96 | *Worcester* | Lieutenant-Commander W. A. Juniper, DSO |
| I.42 | *Windsor* | Lieutenant-Commander D. H. F. Hetherington, DSC |

## 6 : Cruiser Covering Force

Heavy Cruisers :

| C.78 | *Norfolk* | Flag of Vice-Admiral S. S. Bonham-Carter Captain E. G. Bellars |
|------|-----------|----------------------------------------------------------------|
| C.55 | *Suffolk* | Captain R. Shelley |
| C.69 | *London* | Captain R. M. Servaes, CBE |

Destroyers :

| H.91 | *Bulldog* | Commander M. Richmond, DSO, OBE |
|------|-----------|----------------------------------|
| I.75 | *Venomous* | Commander H. W. Falcon-Steward |

## 7 : Reinforcements for Spitzbergen

Heavy Cruiser :

| C.57 | *Cumberland* | Captain A. H. Maxwell-Hyslop, AM |
|------|--------------|----------------------------------|

Light Cruiser:

| C.24 | *Sheffield* | Captain A. W. Clarke |

Destroyer:

| H.08 | *Eclipse* | Lieutenant-Commander E. Mack, DSC |

## 8 : *Heavy Covering Force – Battle Fleet*
Battleships:

| 79 | *Anson* | Flag of Vice-Admiral Sir Bruce Fraser |
| | | Captain H. R. G. Kinahan, CBE |
| 17 | *Duke of York* | Captain G. E. Creasy, DSO, MV |

Light Cruiser:

| C.44 | *Jamaica* | Captain J. L. Storey |

Destroyers:

| I.84 | *Keppel* | Commander J. E. Broome |
| I.01 | *Montrose* | Commander W. J. Phipps |
| I.60 | *Campbell* | Commander E. C. Coates, DSO, DSC |
| I.70 | *Mackay* | Lieutenant J. B. Marjoribanks |
| L.51 | *Bramham* | Lieutenant E. F. Baines |
| I.83 | *Broke* | Lieutenant-Commander A. F. C. Layard |

## 9 : *Minesweeping Flotilla at Archangel*
Minesweepers:

| N.42 | *Halcyon* | Lieutenant-Commander C. H. Corbett-Singleton |
| N.02 | *Hazard* | Lieutenant-Commander J. R. A. Seymour |
| N.86 | *Salamander* | Lieutenant W. R. Muttram |
| N.22 | *Britomart* | Lieutenant-Commander S. S. Stanwitz |

## 10 : *Submarine Forces* (Covering Force)

| P.221 | *Shakespeare* | Lieutenant M. F. R. Ainslie, DSC |
| P.45 | *Unrivalled* | Lieutenant H. B. Turner |
| N.95 | *Unique* | Lieutenant E. R. Boddington |

### (Patrol Force)

| N.76 | *Tribune* | Lieutenant M. C. R. Lumby |
| N.63 | *Tigris* | Lieutenant-Commander G. R. Colvin |
| N.73 | *Sturgeon* | Lieutenant-Commander M. R. G. Wingfield |
| P.54 | *Unshaken* | Lieutenant C. E. Oxborrow, DSO |
| P.41 | *Uredd* | Lieutenant R. O. Rören, RNorN |

### (Minelayer)

| P.14 | *Rubis* | Cap de Corvett H. Rousselot, DSC |

# Appendix Three

## 1 : *RAF Units*

**Group Captain F. L. Hopps, RAF based at Polyarnoe.**

| | | | |
|---|---|---|---|
| 144 Squadron | Hampden | Torpedo Bombers | Afrikanda |
| 455 (RAAF) Squadron | Hampden | Torpedo Bombers | Afrikanda |
| 210 Squadron | Catalina | Flying Boats | Grasnaya |

## 2 : *Luftwaffe Units*

### *Luftflotte V*

| | | | |
|---|---|---|---|
| K.G.30 | Junkers Ju.88 | Bombers | Banak |
| K.G.26 | Junkers Ju.88 & Heinkel He.111 | Torpedo Bombers | Banak & Bardufoss |
| I/St.G.5 | Junkers Ju.87 | Dive Bombers | Kirkenes |
| JG.5 | Messerschmidt Me.109 | Fighters | Various |
| I/K.G.40 | Focke Wulfe FW200 | Long Range Recce | Trondheim |
| I/406 & I/906 | Heinkel He.115 & Blohm & Voss BV.138 | Flying Boats | Tromso & Stavanger |
| I(F)/22 & I(F)/124 | Junkers Ju.88 | Recce Units | Banak, Bardufoss & Kirkenes |

Colonel-General Hans-Jürgen Stumpff – Oslo.
*Fliegerfuhrer Nordost* – Colonel Alexander Holle – Kirkenes.
*Fliegerfuhrer Lofoten* – Colonel Ernst – August Roth – Bardufoss.

# R/T Call Signs

| | | |
|---|---|---|
| 1 | Battlefleet | Bittern |
| 2 | Senior Officer | Dipper |
| 3 | *Anson* | Dabchick |
| 4 | *Duke of York* | Pintail |
| 5 | *Jamaica* | Duck |
| 6 | *Meteor* | Cuckoo |
| 7 | *Montrose* | Merlin |
| 8 | *Keppel* | Nuthatch |
| 9 | *Campbell* | Linnet |
| 10 | *Mackay* | Stonechat |
| 11 | *Vesper* | Magpie |
| 12 | *Vivacious* | Redstart |
| 13 | Spare | Coot |
| 14 | Covering Force | Heron |
| 15 | Senior Officer | Peewit |
| 16 | *Scylla* | Crossbill |
| 17 | *Somali* | Puffin |
| 18 | *Tartar* | Tom-Tit |
| 19 | *Eskimo* | Creeper |
| 20 | *Ashanti* | Sparrow |
| 21 | *Faulknor* | Goose |
| 22 | *Fury* | Owl |
| 23 | *Echo* | Dove |
| 24 | *Intrepid* | Swan |
| 25 | *Impulsive* | Gull |
| 26 | *Onslow* | Bullfinch |
| 27 | *Offa* | Wagtail |
| 28 | *Onslaught* | Robin |
| 29 | *Opportune* | Whinchat |

| 30 | *Milne* | Ivy |
| 31 | Spare | Carrot |
| 32 | Spare | Turtle |
| 33 | Spare | Cabbage |
| 34 | Cruiser Force | Dunlin |
| 35 | Senior Officer | Goldfinch |
| 36 | *Norfolk* | Mallard |
| 37 | *London* | Pipit |
| 38 | *Cumberland* | Crow |
| 39 | *Sheffield* | Nightjar |
| 40 | *Eclipse* | Warbler |
| 41 | *Bulldog* | Dovecot |
| 42 | *Venomous* | Textbook |
| 43 | *Walpole* | Pigeon |
| 44 | Spare | Swallow |
| 45 | Carrier Force | Jackdaw |
| 46 | Senior Officer | Skua |
| 47 | *Avenger* | Bunting |
| 48 | *Wheatland* | Redshank |
| 49 | *Wilton* | Petrel |
| 50 | Spare | Titlark |
| 51 | Minesweepers | Falcon |
| 52 | Senior Officer | Lark |
| 53 | *Harrier* | Buttercup |
| 54 | *Gleaner* | Buzzard |
| 55 | *Sharpshooter* | Diver |
| 56 | Spare | Nettle |
| 57 | Force P | Curlew |
| 58 | Senior Officer, Escort | Snipe |
| 59 | *Worcester* | Blackbird |
| 60 | *Windsor* | Tern |
| 61 | *Oakley* | Redwing |
| 62 | *Cowdray* | Sorrel |
| 63 | Spare | Moorhen |

*Convoys*

| 64 | Escort of PQ 18 | Eagle |
| 65 | Senior Officer | Gannet |
| 66 | *Malcolm* | Handshake |

| | | |
|---|---|---|
| 67 | *Broke* | Whip |
| 68 | *Amazon* | Victor |
| 69 | *Achates* | Tumult |
| 70 | *Camelia* | Compact |
| 71 | *Bryony* | Patent |
| 72 | *Bergamot* | Greenfinch |
| 73 | *Bluebell* | Combat |
| 74 | *Ulster Queen* | Pigmy |
| 75 | *Alynbank* | Football |
| 76 | *Cape Argona* | Plover |
| 77 | *Cape Mariato* | Dogrose |
| 78 | *Daneman* | Wigeon |
| 79 | *St Kenan* | Mustard |
| 80 | *P.614* | Blackcap |
| 81 | *P.615* | Oyster |
| 82 | *Spare* | Scarlet |
| 83 | *Spare* | Ratter |
| 84 | *Spare* | Nectar |
| 85 | *Spare* | Spectrum |
| 86 | Escort of QP 14 | Fulmar |
| 87 | Senior Officer | Woodcock |
| 88 | *Blankney* | Martin |
| 89 | *Middleton* | Spoonbill |
| 90 | *Palomares* | Fisher |
| 91 | *Pozarica* | Riley |
| 92 | *Dianella* | Bunny |
| 93 | *Lotus* | Marrow |
| 94 | *Poppy* | Ticket |
| 95 | *La Malouine* | Palace |
| 96 | *Lord Austin* | Rook |
| 97 | *Lord Middleton* | Raven |
| 98 | *Ayrshire* | Grouser |
| 99 | *Northern Gem* | Waxwing |
| 100 | *Spare* | Heather |
| 101 | *Spare* | Oaktree |
| 102 | *Spare* | Hazel |
| 103 | *Spare* | Nutmeg |

# Fleet Air Arm

## SUMMARY OF AIRCRAFT SORTIES

*SWORDFISH*
Number of Sorties .................................................. 32
U-boats sighted
  On surface .................................................. 12
  Conning Tower awash ................................... 3
  Periscope .................................................... 1
Depth Charge Attacks ..................................... 6
Times Destroyers seen approaching to attack ..................... 6
Other Missions (Search for stragglers) ............................. 3
Rear gun combats (Claim: 1 He 111 damaged) ..................... 2
Swordfish hours flown 90 hours 35 mins ......... 32 deck landings

*HURRICANES*
Fighter sorties ............................................... 59
Number of combats ....................................... 31

| Claims: | Certain | Probable | Damaged |
|---------|---------|----------|---------|
|  | 3 He 111 | 3 He 111 | 12 He 111 |
|  | 2 Ju 88 |  | 2 He 115 |
|  |  |  | 3 Ju 88 |
|  |  |  | 1 BV 138 |
|  | 5 | 3 | 18 |

Hurricane Hours flown 70 hours 10 mins ......... 55 deck landings

*AIRCRAFT LOST OR DAMAGED*
4 Hurricanes shot down. 3 pilots saved.

2 Swordfish broke tail oleo on landing (serviceable within 3 hours)

2 Hurricanes damaged tail oleo (serviceable within 3 hours)

Various minor damage to 5 Hurricanes due to enemy action (repaired within 4 hours)

1 Swordfish smashed rear section of fuselage on landing.

# German Naval Units

**1 :** *Battle Group Altenfiord*
Pocket Battleship:
*Admiral Scheer*  Vice-Admiral Kummetz
Captain Meendsen-Bohlken

Heavy Cruiser:
*Admiral Hipper*  Rear-Admiral Meisel

Light Cruiser:
*Köln*  Captain Baltzer

Destroyers:

| | | |
|---|---|---|
| Z.4 | *Richard Beitzen* | Lieutenant-Commander von Davidson |
| Z.23 | | Lieutenant-Commander Wittig |
| Z.29 | | Lieutenant-Commander Rechel |
| Z.30 | | Lieutenant-Commander Kaiser |
| Z.27 | | Commander Schultz |

Acting as leader with Captain Pönitz, in command of 8th Destroyer Flotilla, embarked.

**2 :** *Submarines for 'Ice Palace' Attack Group*

| | |
|---|---|
| U-88 | Lieutenant-Commander Bohmann |
| U-255 | Lieutenant-Commander Reche |
| U-377 | Lieutenant-Commander Koehler |
| U-378 | Lieutenant-Commander Zetsche |
| U-403 | Lieutenant-Commander Claussen |
| U-405 | Lieutenant-Commander Hopmann |
| U-408 | Lieutenant-Commander von Hymmen |
| U-435 | Lieutenant-Commander Strelow |
| U-457 | Lieutenant-Commander Brandenburg |

| U-589 | Lieutenant-Commander Horrer |
| U-592 | Lieutenant-Commander Bora |
| U-703 | Lieutenant-Commander Bielfeld |

# Sources

*Superior numbers throughout the book refer to the listed sources contained here for easy reference.*

## PRIMARY SOURCES

1   *Operation EV* Report of Commander-in-Chief, Home Fleet, dated 8th October, 1942. (1364/HF01325/5/107).

2   *Operation EV* Report of Rear-Admiral (D), Home Fleet, dated 29th September, 1942. (HD570). Plus Appendices.

3   *Commodore's Report of PQ 18.* (1601/HF1230/119) dated 28th October, 1942. Includes C-in-C Home Fleets covering docket dated 15th November, 1942.

4   Letter from Military Branch, Admiralty to Commander United States Naval Forces in Europe, dated 2nd February, 1943. (M.014755/42) and Reply dated 6th February, 1943. (610/31).

5   Docket on Emergency Turn Procedure from C-in-C, Western Approaches to Secretary of Admiralty dated 9th February, 1943. (M.014755/42).

6   Report of Proceedings of Senior British Naval Officer, Archangel, dated 18th October, 1942. (736/SC.01).

7   Telegrams from SBNO Archangel dated 25th September and 7th October, 1942.

8   Summary of Air Attacks on Convoys PQ 18 and QP 14, dated 13th November, 1942. (M.051890/42).

9   Summary of Submarine Operations during passage of PQ 18 dated 1st November, 1942. Incorporating the attack report of HM Submarine *Tigris*. Dated 1st November, 1942. (2520/SM.4000).

10  Summary of Anti-Submarine Operations during Operation *EV*, dated 27th September, 1942. (M.051890/42).

11 Operation *EV* Appendices to Memorandum HD 00570, dated 29 August, 1942. Covering following facets of planning:
    I    Instructions for Screens.
    II   Screening Diagram 30.
    III  Notes on Screening Diagram 30.
    IV  Screening Diagram 31.
    V   Notes on Screening Diagram 31.
    VI  Screening Diagram 32.
    VII Notes on Screening Diagram 32.
    VIII Rescue Operations.
    IX  Conduct of Submarines.
    X   Surface Action.
    XI  Fuelling Instructions.
    XII Communications.
    XIII Seniority List.
    XIV Approximate times of sunset and sunrise.
    XV Provisional Programme.

12 Report of Battlefleet Operations during *EV*, dated 23rd September, 1942. (2nd B.S. 257/0570).

13 Report of Proceedings HMS *Eskdale*, dated 12th September, 1942. (1364/HF01325/5/107).

14 Report on attack on U-boat, HMS *Farndale*, dated 10th September, 1942. (72/16) Including DA/SW Docket.

15 Memorandum on Operation *EV* dated 24th August, 1942. Containing following facets of intelligence:
    I   Communications.
    II  Navigation.
       North Russian Convoy Instructions.
       Western Approaches Convoy Instructions.
       Weekly Intelligence Reports.
       (HF01325/5/107).

16 Report of Proceedings of HMS *Avenger*, dated 20th September, 1942. (Appendix 2 of HD570/29th).

17 Combat Report of Cam Hurricane V 7653, dated 19th September, 1942. (A11/1).

18 Report of Proceedings of HMS *Harrier*, dated 1st October, 1942. (F02/43).

19 Report on Proceedings of HMS *Bryony*, dated 26th September, 1942. (Unlisted Remarks sheets (2)).

20  Report of Proceedings of HMS *Bluebell*, dated 25th September, 1942. (Unlisted).

21  Report of Proceedings of HMS *Bergamot*, dated 1st October, 1942. (Unlisted).

22  Report of Proceedings of HMS *Cape Argona*, dated 26th September, 1942. (Unlisted).

23  Report of Proceedings of HMS *St Kenan*, dated 26th September, 1942. (Unlisted).

24  Report of Proceedings of HMS *Sharpshooter*, dated 29th September, 1942. (Unlisted).

25  Report of Proceedings of HMS *Ulster Queen*, dated 12th October, 1942. (Unlisted).

26  Report of Proceedings of HMS *Gleaner*, dated 25th September, 1942. (Unlisted).

27  Report of Proceedings of HMS *Malcolm* and the Close Escort, dated 5th November, 1942. (1545/HF01323/5/107).

28  Report of Proceedings of HMS *Achates*, dated 30th September, 1942. (Unlisted).

29  Report of Proceedings of HMS *Bramble*, dated 29th September, 1942. (4A/3772).

30  Armed Guard Report of SS *Exford*, dated 21st September, 1942. (Unlisted).

31  Summary of Statements by survivors of SS *Oliver Ellsworth*, dated 5th November, 1942. (Op-16-B-5).

32  Summary of Statements by survivors of SS *Oregonia*, dated 4th November, 1942. (Op-16-B-5).

33  Summary of Statements of attacks on SS *Nathaniel Greene*, dated 5th May, 1943. (Op-16-B-5).

34  Armed Guard Report of SS *Campfire*, dated 6th October, 1942. (Unlisted).

35  Armed Guard Report of SS *Patrick Henry*, dated 9th January, 1943. (PDNYF 06P56).

36  Armed Guard Report of SS *Virginia Dare*, dated 25th September, 1942. (Op-23L-1-ACK-0669023).

37  Armed Guard Report of SS *Esek Hopkins*, dated 26th September, 1942. (Pers-650-Gd-QB4).

38  Summary of Statements of Survivors of SS *Kentucky*, dated 23rd February, 1943. (Op-16-B-5).

39  Summary of Statements of attacks on SS *Nathaniel Greene*, dated 5th May, 1943. (Op-16-B-5).

40  Armed Guard Report of SS *Nathaniel Greene*, dated 24th September, 1942. (Unlisted).

41  Summary of Statements of survivors of SS *John Penn*, dated 4th November, 1942. (Op-16-B-5).

42  Summary of Statements of survivors of SS *Wacosta*, dated 4th November, 1942. (Op-16-B-5).

43  Summary of Statements of survivors of SS *Macbeth*, dated 10th November, 1942. (Op-16-B-5).

44  Operations Record Book of No. 455 Squadron, RAAF, dated 4th September, 1942 to 25th September, 1942.

45  Operations Record Book of No. 144 Squadron, RAF, dated 1st September, 1942 to 18th September, 1942.

46  Operational Record Book of No. 210 Squadron, RAF, dated 1st September, 1942 to 28th September, 1942.

47  Oberkommando der Kriegsmarine, PQ 18, Unternehmungen: *Eispalast, Meisen-Balz*, Aktz: VIII, 14/16 Jul.-2 Dec., 1942. (PG32509/T1022. Roll 1823-Microfilm US National Archives).

48  I/SK1 Akte Nord, Lage Admiral Norwegan, Mappe 8, I fd, Nr, 1476-1700, 1 Aug.-2 Oct., 1942. PG33141/T1022 T1973. Roll 1973-Microfilm US National Archives).

49  I/Sk1 Akte Nord.F.d.Luft u. Luftflotte 5, Mappe IV, I fd.Nr. 602-761, 14 Aug.-31 Dec., 1942. PG33156/T1022. Roll 1978 US Microfilm US Archives, Washington).

50  Kriegstagebuch der Seekriegsleitung, Teil A, September 1942. (PG32057/T1022. Roll 1676-Microfilm US Archives).

51  Letter to the author from David Kahn, dated 30th December, 1973.

52  Letter to the author from Humphrey R. A. Higgens, dated 27th December, 1973.

53  Letters to the author from Alfred Price, dated 11th December, 1973 and 12th March, 1974.

54  Letter to the author from Edwin Walker, dated 13th January, 1974.

55  Information from Lloyd's Register of Shipping, 31st May, 1974.

56  Files on hand at the Public Record Office include
144 Squadron Air 27/982.
455 Squadron Air 27/1897.
210 Squadron Air 27/1299.

PQ and QP 1942. *Adm* 199/758.
*Gearbox 18.* Adm1/12426.

## SECONDARY (PUBLISHED) SOURCES

57   *Through the Waters*; Robert Hughes; William Kimber, 1956.
58   *The Russian Convoys*; B. B. Schofield; Batsford, 1964.
59   *With the Red Fleet*; Admiral Arseni Golovko; Putnam, 1965.
60   *The War at Sea, Volume Two*; Captain S. W. Roskill, HMSO, 1960.
61   *The Second World War, Volume IV, The Hinge of Fate*; W. S. Churchill; Cassell, 1951.
62   *The Rise and Fall of the German Air Force, 1939-45*; Air Ministry (ACAS(1)), 1948.
63   *Convoy is to Scatter*; Captain Jack Broome; William Kimber, 1972.
64   *Liberty Ships*; John Gorley Bunker, USNI, 1972.
65   *Max Horton and the Western Approaches*; Rear-Admiral W. S. Chalmers; Hodder & Stoughton, 1954.
66   *Goering; Air Leader*; Asher Lee; Duckworth, 1972.
67   *Sea Warfare*; Vice-Admiral Fredrich Ruge; Cassell, 1957.
68   *The Tirpitz*; David Woodward; William Kimber, 1953.
69   *The Luftwaffe War Diaries*; Cajus Bekker, Macdonald, 1966.

# PQ17 - CONVOY TO HELL

## by Paul Lund and Harry Ludlam

In June, 1942, Convoy PQ17, consisting of thirty-five merchant ships, set out for Russia with an escort of cruisers and destroyers. They had a reasonable chance of success until the order came to 'Scatter!'

What followed represents one of the most terrible and tragic blunders of the Second World War.

Authors Ludlam and Lund give a first hand account of the horror and despair that faced the men left to the mercy of a cruel enemy. From thousands of sources and recollections they have built up an unforgettable picture of what it was like to be in PQ17 – and survive . . .

**NEW ENGLISH LIBRARY**

# NEL BESTSELLERS

**Crime**

| T026 663 | THE DOCUMENTS IN THE CASE | Dorothy L. Sayers | 50p |
| T027 821 | GAUDY NIGHT | Dorothy L. Sayers | 75p |
| T030 180 | UNNATURAL DEATH | Dorothy L. Sayers | 60p |
| T026 671 | FIVE RED HERRINGS | Dorothy L. Sayers | 50p |
| T025 462 | MURDER MUST ADVERTISE | Dorothy L. Sayers | 50p |

**Fiction**

| T030 199 | CRUSADER'S TOMB | A. J. Cronin | £1.25 |
| T029 522 | HATTER'S CASTLE | A. J. Cronin | £1.00 |
| T027 228 | THE SPANISH GARDNER | A. J. Cronin | 45p |
| T013 936 | THE JUDAS TREE | A. J. Cronin | 50p |
| T015 386 | THE NORTHERN LIGHT | A. J. Cronin | 50p |
| T031 276 | THE CITADEL | A. J. Cronin | 95p |
| T027 112 | BEYOND THIS PLACE | A. J. Cronin | 60p |
| T016 609 | KEYS OF THE KINGDOM | A. J. Cronin | 60p |
| T029 158 | THE STARS LOOK DOWN | A. J. Cronin | £1.00 |
| T022 021 | THREE LOVES | A. J. Cronin | 90p |
| T022 536 | THE HARRAD EXPERIMENTS | Robert H. Rimmer | 50p |
| T022 994 | THE DREAM MERCHANTS | Harold Robbins | 95p |
| T023 303 | THE PIRATE | Harold Robbins | 95p |
| T022 986 | THE CARPETBAGGERS | Harold Robbins | £1.00 |
| T031 667 | WHERE LOVE HAS GONE | Harold Robbins | £1.00 |
| T023 958 | THE ADVENTURERS | Harold Robbins | £1.00 |
| T025 241 | THE INHERITORS | Harold Robbins | 90p |
| T025 276 | STILETTO | Harold Robbins | 50p |
| T025 268 | NEVER LEAVE ME | Harold Robbins | 50p |
| T025 292 | NEVER LOVE A STRANGER | Harold Robbins | 90p |
| T022 226 | A STONE FOR DANNY FISHER | Harold Robbins | 80p |
| T031 640 | 79 PARK AVENUE | Harold Robbins | 80p |
| T027 945 | THE BETSY | Harold Robbins | 90p |
| T029 557 | RICH MAN, POOR MAN | Irwin Shaw | £1.25 |
| T031 241 | EVENING IN BYZANTIUM | Irwin Shaw | 75p |
| T021 025 | THE MAN | Irving Wallace | 90p |
| T022 897 | THE PRIZE | Irving Wallace | £1.00 |
| T027 082 | THE PLOT | Irving Wallace | £1.00 |
| T030 253 | THE THREE SIRENS | Irving Wallace | £1.25 |
| T020 916 | SEVEN MINUTES | Irving Wallace | 90p |

**Historical**

| T022 196 | KNIGHT WITH ARMOUR | Alfred Duggan | 50p |
| T022 250 | THE LADY FOR RANSOM | Alfred Duggan | 50p |
| T017 958 | FOUNDING FATHERS | Alfred Duggan | 50p |
| T022 625 | LEOPARDS AND LILIES | Alfred Duggan | 60p |
| T023 079 | LORD GEOFFREY'S FANCY | Alfred Duggan | 60p |
| T024 903 | THE KING OF ATHELNEY | Alfred Duggan | 60p |
| T020 169 | FOX 9: CUT AND THRUST | Adam Hardy | 30p |
| T021 300 | FOX 10: BOARDER'S AWAY | Adam Hardy | 35p |
| T023 125 | FOX 11: FIRESHIP | Adam Hardy | 35p |
| T024 946 | FOX 12: BLOOD BEACH | Adam Hardy | 35p |
| T027 651 | FOX 13: SEA FLAME | Adam Hardy | 40p |

**Science Fiction**

| T027 724 | SCIENCE FICTION ART | Brian Aldiss | £2.95 |
| T030 245 | TIME ENOUGH FOR LOVE | Robert Heinlein | £1.25 |
| T029 492 | STRANGER IN A STRANGE LAND | Robert Heinlein | 80p |
| T029 484 | I WILL FEAR NO EVIL | Robert Heinlein | 95p |
| T026 817 | THE HEAVEN MAKERS | Frank Herbert | 35p |
| T031 462 | DUNE | Frank Herbert | £1.25 |
| T022 854 | DUNE MESSIAH | Frank Herbert | 60p |
| T023 974 | THE GREEN BRAIN | Frank Herbert | 35p |
| T015 270 | THE WEAPON MAKERS | A. E. Van Vogt | 30p |
| T023 265 | EMPIRE OF THE ATOM | A. E. Van Vogt | 40p |
| T027 473 | THE FAR OUT WORLD OF A. E. VAN VOGT | | |
| | | A. E. Van Vogt | 50p |